AMERICAN
WAYS

AMERICAN WAYS

A Cultural Guide to the United States

Third Edition

GARY ALTHEN

WITH JANET BENNETT

INTERCULTURAL PRESS
an imprint of Nicholas Brealey Publishing

BOSTON • LONDON

This edition first published by Intercultural Press, an imprint of Nicholas Brealey
Publishing, in 2011.

53 State Street, 9th Floor	3-5 Spafield Street, Clerkenwell
Boston, MA 02109, USA	London, EC1R 4QB, UK
Tel: + 617-523-3801	Tel: +44-(0)-207-239-0360
Fax: + 617-523-3708	Fax: +44-(0)-207-239-0370
www.interculturalpress.com	www.nicholasbrealey.com

Printed in the United States of America

20 19 18 17 16   7 8 9 10

ISBN: 978-0-98424-717-2

CONTENTS

Contents

Contents

Contents

PREFACE TO THE
THIRD EDITION

Some things change, while others remain the same. So it is with American ways.

When the first edition of *American Ways* appeared in 1988, the United States was experiencing what was considered a "normal" year for that era. There was a presidential election (George H. W. Bush was chosen over Michael Dukakis); a political scandal (Iran-Contra); the Dow Jones Industrial Average (a widely used indicator of stock market performance) rose by about 15 percent; and the Cold War was in progress, with few in the United States suspecting that it would end in the following year (with the fall of the Berlin Wall). Popular musicians included Michael Jackson, George Harrison, Enya, Paul Simon, and the group Guns N' Roses. The Los Angeles Dodgers won the World Series.

By 2003, when the second edition appeared, the country had experienced the terrorist attacks of what became known as 9/11, and problems were rampant. The economy had yet to recover from the shock of the hijacked airplanes being directed into three iconic buildings. President George W. Bush, whose accession to the presidency took place under a legal cloud, had declared a "Global War on Terror" and had ordered an attack on Iraq. Assorted "security measures" had become controversial. Dissension was widespread. People were confused and insecure about their future.

At the time of this third edition of *American Ways*, the United States seems to be at a major turning point. Concern about terrorism and security continues to be high. The war in Iraq seems to be winding down, while the war in Afghanistan is absorbing more and more resources. The country faces other grave problems, including an economic recession (or worse), an enormous and growing national debt, and a society and political system seemingly paralyzed by partisan divisions. Meanwhile, the country is experiencing some significant demographic and social shifts:

- An aging population
- An increasingly diverse population
- Greater equality for females in segments of society formerly dominated by males
- An increasing gap between the wealthy and the less well-off
- Assorted developments in electronic communication and social media that are reshaping the way people do business, interact with others, and, some suggest, mentally process the information they receive

Taken together, these current developments, pervasive demographic changes, and social transformation seem to have the country at a crossroads.

Pessimistic observers believe the United States is on the path toward breakdown, following the pattern of history's previous imperial powers. Faced with a huge debt to foreign creditors, global climate change, a predicted decline in production of fossil fuels, massive commitment to military expenditures, a deteriorating infrastructure, growing social and economic divisions, and a seemingly paralyzed political system, the country will experience some form of radical transformation.

Optimistic observers, by contrast, say that "we've weathered hard times before, and we will do so again." Somehow Americans' intelligence, ambition, inventiveness, pragmatism, organizational ability, willingness to experiment, and technological sophistication will enable their country to solve whatever problems come its way. All that's needed is the resolve to confront those problems. That resolve will come, according to this line of thought, when the problems become truly serious.

Beneath all these and many other issues and arguments, at least some essentials of U.S. American culture persevere. Sociologist Claude Fischer summarizes his findings from an exhaustive study of American culture and character with these words:

> . . . continuity is a striking feature of American culture. To be sure, there have been important changes, spikes, sideways moves, and reversals, but what seemed socially distinctive about America in the eighteenth century still seems distinctive in the twenty-first. The major change has been the broadening and deepening of that distinctive culture and the incorporation into it of more Americans who had been—because of gender, race, age, servitude, poverty, and isolation—less than full participants. (2010, 241)

These distinctive characteristics, according to Fischer, include an emphasis on individualism, voluntarism, material progress, and religiosity.

A faith in science and technology also continues to distinguish U.S. American culture from most others. People from all parts of the American political spectrum trumpet their concern with "freedom." The idea that one's own hard work can improve one's economic and social standing perseveres. The notion that the United States is the greatest country in the world seems to have been strengthened in some people's minds but weakened in the minds of others. Readers of this third edition of *American Ways* will find elaboration on these and many other aspects of American life in the pages that follow.

First, though, a few words about terms.

Americans have a fondness for euphemisms—that is, gentle, indirect words or expressions used in place of words or expressions that refer clearly to unpleasant topics or that may imply something negative. For example, instead of saying that someone *died*, Americans are likely to say that the person *passed away, passed on, went to her final reward,* or some such soft-sounding expression. Many stores that used to have *clerks* now have *associates*. In such stores, people who come to shop may be called *guests* rather than *customers*. People employed to clean buildings (mop floors, empty rubbish containers, etc.) used to be called *janitors*. They are now commonly called *sanitary engineers* to avoid the implication that they occupy a lowly station.

Without going into details about a complex issue, suffice it to say here that America's "culture wars" of the 1980s produced a heightened sensitivity to terms used to refer to people or groups often perceived to be socially marginalized or discriminated against. The idea, held dear by some and ridiculed by others, was that everyone ought to use terminology that conveys respect for such people and groups, rather than terminology that might insult them or reinforce their possible feelings of exclusion. Here are some examples of "politically correct" terminology, furnished by the online encyclopedia *Wikipedia*:

- *African-American* in place of *Black*, *Negro*, and other terms
- *Native American* (or in Canada *First Nations*) in place of *Indian*
- "Gender-neutral" terms such as *firefighter* in place of *fireman*
- Terms relating to disability, such as *visually challenged* or *hearing impaired* in place of *blind* or *handicapped*

("Political Correctness," 2010)

Visitors from abroad will probably notice that U.S. Americans exhibit a certain caution when choosing words that refer to race, gender, disability, and sexual orientation.

For this book, one application of the heightened attention to word choice has to do with *foreign*. For decades (or longer), *foreign* referred to people from one country who were temporarily in another. For others, though, *foreign* implied strangeness, or being out of place. A more sensitive term, from this point of view, is *international*. In this edition, *foreign* and *international* are used interchangeably.

People who consider themselves sensitive to the feelings of citizens of the Western Hemisphere outside the United States of America argue that it is unacceptably arrogant for people in the United States to refer to themselves as *Americans*. Everyone from the Western Hemisphere is American, they say. People in the United States should refer to themselves as *U.S. Americans* or *U.S. citizens*.

In this book, people who live in or are from the United States of America are called *Americans* or *U.S. Americans*. Caucasian U.S. Americans are referred to as *European Americans*, to distinguish them from African Americans, Asian Americans, and other groups that comprise the country's quite diverse population.

Next, a few words on the style in which this book is written. *American Ways* exemplifies the typical organization and writing style of American nonfiction writing. Thoughts are presented in a linear way, within chapters, within subsections, and even within paragraphs, like this one. There is usually a main idea or other form of introduction at the beginning, then some elaboration, then a conclusion.

Ideas are made explicit. There are few digressions from the main topic. For more on the way U.S. Americans typically organize their presentations, see chapter 3.

In conclusion, some words about culture change. Social scientists argue about the notion of "culture change": Do cultures actually change, or is it only that people's superficial behaviors seem to alter over time? If cultures do change, what is it that actually becomes different? What causes the changes? How fast does change occur?

This book does not explore these interesting but difficult questions. Rather, it offers a large set of generalizations—with many, many qualifications—about the assumptions, values, and behaviors that seem typical of the people who live in the United States of America. Readers are encouraged to compare what they read in this book with what they observe for themselves during their time in the United States. What seems accurate? What may be changing? What remains distinctively "American" about the way U.S. Americans are living their lives? Exploring such questions can ensure that your time in the United States will be stimulating and rewarding.

—Gary Althen
Grand Lake, Colorado

ACKNOWLEDGMENTS

Countless people contributed to this book. Most were international students, scholars, and visitors with whom I talked during my 30-plus years in international education. What stood out to them as they entered a new culture? What did they find most difficult to understand and accommodate?

There were also fellow Americans I heard and watched while working overseas myself. Seeing the patterns in their responses to another culture was highly illuminating.

Others to whom I am indebted:

- Professional colleagues who shared my interest in intercultural communication and in helping people from overseas understand their host society. One particular colleague, Nancy Young of New York University, offered detailed suggestions for this revision.
- Authors of books and articles about intercultural communication, American culture, and the cultures of other countries.
- Colleagues overseas who found earlier editions of *American Ways* worthy of being translated into their languages.
- Intercultural Press cofounder David Hoopes and his colleagues, particularly Toby Frank, Patty Topel, and Judy Carl-Hendrick, who were instrumental in producing the first two editions of this book.

Acknowledgments

Amanda Doran and Susan Szmania, then at the University of Texas at Austin, provided the impetus and many ideas for this book's second edition, a project too time-consuming for me to undertake on my own.

For this third edition, I've been privileged to have the help of the very respected interculturalist Janet Bennett. Unlike me, she is still active—to say the least—in the field. She provided information and ideas that permeate this edition. Also, she brought a more current sensibility to some of the commentary in these pages.

At Nicholas Brealey Publishing, now the owner of Intercultural Press, Erika Heilman and Jennifer Olsen have been supportive and responsive. Copy editor Renee Nicholls' astute observations made this a better book.

My wife, Sandy, has helped me find the time and space necessary for preparing this new edition. I am deeply grateful to her.

—Gary Althen
Grand Lake, Colorado

INTRODUCTION

Most U.S. Americans see themselves as open, frank, and fairly friendly. If you ask them a question, they will answer it. They have nothing to hide. They cannot understand why people from other countries should have any difficulty understanding them. Unless, of course, there are language problems.

But most people from other countries do have trouble understanding Americans. Even if they have a good command of English, most foreigners have at least some difficulty understanding what the Americans they encounter are thinking and feeling. What ideas and attitudes underlie their actions? What motivates them? What makes them talk and act the way they do? This book addresses those questions. It is intended to help international visitors—both those staying for a long time and those here for short visits—to understand the natives.

ON UNDERSTANDING

This book is not intended to encourage foreigners to like U.S. Americans or want to imitate them. Some visitors from abroad will have positive feelings toward most of the Americans they meet. Others will not. Some will want to remain for a long time in the United States while others will want to go home as soon as possible. People in both groups, however, will be more likely to benefit from their stays in the States if they understand the natives. *Understand* here means having a reasonably accurate set of ideas for interpreting the behavior they see.

Let's look at an example, one that causes many foreigners to have negative feelings toward U.S. Americans.

Tariq Nassar is Egyptian. In his society, people place a high premium on family loyalty. Obligations to parents and siblings are an important part of daily life. Tariq has come to the United States to earn a master's degree in civil engineering. Through the U.S. university he is attending, he has a "host family," a local family that periodically invites him to their home for dinner or some other activity. The family's name is Wilson. Mr. Wilson is a middle-aged engineer. His wife works part-time as a paralegal. Their two children, a daughter who is twenty-two and a son who is nineteen, are both college students, one attending a university in a distant state, the other a local community college.

Mr. Wilson's father died two years ago. His mother, Tariq learns, lives in a nursing home. One Sunday after having dinner with the Wilsons, Tariq goes with them to visit Mr. Wilson's mother. The nursing home is full of frail, elderly people, most of whom are sitting silently in lounge areas or lying in their rooms. A few are playing cards or dominoes in the game room or are watching television.

Mr. Wilson's mother is obviously old, but she can move around reasonably well and can carry on a normal conversation with anyone who talks a bit louder than usual. Mr. Wilson says he visits his mother once a week if at all possible. Sometimes he has to go out of town, so two weeks will pass between visits. His wife sometimes goes along on these visits; the children rarely do, since one lives far away and the other is usually busy studying.

Tariq is horrified. How can Mr. Wilson, who otherwise seems like a pleasant and generous person, stand to have his mother living in such a place? Why doesn't she live with Mr. Wilson?

How can Tariq interpret Mr. Wilson's behavior? There are several possibilities.

- Mr. Wilson is a selfish, irresponsible person who does not understand children's obligations toward their parents.

- Mr. Wilson's mother has a medical or psychological problem that is not evident to him and that requires special care she could not get in Mr. Wilson's home.
- Mr. Wilson's wife is a domineering woman who, for selfish reasons, refuses to have her husband's mother living in her house.

Any of these interpretations might be correct, but there are others that are more likely to explain the situation. If Tariq understood the way in which Americans are trained to behave as independent, self-reliant individuals, he would be more likely to understand why Mr. Wilson's mother is in the nursing home. He might realize that the mother may actually prefer to be in the nursing home rather than "be a burden" to her son and his family. Tariq might understand, at least to some degree, the concern for privacy that leads Americans to keep to themselves in ways people in his own country would rarely do.

If Tariq misinterpreted this situation, he might well become unfriendly and even hostile to Mr. Wilson and his wife. His host family relationship would end. He would then lose a good opportunity to socialize, to meet Americans in age groups other than that of his fellow students, and to learn from Mr. Wilson about the engineering profession as it is practiced in the United States.

If, on the other hand, Tariq understood the nursing home situation in the same way the Wilsons probably do, he might go on to develop a closer and more rewarding relationship with the Wilson family.

So, understanding Americans can be beneficial. Misunderstanding them can eliminate opportunities and produce unwarranted negative feelings. This book can help foreign visitors understand U.S. Americans and thereby better achieve their own goals while in the United States.

HOW MUCH GENERALIZING
IS ACCEPTABLE?

Who are these Americans? The United States of America covers a land area of 3,531,901 square miles (9,147,582 sq. km.) and is inhabited by some 310,000,000 individuals. According to 2009 census estimates, population density ranges from 1,184 people per square mile (438 per sq. km.) in the state of New Jersey to 1.2 per square mile (0.46 per sq. km.) in the state of Alaska. There are deserts, plains, wetlands, tundra, forests, and snow-covered mountains.

America's population reflects remarkable ethnic diversity. While the majority of Americans are non-Hispanic white (to use the official terminology), about 15 percent of the population is Hispanic, another 13 percent is African American, about 5 percent is Asian, and about 1 percent is Native American. In the year 2007, there were 38.1 million foreign-born residents in the United States, representing 12.6 percent of the total population. Terms such as *Asian American*, *Italian American*, and *Arab American* are commonly used and reflect the persistence of various ethnic heritages within the country.

America's population includes Catholics, Protestants of many denominations, Jews of several persuasions, Muslims, Buddhists, animists, and others. Some people believe in no Supreme Being or higher power. There are people who have many years of formal education and people who have nearly none. There are the very rich as well as the very poor. There are Republicans, Democrats, independents, libertarians, socialists, Communists, and adherents of other political views as well. There are people in thousands of lines of work, from abalone divers to zoo attendants. Some live in urban areas, some in rural locations.

Given all this diversity, can one meaningfully talk about Americans? Probably so, if one is careful. Consider it this way:

- *In some ways all people are alike.* Anatomists and physiologists study ways in which the structure and functions of the human body operate, regardless of race, religion, income, or political opinion. A human pancreatic gland knows no political persuasion.
- *In some ways every person is unique.* Psychologists study the manner in which each person's characteristics and experiences give rise to his or her particular attitudes and behavior. Some social scientists use the term "multilayered self" to refer to the idea that each person embodies a unique combination of factors such as nationality, regional background, ethnicity, physical traits, economic status, religion, level of education, sexual orientation, occupation, and group memberships.

■ *In some ways groups of people resemble each other.* One can find common characteristics among such groups as physicists, mothers, Olympic athletes, and farm laborers. One can also find common characteristics among nationality groups—U.S. Americans, Nigerians, Irish, Egyptians, and so on. Members of these nationality groups share certain common experiences that result in similarities among them—even if, like many Americans, they do not recognize those similarities themselves. U.S. Americans might all seem different from each other until you compare them as a group with the Japanese, for example. Then it becomes clear that certain attitudes and behaviors are much more characteristic of the Americans and others are far more typical of the Japanese.

The ideas, values, and behaviors that comprise "American culture" are generally those of the European American, middle-class, Protestant males who long dominated the society. Until fairly recently, people in that category held the large majority of the country's most influential positions. They have been the political, business, and military leaders, the university presidents, the scientists, the journalists, and the novelists who have successfully exerted influence on the society.

Obviously, not all Americans are such people. Catholics and Jews have become noticeably more integrated into the society in the past fifty years or so. The non–European American portion of the population is growing, and in fact some demographers predict that by the middle of the twenty-first century European Americans will be in the minority, as is the case even now in some large American cities. That shift has already had some effects on the general culture. An increasing number of non–European Americans, non-Protestants (mainly Catholics and Jews and, increasingly, Mormons), and women have achieved influential positions. Nevertheless, society's main ideals have been forged by that middle-class, European American, Protestant group. Members of other groups usually (not always) agree with those ideals, at least on some level. Historically, millions of immigrants have, at least over the space of a generation or two, accommodated themselves to them. International visitors can, though, find Americans who actively oppose the ideas and behaviors that generally define American culture.

Foreign visitors will find many variations on the "American culture" portrayed in this book. There are, as has already been suggested, regional, ethnic, family, and individual differences. Southerners (which really means people from the southeastern states, except Florida, which is home to many transplants from northern states and from Cuba) are known for their hospitality, relatively slow pace of life, and respect for tradition. New Englanders are often regarded as relatively quiet and inexpressive. Texans are deemed more forceful and openly self-confident than their relatively self-effacing Midwestern compatriots.

Variations related to ethnic background are also noticeable. Chinese Americans seem to place a higher value on education than do Americans in general. African Americans, at least those who live in mainly black communities, tend to be more verbally and physically expressive than European Americans. So do Italian Americans.

Growing up in ethnically and culturally different situations, Americans learn the attitudes and behaviors of their families. Families vary in many ways, such as how they deal with disagreement or conflict, the degree to which they share their thoughts and feelings, and their level of comfort with being touched by other people. ("I grew up in a family where people didn't touch each other much," you may hear an American explain.)

And, of course, there are individual differences. Some people are more outgoing than others, or more aggressive, more adventurous, more contemplative, or more focused on their own inner feelings.

Generalizations such as the ones in this book are subject to exception and refinement. Readers ought not to believe that this book will enable them to understand all U.S. Americans. It will not. Readers are advised to observe Americans with their minds open to new observations and new interpretations.

ON ASKING "WHY?"

This is not a philosophical or political book. It is intended to be a practical guide for understanding U.S. American culture. It barely concerns itself with the question of *why* Americans act as they do. There is a great temptation among people who encounter cultural differences to ask why those differences exist. "Why do they talk so loud?" "Why do they love their dogs more than their children?" "Why are they so hard to get to know?" "Why do they smile and act so friendly when they can't even remember my name?" And there are countless other such questions, most of them ultimately unanswerable. The fact is that people do what they do. The "whys"—the reasons—probably cannot be determined. The general characteristics of American culture have been ascribed by various observers to such factors as its temperate climate; its nineteenth-century history as a large country with an open frontier to the west, its rich natural resources; its citizens' origins among dissenters and the lower classes in Europe; its high level of technological development; the influence of Christianity; the declining influence of Christianity; its capitalist economic system; and "God's benevolent attention."

No one can say which of the many explanations of American cultural patterns is correct. The late James Bostain, who trained U.S. Department of State officers and others bound for overseas assignments, said in his lectures that the only answer to "why" questions about cultural differences is "Because . . . ." You might ask, for example, "Why are Americans so practical?" Because their educational system emphasizes practice more than theory. Why does their educational system emphasize practice over theory? Because Americans tend to believe that theory is less important than what really works. Why do Americans tend to believe that theory is less important than what really works? Because . . . . Because . . . . Because.

Although it may be interesting to speculate about the "why" questions (especially for people from places where theory is considered more important than practice!), it is not necessary in daily dealings with Americans to understand the ultimate explanations for their behavior. This book, therefore, does not examine that topic in depth.

The assumption underlying this book's discussion of U.S. American and other cultures is that, as James Bostain put it, "People act the way they were taught to act, and they all have different teachers." There are reasons for the way people behave, even if we can't be certain what those reasons are. People who have grown up in the United States have been taught, or trained, to act in some ways and not in others. They share a culture. We will begin exploring that culture after a few words about Americans' conceptions of themselves and their attitudes toward foreigners.

HOW AMERICANS SEE THEMSELVES

It is usually helpful, when trying to understand others, to understand how we see ourselves. A few comments about Americans' self-perceptions appear here; others come later.

Americans do not usually see themselves, when they are at home, as representatives of their country, even though they are quite patriotic at times. Their government's 2003 invasion of Iraq brought forth a widespread display of American flags, which people mounted on their porches, in their front windows, and even on their cars. Usually, Americans see themselves as individuals (we will stress this point later) who are different from all other individuals, American or foreign. U.S. Americans often say they have no culture, since they often conceive of culture as an overlay of arbitrary customs to be found only in other countries. Individual Americans may think they chose their own values rather than having had their values and the assumptions on which they are based imposed on them by the society into which they were born. If asked to say something about American culture, they may be unable to answer and they may even deny that there is an American culture and become annoyed at being asked the question. "We're all individuals," they will say.

Because they think they are responsible as individuals for having chosen their basic values and their way of life, many Americans resent generalizations others make about them. Generalizations such as the ones in this book may disturb them. They may be offended by the notion that they hold certain ideas and behave in certain ways simply because they were born and raised in the United States and not because they had consciously thought about those ideas and behaviors and chosen the ones they preferred.

At the same time, Americans will readily generalize about various subgroups within their own country. Northerners have stereotypes (that is, rigid, overgeneralized, simplified notions) about Southerners, and vice versa. There are stereotypes of people from the Appalachian region and from the Midwest, feminists, European American men, politicians, rich people, minority ethnic groups, minority religious groups, Texans, New Yorkers, Californians, Iowans, and so on. We have already commented on a few of these differences and will mention more later. The point is to realize that Americans acknowledge few generalizations that can safely be made about themselves, in part because they are so individualistic and in part because they think regional and other kinds of differences completely distinguish Americans of various groups from each other.

HOW AMERICANS SEE FOREIGNERS

Like people everywhere else, Americans, as they grow up, are taught certain attitudes toward other countries and the people who live in them. Parents, teachers, schoolbooks, and the media are principal sources of information and attitudes about foreigners and foreign countries.

Americans generally believe that theirs is a superior country, probably the greatest country in the world. It is economically and militarily powerful, even if it suffers temporary setbacks; its people are creative and energetic; its influence extends to all parts of the globe. Americans generally believe their democratic political system is the best possible one, since it gives all citizens the right and opportunity to try to influence government policy and since it protects citizens from arbitrary government actions. They also believe the system is superior because it gives them the freedom to complain about its failings. Americans generally believe their country's free-market economic system has enabled them to enjoy one of the highest standards of living ever.

Travel writer Bill Bryson puts it this way:

> When you grow up in America you are inculcated from the earliest age with the belief—no, the understanding—that America is the richest and most powerful nation on earth because God likes us best. It has the most perfect form of government, the most exciting sporting events, the tastiest food and amplest portions, the largest cars, most productive farms, the most devastating nuclear arsenal and the friendliest, most decent and most patriotic folks on earth. Countries just don't come any better. (1989, 270–271)

Even during the worldwide economic recession of the late 2000s—with its high unemployment, two continuing wars, and partisan gridlock in Washington, D.C.—polls showed that most Americans remained optimistic about their country's future. And they continued to believe that their country was better off than others. They continued to believe in the idea of "American exceptionalism"—that is, the idea that America has a special, enlightened place among nations.

If Americans consider their country to be superior, then it cannot be surprising that they often consider other countries to be inferior. The people in those other countries are assumed to be less intelligent, hardworking, and sensible than Americans are. Political systems in other countries are often assumed to be inadequately responsive to the public and excessively tolerant of corruption and abuse; other economic systems are regarded as less efficient than that of the United States. People from other countries (with the exception of Canadians and Northern Europeans, who are generally viewed with respect) tend to be perceived as underdeveloped Americans, prevented by their "primitive" or inefficient economic and social systems and by their quaint cultural customs from achieving what they could if they were Americans. U.S. Americans tend to suppose that people born in other countries are less fortunate than they are and that most would prefer to live in the United States. The fact that millions of foreigners do seek to enter or remain in the U.S. illegally every year supports this view. (The fact that billions of foreigners do not seek entry is ignored or discounted.)

Visitors from abroad often find that Americans in general are condescending to them, treating them a bit (or very much) like children who have limited experience and perhaps limited intelligence. International visitors are well advised to remember that it is not malice or intentional ignorance that leads so many Americans to treat them like inferior beings. The Americans are, once again, acting the way they have been taught to act. They have been taught that they are superior, and they have learned the lesson well.

There are obviously many exceptions to the preceding generalizations. The main exceptions are those Americans who have lived or at least traveled extensively in other countries and those who have in some other way had extensive experience with people from abroad. Many Americans will also make an exception for a foreigner who has demonstrated some skill, personality trait, or intellectual capability that commands respect. British writers, German scientists, Korean martial arts specialists, and Kenyan runners, among others, readily have many Americans' respect.

ON DESCRIBING AMERICANS

If you ask a Turk, for example, who is visiting the United States whether the Americans she has met think and act the way Turks normally do, she'll probably say, without any hesitation, "No!" If you then ask her to explain how the Americans differ from the Turks, she will probably hesitate and then offer something like, "Well, that's hard to say."

It is indeed difficult to explain how one cultural group differs from another. Anthropologists, psychologists, sociologists, journalists, commu nication experts, and others have tried various approaches to explaining the distinctive features of different cultures. There is no single best way to proceed.

Our approach to helping international visitors understand Americans is divided into three parts. Part I presents some general ideas (or theories) about cultural differences and American culture as it compares with others. Part II gives information about specific aspects of American life, including friendships, social relationships, politics, religion, and the media. Part III concludes the book by offering guidelines for responding constructively to cultural differences.

PART I

General Ideas About American Culture

How does U.S. American culture differ from others? There are several ways to address that question. The first way we will use, in chapter 1, is to consider the values and assumptions that Americans live by. The second is to examine their "communicative style;" we do this in chapter 2. Chapter 3 is about the way Americans reason and think about things. Chapter 4, the last in Part I, addresses U.S. American customs.

American Values and Assumptions

As people grow up, they learn certain values and assumptions from their parents and other relatives, their peers, teachers, religious officials, the Internet, television, movies, books, newspapers, and perhaps other sources. Values and assumptions are closely related, but there are some differences between them. The ways in which different cultures approach the issue of appropriate roles for men and women provide a good example of the relationship between values and assumptions. Values are ideas about what is right and wrong, desirable and undesirable, normal and abnormal, proper and improper. In some cultures, for example, people are taught that men and women should inhabit separate social worlds, with some activities clearly in the men's domain and others clearly in the women's. In other cultures men and women are considered to have more or less equal access to most social roles.

Assumptions, as used here, are the postulates—the unquestioned givens—about people, life, and the way things are. People in some societies assume, for example, that family life proceeds most harmoniously when women stay at home with their children and men earn money by working outside the home. In other societies people assume that family life works best when outside work and child-rearing responsibilities are shared by men and women. In some societies people assume that when a mature man and woman are alone together, sexual activity will almost certainly occur. In others, platonic (that is, lacking a sexual element) friendship between unmarried men and women is assumed to be possible.

Scholars discuss the definition of values, assumptions, and other terms that appear in this book. But this book is not for scholars. It is for international visitors who want some basic understanding of U.S. Americans. Readers who want to explore more scholarly works on the issues raised here can refer to the References and Suggested Readings section at the end of this book.

People who grow up in a particular culture share certain values and assumptions. That does not mean they all share exactly the same values to exactly the same extent. It does mean that most of them, most of the time, agree with each other's ideas about what is right and wrong, desirable and undesirable, and so on. They also agree, mostly, with each other's assumptions about human nature, social relationships, and so on.

Any list of values and assumptions is inherently arbitrary. Depending on how one defines and categorizes things, one could make a three-item or a thirty-item list of a country's major values and assumptions. The list offered here has eight entries, each covering a set of closely related values and assumptions commonly held by U.S. Americans:

- Individualism, freedom, competitiveness, and privacy
- Equality
- Informality
- The future, change, and progress
- Goodness of humanity
- Time
- Achievement, action, work, and materialism
- Directness and assertiveness

Because individualism is so vital to understanding American society and culture, it receives more attention than the other values discussed here.

INDIVIDUALISM, FREEDOM, COMPETITIVENESS, AND PRIVACY

Individualism

The most important thing to understand about Americans is probably their devotion to individualism. They are trained from very early in their lives to consider themselves as separate individuals who are responsible for their own situations in life and their own destinies. They are not trained to see themselves as members of a close-knit, interdependent family, religious group, tribe, nation, or any other collective.

You can see it in the way Americans treat their children. One day I was at a local shopping mall, waiting in line to buy an Orange Julius (a cool drink made in a blender with orange juice, ice, and some other ingredients). Behind me in the line was a woman with two children, a boy who was about three years old and a girl who was about five. The boy had his hand in a pocket of his blue jeans, and I could hear that he had some coins in there.

The boy asked his mother, "Can I get an Orange Julius?"

"No," she said to him. "You don't have enough money left for an Orange Julius. Remember you bought that cookie a while ago. You do have enough money for a hot dog. So you could get a hot dog now if you want to. Or, you could save your money, and sometime later when you have enough money, we could come back here and you could get an Orange Julius."

When I tell this story to people from other countries, they usually react with disbelief. The idea that a child so young would even have his own money to spend, let alone be expected to decide how to spend it, seems beyond their comprehension. Here is a young boy whose own mother is forcing him to make a decision that affects not just his situation at the moment—whether or not to get a hot dog—but will also affect him at some unspecified time in the future, when he will have more money.

But when Americans hear this story, they usually understand it perfectly well. This mother is helping her son learn to make his own decisions and to be accountable for his own money. Some American parents might not expect a three-year-old to make a decision about how to spend money, but they certainly understand what the mother is doing. She is getting her son ready for a world in which he will be responsible for his choices and their consequences. Even his own mother won't be helping him later in life, and he needs to be prepared.

This particular mother may or may not have owned a copy of Dr. Benjamin Spock's famous book, *Dr. Spock's Baby and Child Care*, to which millions of American parents have long turned for information and advice on raising their children. A recent version of the book makes this observation:

> In the United States . . . very few children are raised to believe that their principal destiny is to serve their family, their country, or their God [as is the practice in some other countries]. Generally children [in the United States] are given the feeling that they can set their own aims and occupation in life, according to their inclinations. We are raising them to be rugged individualists . . . (1998, 7)

The ideal U.S. American rugged individualist moves out of his or her parents' home after completing secondary school, either to go to college or take on a job. A major consequence of the early-2000s economic depression was the large number of young people who were compelled by financial difficulties to remain in, or move back into, their parents' home. Most Americans consider such situations deeply unfortunate.

Research by social scientists indicates that the culture of the United States is among the most individualistic in the world. From the viewpoint of many international visitors, American individualism is well exemplified by the phenomenon of the "vanity" license plate. Instead of settling for a license plate that contains whatever random letters and numbers their state sends them, automobile owners can pay an extra fee and get a license plate that conveys a message of their own choosing. The plate might convey something about their outlook on life (such as O2 BE ME), political opinion (BUSHLIES), religious views (ATHIEST), hobby (DANCR), or self-image, (STUDLY). Vanity plates enable a person to stand out from the crowd.

Americans are trained to conceive of themselves as separate individuals, and they assume everyone else in the world is too. When they encounter a person from abroad who seems to them excessively concerned with the opinions of parents, with following traditions, or with fulfilling obligations to others, they assume that the person feels trapped or is weak, indecisive, or "overly dependent." They assume all people must resent being in situations where they are not "free to make up their own minds." They assume, furthermore, that after living for a time in the United States, people will come to feel "liberated" from constraints arising from outside themselves and will be grateful for the opportunity to "do their own thing" and "have it their own way." As indeed, many are.

Margaret Wohlenberg was the only American student among about nine hundred Malays enrolled at the branch campus of Indiana University in Shah Alam, Malaysia. She took Psychology 101, an introductory psychology course from the Indiana University curriculum and earned a grade of A+. The other students' grades were lower. In her assessment of the class, she wrote,

> I do not think that Psych 101 is considered a very difficult course for the average freshman on the Bloomington campus [Indiana University's main location], but it is a great challenge to these [Malay] kids who have very little, if any, exposure to the concepts of Western psychology. . . . The American [while growing up] is surrounded, maybe even bombarded, by the propaganda of self-fulfillment and self-identity. Self-improvement and self-help—doing my own thing—seem at the core of American ideology.

But these are "quite unfamiliar ideas to the Malay students," Ms. Wohlenberg said. The Malay students' upbringing emphasizes the importance of family relationships and individual subservience to the family and the community.

It is this concept of themselves as individual decision makers that blinds at least some Americans to the fact that they share a culture with each other. They often have the idea, as mentioned above, that they have independently made up their own minds about the values and assumptions they hold. The notion that social factors outside themselves have made them "just like everyone else" in important ways offends their sense of dignity.

Americans, then, consider the ideal person to be an individualistic, self-reliant, independent person. They assume, incorrectly, that people from elsewhere share this value and this self-concept. In the degree to which they glorify "the individual" who stands alone and makes his or her own decisions, Americans are quite distinctive.

The individual that Americans idealize prefers an atmosphere of freedom, where neither the government nor any other external force or agency dictates what the individual does. For Americans, the idea of individual freedom has strong, positive connotations.

By contrast, people from many other cultures regard some of the behavior Americans legitimize with the label "individual freedom" to be self-centered and lacking in consideration for others. Mr. Wilson (see pages xx) and his mother are good American individualists, living their own lives and interfering as little as possible with others. Tariq Nassar found their behavior almost immoral.

Foreign visitors who understand the degree to which Americans are imbued with the notion that the free, self-reliant individual is the ideal kind of human being will be able to understand many aspects of American behavior and thinking that otherwise might not make sense. A very few of many possible examples:

- Americans see as heroes those individuals who "stand out from the crowd" by doing something first, longest, most often, or otherwise "best." Real-life examples are President Abraham Lincoln, aviators Charles Lindbergh and Amelia Earhart, civil-rights leader Martin Luther King, Microsoft founder Bill Gates, Apple founder Steve Jobs, and football player Tom Brady. Perhaps the best example from the world of fiction is the American cowboy as portrayed by such motion-picture actors as John Wayne and Clint Eastwood.
- Americans admire people who have overcome adverse circumstances (for example, poverty or a physical handicap) and "succeeded" in life. Barack Obama is one example (although not everyone agrees with his ideas). Media mogul Oprah Winfrey is another.
- Many Americans do not display the degree of respect for their parents that people in more traditional or family-oriented societies commonly do. From their point of view, being born to particular parents is a sort of historical or biological accident. The parents fulfill their responsibilities to their children while the children are young, but when the children reach "the age of independence," the close child-parent tie is loosened, occasionally even broken.
- It is not unusual for Americans who are beyond the age of about twenty-two (and sometimes younger) and who are still living with their parents to pay their parents for room and board. Elderly parents living with their

grown children may do likewise. Paying for room and board is a way of showing independence, self-reliance, and responsibility for oneself.

- Americans buy huge numbers of self-help and how-to books, reflecting their inclination to do things for themselves rather than seek help from others. Foreign visitors are often struck by the frequency with which their requests for help are greeted not with offers of the desired help but with instructions for helping themselves.

Certain phrases common among Americans capture their devotion to individualism: "You'll have to decide that for yourself." "If you don't look out for yourself, no one else will." "Look out for Number One" (or, reflecting the growing influence of Hispanics in the country, "Look out for *Numero Uno*"). "Be your own best friend."

In the late 1900s, social scientists who studied cultural differences published extensively about differences between individualistic and collectivistic societies. Some of their articles offered observations that can be quite helpful to collectivists and others trying to understand American culture. Two examples follow; both mention ideas that are addressed elsewhere in this book. The first passage is from Richard Brislin:

> To transcend the distance between self and others, people in individualistic societies have to develop a certain set of social skills. These include public speaking, meeting others quickly and putting them at ease . . . , making a good first impression, and being well mannered, cordial, and verbally fluent during initial encounters with others. These skills are not as necessary for collectivists. When it comes time for a person to meet unknown others in the larger society, members of the collective act as go-betweens and make introductions, describe the person's accomplishments and abilities, and so forth. . . . In short, individualists have to rely on themselves and to develop skills that allow them to branch out in society. Collectivists have a supportive group that assists in this same goal. (1990, 21–22)

Collectivists will want to understand that individualists are, according to Harry Triandis, Richard Brislin, and C. H. Hui, likely to:

- pay relatively little attention to groups (including families) they belong to

- be proud of their accomplishments and expect others to feel proud of their own accomplishments
- be more involved with their peers and less involved with people who are older or more senior in an organization, and be more comfortable in social relationships with those who are their equals and less comfortable in relationships with people of higher or lower status than themselves
- act competitively
- define status in terms of accomplishments (what they have achieved through their own efforts) rather than relationships or affiliations (the family or other group to which they belong)
- seem relatively unconcerned about being cooperative or having smooth interpersonal relations
- seem satisfied with relationships that appear superficial and short-term
- be ready to "do business" very soon after meeting, without much time spent on preliminary getting-acquainted conversation
- place great importance on written rules, procedures, and deadlines, such as leases, contracts, and appointments
- be suspicious of, rather than automatically respectful toward, people in authority
- assume that people in general need to be alone some of the time and prefer to take care of problems by themselves. (1988, 271)

Let's elaborate for a moment on just one of these ideas: act competitively. Individualistic Americans naturally see themselves as being in competition with others. Competitiveness pervades U.S. society. It is obvious in the attention given to athletic events and to star athletes, who are praised for being "real competitors." It is also obvious in schools and co-curricular activities for children, where games and contests are assumed to be desirable and beneficial. Competitiveness is less obvious when it is in the minds of people who are persistently comparing themselves with others: who is faster, smarter, richer, better-looking; whose children are the most successful; whose husband is the best provider or the best cook or the best lover; which salesperson sold the most during the past quarter; who earned his first million dollars at the earliest age; and so on. People who are competing with others are essentially alone, trying to maintain their superiority and, implicitly, their separateness from others.

Closely associated with the idea of the self-sufficient individual is the typical U.S. American assumption that each individual has a fundamental identity: a core of ideas, attitudes, and behaviors that make up the "self." Along with that comes the assumption that people everywhere have a similar view of themselves and their "personal identities."

But that is not the case. "One of the things I've learned to love about Japan," wrote an American visiting professor in that country,

> is its freedom from the classic Western notion that a person is a stable, unchanging, continuous entity, some essential self. In Japan, behavior and even personality depend partly on context, on the rules of a given situation. (Davidson, 101–102)

Privacy

Also closely associated with the value they place on individualism is the importance Americans assign to privacy. U.S. Americans tend to assume that most people "need some time to themselves" or "some time alone" to think about things or recover their spent psychological energy. Most Americans have great difficulty understanding people who always want to be with another person, who dislike being alone. Americans tend to regard such people as weak or dependent.

If the parents can afford it, each child will have his or her own bedroom. Having one's own bedroom, even as an infant, inculcates in a person the notion that she is entitled to a place of her own where she can be by herself and—notice—keep her possessions. She will have her clothes, her toys, her books, and so on. These things will be hers and no one else's.

Americans assume that people have their "private thoughts" that might never be shared with anyone. Doctors, lawyers, psychiatrists, and others have rules governing "confidentiality" that are intended to prevent information about their clients' personal situations from becoming known to others. Corporations and other organizations have "privacy policies" intended to assure that information they obtain about individual clients or members will not be made known to others. "Hacking" into computer systems to obtain information about other people is illegal.

Americans' attitudes about privacy can be difficult for people from other countries to understand. For example, Americans will often give visitors a tour of their house, including the bedrooms, which people from many other places consider private. They may speak quite openly, even to strangers, about personal or family problems that would be kept confidential elsewhere. Yet, in Americans' minds, there are boundaries that other people are simply not supposed to cross. When such boundaries are crossed, the Americans' bodies will visibly stiffen and their manner will become cool and aloof.

On the other hand, users of the social-networking site Facebook will often reveal information about themselves that, outside the environment of a computer network, they would probably keep to themselves.

EQUALITY

Americans are also distinctive in the degree to which they believe in the ideal, as stated in their Declaration of Independence, that "all men are created equal." Although they sometimes violate the ideal in their daily lives, particularly in matters of interracial relationships and sometimes relationships among people from different social classes, U.S. Americans have a deep faith that in some fundamental way all people (at least all American people) are of equal value, that no one is born superior to anyone else. "One person, one vote," they say, conveying the idea that any person's opinion is as valid and worthy of attention as any other person's opinion. U.S. Americans generally admire a higher-status person who acts "down to earth" or does not "put on airs." By wearing blue jeans in his public appearances, for example, multimillionaire Apple founder Steve Jobs can appear to be a "regular guy."

Americans are usually uncomfortable when someone treats them with obvious deference. They dislike being the subjects of open displays of respect—being bowed to, deferred to, or treated as though they could do no wrong or make no unreasonable requests. They may even be offended at the suggestion that there are social classes in the United States, so strong is their belief in the ideal of equality.

It is not just males who are created equal, in the American mindset, but females too. While Americans may violate the ideal in practice (for example, women continue to be paid less, on average, than do men in similar jobs), they do generally assume that women and men are equal, deserving of the same level of respect. Women may be different from men but are not inferior to them. In fact, as women in the early 2000s came to hold a larger portion of jobs, get more formal education, and attain more influential positions, concern arose in some circles that men were inferior to women, or at least less able to adjust their behavior and attitudes to the modern era.

This is not to say that Americans make no distinctions among themselves as a result of such factors as gender, age, wealth, occupation, level of education, or income. They do. But the distinctions are acknowledged in relatively subtle ways. Tone of voice, order of speaking, choice of words, seating arrangements—such are the means by which Americans acknowledge status differences among themselves. People of higher status are more likely to speak first, louder, and longer. They sit at the head of the table or in the most comfortable chair. They feel free to interrupt other speakers more than others feel free to interrupt them. The higher-status person may put a hand on the shoulder of the lower-status person. If there is touching between the people involved, the higher-status person will touch first.

Foreigners who are accustomed to more obvious displays of respect (such as bowing, averting eyes from the face of the higher-status person, or using honorific titles) often overlook the ways in which Americans show respect for higher-status people. They think, incorrectly, that Americans are generally unaware of status differences and disrespectful of other people. What is distinctive about the American outlook on the matter of equality are the underlying assumptions that (1) no matter what a person's initial station in life, he or she has the opportunity to achieve high standing and (2) everyone, no matter how unfortunate, deserves some basic level of respect.

Although some research indicates that it is less and less the case, U.S. Americans in general hold to the idea that they can move up the social ladder if they get a good education and work hard enough (*The New York Times*, 2005).

INFORMALITY

Their notions of equality lead Americans to be quite informal in their general behavior and in their relationships with other people. Store clerks and restaurant servers, for example, may introduce themselves by their first (given) names and treat customers in a casual, friendly manner. American clerks, like other Americans, have been trained to believe that they are as valuable as anyone else, even if they happen to be engaged at a given time in an occupation that others might consider lowly. This informal behavior can outrage visitors from abroad who hold high status in countries where people do not assume that "all men are created equal." Meanwhile, that American clerk is likely to feel offended by a customer who treats her "disrespectfully," speaking to her brusquely or seeming to order her about.

Relationships among students, teachers, and coworkers in American society are often quite informal, as the following example illustrates. Liz, a staff member at a university international office, invited a group of French exchange students along with their American teachers and several coworkers to her home for dinner. When the guests arrived, she welcomed them by saying, "Make yourselves at home." She showed them where to find the food and drinks in the kitchen and introduced them to some of the other guests. The French students then served themselves and sat with the other guests in small groups throughout the house, eating and talking. The young son of one of the American guests entertained them with jokes. When it was time to leave, several of the American guests stayed to help Liz clean up.

Later, in describing the dinner party, the French students remarked that such an event would almost never happen in their country. First, they were surprised that Liz, whom they had met only twice before, had invited them into her home. Moreover, they were impressed that the teachers and students and the international office coworkers and their family members socialized so easily. Even though they held positions of different status at work and were of different ages, they seemed to interact effortlessly.

People from societies where general behavior is more formal than it is in the United States are struck by Americans' informal speech, dress, and body language. Americans use idiomatic speech and slang on most occasions, reserving formal speech for public events and fairly formal situations. Even while giving a formal speech or presentation they may move about—behavior that, in some cultures, is seen as disrespectful toward the audience. U.S. Americans of almost any station in life can be seen in public wearing jeans, sandals, or other informal clothing. People slouch in chairs or lean on walls or furniture when they talk, rather than maintaining an erect posture.

A brochure advertising a highly regarded liberal arts college contained a photograph of the college president, dressed in shorts and an old T-shirt, jogging past one of the classroom buildings on his campus. Americans are likely to find the photograph appealing: "Here is a college president who's just like anyone else. He doesn't think he's too good for us."

Similarly, U.S. President George W. Bush frequently allowed himself to be photographed in his jogging clothes while out for one of his frequent runs or in work clothes while clearing weeds at his Texas ranch. President Barack Obama was often photographed playing basketball, wearing shorts and a T-shirt.

The superficial friendliness for which Americans are so well known is related to their informal, egalitarian approach to other people. "Hi!" they will say to just about anyone, or "Howya doin?" (that is, "How are you doing?" or "How are you?"). This behavior reflects not so much a special interest in the person addressed as a concern (not conscious) for showing that one is a "regular guy," part of a group of normal, pleasant people—like the jogging college president and the jogging president of his superpower country.

More ideas about American notions of friendship appear in Part II.

THE FUTURE, CHANGE, AND PROGRESS

Americans are generally less concerned about history and traditions than are people from older societies. "History doesn't matter," many of them will say, or "It's the future that counts." They look ahead. They have the idea that what happens in the future is within their control, or at least subject to their influence. The mature, sensible person, they think, sets goals for the future, writes them down, and works systematically toward them. When asked about their goals, as they commonly are in job interviews ("Where do you want to be in ten years?"), most Americans have a ready reply. If they don't, they are likely to apologize for their apparent inadequacy ("I'm sorry, but I haven't figured that out yet.").

Americans believe that people, as individuals or working cooperatively together, can change most aspects of their physical and social environments if they decide to do so, then make appropriate plans and get to work. Changes will presumably produce improvements. New things are better than old things.

Closely associated with their assumption that they can bring about desirable changes in the future is the Americans' assumption that their physical and social environments are subject to human domination or control. Early Americans cleared forests, drained swamps, and altered the course of rivers in order to "build" the country. Contemporary Americans have gone to the moon in part just to prove they could do so. "If you want to be an American," says cross-cultural trainer L. Robert Kohls, "you have to believe you can fix it." Crooked teeth, bulging waistlines, and wrinkled faces are all subject to improvement. Witness the amount of money Americans spend on orthodontics, diets and weight-loss products, and plastic surgery.

"The difficult takes a while," according to a saying often attributed to the United States Marine Corps. "The impossible takes a little longer."

The typical American sense of personal power—the belief that they can and should make things happen—does not exist in many other cultures. The fundamental American belief in progress and a better future contrasts sharply with the fatalistic (Americans are likely to use that term with a negative or critical connotation) attitude that characterizes people from many other cultures, notably Latin American, Asian, and Middle Eastern, where there is a pronounced reverence for the past. In those cultures the future is often considered to be in the hands of fate, God, or at least the few powerful people or families that dominate the society. The idea that people in general can somehow shape their own futures seems naïve, arrogant, or even sacrilegious.

Americans are generally impatient with people they see as passively accepting conditions that are less than desirable. "Why don't they do something about it?" Americans will ask. Americans don't realize that a large portion of the world's population sees the world around them not as something they can change, but rather as something to which they must submit, or at least something with which they must seek to live in harmony.

GOODNESS OF HUMANITY

The future cannot be better if people in general are not fundamentally good and improvable. Americans assume that human nature is basically good, not basically evil. International visitors will see them doing many things that are based on this assumption. Some examples will help.

Getting More Education or Training. Formal education is not just for young people. It's for everyone. Many postsecondary students are adults who seek to "improve themselves" or to change careers by learning more or earning a degree. Newspaper articles at graduation time often feature grandmothers or grandfathers who have returned to school late in life and earned a college diploma. Educational institutions offer online courses, night and weekend classes, and correspondence courses so that people who have full-time jobs or who live far from a college or university have the opportunity to get more education.

"Continuing" educational opportunities in the form of workshops, seminars, or training programs are widely available. Through them people can learn about a huge array of topics, from being a better parent to investing money wisely to behaving more assertively. Professional development in many lines of work, such as teaching, nursing, and law, comes in the form of workshops or seminars.

Rehabilitation. Except in extreme cases where it would clearly be futile, efforts are made to rehabilitate people who have lost some physical capacity as a result of injury or illness. A person who learns to walk again after a debilitating accident is widely admired. Bicycle racer Lance Armstrong was acclaimed for continuing his career after overcoming testicular cancer.

Rehabilitation is not just for the physically infirm but for those who have failed socially as well. Jails, prisons, and detention centers are intended at least as much to train inmates to be socially useful as they are to punish them. A widespread (but not universally held) assumption is that people who violate the law do so more because of adverse environmental conditions such as poverty, domestic violence, or the media than because they themselves are irredeemably evil individuals.

Belief in Democratic Government. We have already discussed some of the assumptions that underlie the American belief that a democratic form of government is best—assumptions about individualism, freedom, and equality. Another assumption is that people can make life better for themselves and others through the actions of governments they choose.

Voluntarism. It is not just through the actions of governments or other formal bodies that life can be improved but through the actions of citizen volunteers as well. Many international visitors are awed by the array of activities Americans support on a voluntary basis: parent-teacher organizations in elementary and secondary schools, community "service clubs" that raise money for worthy causes, organizations of families that play host to foreign students, "clean-up, paint-up, fix-up" campaigns to beautify communities, organizations working to preserve wilderness areas, and on and on.

I myself volunteer with the National Park Service. In Rocky Mountain National Park, which is near my summer home, I have painted picnic tables, repaired fences, cleared fallen trees from roadsides, answered visitors' questions about hiking trails, and helped collect water samples from creeks for scientists to study. My wife volunteers in the local public library, where she checks in and reshelves books, searches for lost or misshelved items, and generally puts things back in their proper places. Sociologist Claude Fischer goes so far as to assert that such voluntarism is "a central feature of American culture and character" (2010, 10).

International visitors who plan to be in the United States for an extended period will find that volunteering with a service organization will afford them a more sophisticated understanding of at least a subset of Americans, as well as opportunities to establish closer relationships with some natives.

Educational Campaigns. When Americans perceive a social problem, they are likely (often on a voluntary basis) to establish an "educational campaign" to "make the public aware" of the dangers of something and to induce people to take preventive or corrective action. Thus there are campaigns concerning tobacco, addictive drugs, alcohol, domestic abuse, handguns, and many specific diseases. Often these groups are started by someone who has either suffered personally from the problem or lost a loved one to it.

Self-help. Americans assume themselves to be improvable. We have already mentioned their participation in various educational and training programs. Mention has also been made of the array of "self-help" and "how-to" books Americans buy as well as of the number of group activities they join in order to make themselves "better." Through things they read or groups they join, Americans can stop smoking, stop using alcohol, lose weight, improve their physical condition or memory or reading speed, manage their time and money more effectively, become better at their jobs, and seek to improve themselves in countless other ways.

"Where there's a will, there's a way," U.S. Americans say. People who want to make things better can do so if only they have a strong enough motivation.

"Just do it!"—the Nike slogan—has an all-American sound.

TIME

For Americans, time is a resource that, like water or coal, can be used well or poorly. "Time is money," they say. "You only get so much time in this life; you'd best use it wisely." As Americans are trained to see things, the future will not be better than the past or the present unless people use their time for constructive, future-oriented activities. Thus, Americans admire a "well-organized" person, one who has a list of things to do—either on a piece of paper or in a personal digital assistant—and a schedule for doing them. The ideal person is punctual (that is, arrives at the scheduled time for a meeting or event) and is considerate of other people's time (that is, does not "waste people's time" with conversation or other activity that has no visible, beneficial outcome).

Early in his long and productive career, American anthropologist Edward T. Hall lived and worked on reservations belonging to two Native

American Indian groups, the Navajo and the Hopi. He discovered that the Native American's notion of time was very different from the one he learned growing up as a European American man. In describing his experience on the reservation, Hall later wrote,

> During my five-year stay on the reservations, I found that, in general, the Indians believed that whites were crazy, although they didn't tell us that. We were always hurrying to get someplace when that place would still be there whenever we arrived. Whites had a kind of devil inside who seemed to drive them unmercifully. That devil's name was Time. (1992, 218)

The American attitude toward time is not necessarily shared by others, especially non-Europeans. Most people on our planet are more likely to conceive of time as something that is simply there, around them, not something to "use." One of the more difficult things many international businesspeople and students in the United States must adjust to is the notion that time must be saved whenever possible and used wisely every day.

In their efforts to use their time wisely, Americans are sometimes seen by international visitors as automatons, inhuman creatures who are so tied to their clocks, their schedules, and their daily planners that they cannot participate in or enjoy the human interactions that are necessary to a fulfilling life. "They are like little machines running around," one international visitor said.

The premium Americans place on efficiency is closely related to their concepts of the future, change, and time. To do something efficiently is to do it in the way that is quickest and requires the smallest expenditure of resources. This may be why e-mail and text messages have become such popular means of communication in American society. Students commonly correspond with their professors by e-mail or text message rather than waiting to talk with them during their office hours. Likewise, businesspeople frequently check their electronic mail not just while on the job but also before and after work, on weekends, and even while on vacation. Popular magazines offer suggestions for more efficient ways to shop, cook, clean house, do errands, raise children, tend the yard, and on and on. The Internet provides immediate access to all kinds of information and products. Americans have come to expect instant responses to phone calls, e-mails, text messages, faxes, and other forms of communication. Many quickly become impatient if the responses aren't immediate, even when there is no apparent urgency.

In this context the "fast-food industry" is an excellent example of an American cultural product. McDonald's, KFC, Pizza Hut, and other fast-food establishments prosper in a country where many people want to minimize the amount of time spent preparing and eating meals. The millions of Americans who take their meals at fast-food restaurants cannot be interested in lingering over their food while talking with friends, in the way millions of Europeans do. As McDonald's restaurants have spread around the world, they have come to symbolize American culture, bringing not just hamburgers but an emphasis on speed, efficiency, and shiny cleanliness. The typical American food, some observers argue, is fast food.

Also in this context, it will surprise many visitors from Europe or Japan to see that some of the newer electronic communications devices commonly used in their countries, such as wands to pay for purchases, are not widespread in the United States. Their admiration for technology and efficiency does not necessarily mean that U.S. Americans always have the most advanced technological devices at their disposal.

ACHIEVEMENT, ACTION, WORK, AND MATERIALISM

"He's a hard worker," one American might say in praise of another. Or, "She gets the job done." These expressions convey the typical U.S. American's admiration for a person who approaches a task conscientiously and persistently, seeing it through to a successful conclusion. More than that, these expressions convey an admiration for achievers, people whose lives center on accomplishing some physical, measurable task. Social psychologists use the term *achievement motivation* to describe people who place a high value on getting things done. Affiliation is another type of motivation, shown by people whose main intent is to establish and maintain relationships with other people. Obviously, the achievement motivation predominates in America.

Visitors from abroad commonly remark, "Americans work harder than I expected them to." (Perhaps these visitors have been excessively influenced by American movies and television programs, which are less likely to show people working than driving around in fast cars or pursuing members of the opposite sex.) While the so-called "Protestant work ethic" may have lost some of its hold on Americans, there is still a strong belief that the ideal person is a hard worker. A hard worker is one who "gets right to work" on a task, works efficiently, and completes the task in a timely way that meets reasonably high standards of quality.

Hard workers are admired not just on the job but in other aspects of life as well. Housewives, students, and people volunteering their services to charitable organizations are praised as hard workers if they achieve something noteworthy.

More generally, Americans like *action*. They do indeed believe it is important to devote significant energy to their jobs or to other daily responsibilities. Beyond that, they tend to believe they should be *doing* something most of the time. They are usually not content, as people from many countries are, to sit for long periods and talk with other people. They get restless and impatient. If they are not doing something at the moment, they should at least be making plans and arrangements for doing something later.

People without the Americans' action orientation often see Americans as frenzied, always "on the go," never satisfied, compulsively active, and often impatient. Beyond that, they may evaluate Americans negatively for being unable to relax and enjoy life's pleasures. Even recreation, for Americans, is often a matter of acquiring lavish equipment, making elaborate plans, then going somewhere to do something.

U.S. Americans tend to define and assess people according to the jobs they have. ("Who is she?" "She's the vice president in charge of personal loans at the bank.") Family backgrounds, educational attainments, and other characteristics are considered less important in identifying people than the jobs they hold.

There is usually a close relationship between the job a person has and the level of the person's income. Americans tend to measure a person's success in life by referring to the amount of money he or she has acquired and to the title or position that person has achieved. Being a bank vice president is quite respectable, but being a bank president is more so. The president gets a higher salary and more prestige. The president can also buy more things that reflect well on his or her status: a bigger house, a sports car, a boat, a vacation home, and so on.

For decades, three-quarters of incoming university students in the United States have told pollsters that earning "a lot of money" was a "very important" goal for them.

Regardless of income, Americans tend to spend money rather freely on material goods. Items that they once considered luxuries, such as personal electronic devices, large-screen television sets, cellular telephones, and electric garage-door openers are now considered necessities. Credit cards, which are widely available even to teenagers, encourage spending, and of course the scale and scope of the advertising industry is well known. Americans are often criticized for being so "materialistic," so concerned with acquiring possessions. For Americans, though, this materialistic bent is natural and proper. They have been taught that it is good to achieve, to work hard, and to acquire more material badges of their success and in the process ensure a better future for themselves and their families. And, like people elsewhere, they do what they are taught. No wonder that the high unemployment rate marking a financial recession causes a high incidence of mental health problems among Americans.

DIRECTNESS AND ASSERTIVENESS

Americans, as we've said before, generally consider themselves to be frank, open, and direct in their dealings with other people. "Let's lay our cards on the table," they say. Or, "Let's stop playing games and get to the point." These and many other common expressions convey the American's general idea that people should explicitly state what they think and what they want from other people.

Americans usually assume that conflicts or disagreements are best settled by means of forthright discussions among those involved. If I dislike something you are doing, I should tell you about it directly so you will know, clearly and from me personally, how I feel about it. Bringing in other people to mediate a dispute is commonly considered cowardly, the act of a person without enough courage to speak directly to someone else.

The word *assertive* is the adjective Americans commonly use to describe the person who plainly and directly expresses feelings and requests. People who are inadequately assertive can take "assertiveness-training classes." What many Americans consider assertive is, however, often judged as aggressive by some non-Americans and sometimes by other Americans— particularly if the person referred to is a woman.

Levels of directness, like most other aspects of interpersonal relationships, vary not just according to cultural background but also according to personalities and context. Some people are more blunt than others. Bosses can generally be more direct with subordinates than vice versa. Parents are likely to be more direct with their children than with their own parents.

Americans will often speak openly and directly to others about things they dislike, particularly in a work situation. They will try to do so in a manner they call "constructive"—that is, a manner the other person will not find offensive or unacceptable. If they do not speak openly about what is on their minds, they will often convey their reactions through facial expressions, body positions, and gestures. Americans are not taught, as people in many Asian countries are, that they should mask their emotional responses. Their words, the tone of their voices, or their facial expressions will usually reveal their feelings: anger, unhappiness and confusion, or happiness and contentment. They do not consider it improper to display these feelings, at least within limits. Many Asians feel embarrassed around Americans who are exhibiting a strong emotional response. On the other hand, as we will see in Part II, Latin Americans and Middle Easterners are generally inclined to display their emotions more openly than Americans do and view Americans as unemotional and "cold."

U.S. Americans, though, are often less direct and open than they realize. There are in fact many restrictions on their willingness to discuss things openly. It is difficult to categorize those restrictions, which are often not "logical" in the sense of being consistent with each other. Generally, though, Americans are reluctant to speak openly when:

- the topic is in an area they consider excessively personal, such as unpleasant body or mouth odors, sexual functioning, mental illness, or personal inadequacies;

- they want to decline a request that has been made of them but do not want to offend or hurt the feelings of the person who made the request;
- they are not well enough acquainted with the other person to be confident that direct discussion will be accepted in the constructive way that is intended; paradoxically,
- they know the other person very well (it might be a spouse or close friend) and they do not wish to risk giving offense and creating negative feelings by talking about some delicate problem.

A Chinese visitor invited an American couple to his apartment to share a dinner he had prepared. They complimented him warmly about the quality of his meal. "Several Americans have told me they like my cooking, " he replied, "but I cannot tell whether they are sincere or are just being polite. Do you think they really like it?" His question reflects a common confusion about when Americans can and cannot be "taken at their word."

All of this is to say that Americans, even though they see themselves as properly assertive and even though they often behave in open and direct ways, have limits on their openness. It is not unusual for them to try to avoid direct confrontations with other people when they are not confident that the interaction can be carried out in a constructive way that will result in an acceptable compromise. (Americans' ideas about the benefits of compromise are discussed later.)

There are regional variations within the United States regarding people's willingness to speak openly and directly with others. Urban Easterners have a reputation for being more blunt than people from other parts of the country, particularly the Midwest and the South, where being "nice" might be considered more important than being "honest."

International visitors often find themselves in situations where they are unsure or even unaware of what the Americans around them are thinking or feeling and are unable to find out because the Americans will not tell them directly what they have on their minds. Two examples:

Sometimes a person from another country will "smell bad" to Americans because he or she does not follow the hygienic practices, including daily bathing and the use of deodorants, that most Americans consider necessary (see chapter 16). But Americans will rarely tell another person (American or otherwise) that he or she has "body odor" because that topic is considered too sensitive.

A foreigner (or another American, for that matter) may ask a "favor" of an American who considers it inappropriate, such as wanting to borrow some money or a car or asking for help with an undertaking that will require more time than the American thinks she or he has available. The American will want to decline the request but will be reluctant to say no directly.

Americans might feel especially reluctant to refuse someone from another country directly for fear of making the person feel unwelcome or discriminated against. They will often try to convey their unwillingness indirectly by saying such things as "it's not convenient now" or by repeatedly postponing an agreed-upon time for doing something.

Despite these limitations, Americans are generally more direct and open than people from almost all other countries with the exception of Israel and Australia. They will not try to mask their emotions, as Scandinavians or Japanese tend to do. They are much less concerned with "face" (that is, avoiding embarrassment to themselves or others) than most Asians are. To them, being honest is usually more important than preserving harmony in interpersonal relationships.

Americans use the words *pushy* or *aggressive* to describe a person who is excessively assertive in voicing opinions or making requests. The line between acceptable assertiveness and unacceptable aggressiveness is difficult to draw. Iranians and people from other countries where forceful arguing and negotiating are typical forms of interaction risk being seen as aggressive or pushy when they treat Americans in the way they treat people at home. This topic is elaborated upon in chapter 2.

The Communicative
Style of Americans

Pushy Greeks. Shy Taiwanese. Opinionated Germans. Emotional Mexicans, Brazilians, and Italians. Cold British. Loud Nigerians. These are among the stereotypes or general ideas U.S. Americans have about some other nationalities. In part these stereotypes arise from differences in what the communications scholar Dean Barnlund called "communicative style."

When people communicate with each other, they exhibit a style that is strongly influenced by their culture. "Communicative style" refers to several characteristics of conversations between individuals, according to Barnlund (1989): (1) the topics people prefer to discuss, (2) their favorite forms of interaction in conversation, (3) the depth to which they want to get involved with each other, (4) the communication channels (verbal or nonverbal) on which they rely, and (5) the level of meaning (factual versus emotional) to which they are most attuned. Each of these is discussed here.

Naturally, people prefer to use their own communicative styles. Issues about communicative style rarely arise when two people from the same culture—and the same age category and gender—are together because their styles generally agree. Most people—including most Americans—are as unaware of their communicative style as they are of their basic values and assumptions. International visitors who understand something about the Americans' communicative style will be less likely to misinterpret or misjudge Americans than will those who don't know the common characteristics of interpersonal communication among Americans. They will also have a better understanding of some of the stereotypes Americans have about other nationality groups.

PREFERRED DISCUSSION TOPICS

When they first encounter another person, Americans engage in a kind of conversation they call *small talk*. The most common topic of small talk is the weather. Another very common topic is what the speakers "do," meaning, normally, what jobs they have. They may discuss their current physical surroundings—the room or building they are in, the area where they are standing, or whatever is appropriate. Later, after the preliminaries, Americans may talk about past experiences they have both had, such as watching a particular TV program, seeing a certain movie, traveling to a certain place, or eating at a particular restaurant.

Beyond these very general topics of small talk, there is variation according to the life situations of the people involved and the setting in which the conversation is taking place. Students are likely to talk about their teachers and classes; if they are of the same gender, they are likely to discuss their social lives. Adults may discuss their jobs, recreational interests, houses, or family matters. Men are likely to talk about sports or cars. Women are likely to talk about interpersonal relationships or their children or grandchildren, if they have any. It is important to remember that these are general observations and that individual Americans will differ in their preferred topics of conversation. Some men are not interested in sports, for example, and some women are.

U.S. Americans are explicitly taught not to discuss religion and politics unless they are fairly well acquainted with the people they are talking to. In public meetings Americans will openly debate political matters, but we are talking here about communicative style in interpersonal situations. Politics and religion are thought to be "controversial," and discussing a controversial topic can lead to an argument. Americans, as we will discuss under "Favorite Forms of Interaction," are taught to avoid arguments.

Unlike Americans, people from Germany, Iran, Brazil, and many other countries consider politics, and sometimes religion, to be excellent topics for informal discussion and debate. For them, discussing—and arguing about—politics is a favorite way to pass the time and to get to know other people better.

Americans generally avoid some topics because they are "too personal." Financial matters is one. To many foreigners, this may seem contradictory because Americans seem to value material wealth so highly. However, inquiries about a person's earnings or about the amount someone paid for an item are usually beyond the bounds of acceptable topics. So are body and mouth odors (as already mentioned), bodily functions, sexual behavior and responses, and fantasies. Another sensitive topic for many Americans is body weight. It is considered impolite to tell someone, especially a woman, that he or she has gained weight. On the other hand, saying that someone has lost weight or that he or she "looks slim" is a compliment. Mary, an American woman married to Dieter, a German, told me she encountered a different attitude toward body weight while visiting her husband's family in Bavaria. She was shocked that Dieter's friends and family commented so openly about how much weight he had gained while living in the United States. "If my family said that about me, I would be very insulted!" Mary exclaimed.

Upon first meeting, people from Latin America and Spain may have long interchanges about the health and well-being of each other's family members. Saudis, by contrast, often consider questions about family members, particularly women, inappropriate unless the people talking know each other well. Americans might inquire briefly about family members ("How's your wife?" or "How're the kids?"), but politeness in brief and casual encounters does not require dwelling on the subject.

As was already said, people prefer to use their own communicative styles. That means, among other things, they prefer to abide by their own ideas about conversation topics that are appropriate for a given setting.

People from other countries who have different ideas from Americans about what topics are appropriate for a particular context are likely to feel uncomfortable when they are talking with Americans. They may not feel they can participate in the conversation on an equal footing, and Americans often resist (quite unconsciously) foreigners' attempts to bring up a different topic.

Listening to American small talk leads some people from other societies to the erroneous conclusion that Americans are intellectually incapable of carrying on a discussion about anything significant. Some foreigners believe that topics more complex than weather, sports, or social lives are beyond the Americans' ability to comprehend. Foreigners should keep in mind that this is the communicative style that Americans are accustomed to; it does not necessarily reflect their level of intelligence.

FAVORITE FORMS OF INTERACTION

The typical conversation between two U.S. Americans takes a form that can be called *repartee*. No one speaks for very long. Speakers take turns frequently, often after speaking only a few sentences. "Watching a conversation between two Americans is like watching a table tennis game," a British observer said. "Your head goes back and forth and back and forth so fast it almost makes your neck hurt."

Americans tend to be impatient with people who take long turns. Such people are said to "talk too much." Many Americans have difficulty paying attention to someone who speaks more than a few sentences at a time, as Nigerians, Egyptians, and some others typically do. Americans admire conciseness, or what they call "getting to the point" (about which more is said in the next chapter).

Americans engage in far less *ritual* interaction than do many other cultural groups. Only a few ritual interchanges are common: "How are you?" "I'm fine, thank you," "Nice to meet you," "Hope to see you again," and "We'll have to get together." These things are said under certain circumstances Americans learn to recognize and, like any ritual interchange, are concerned more with form than with substance. That is, the questions are supposed to be asked and the statements are supposed to be made in particular circumstances, no matter what the people involved are feeling or what they really have in mind.

Among American women, ritual interchanges often entail compliments: "I like your hair that way," or "That dress looks good on you." Among men, gentle insults are a frequent form of interaction: "Are you still driving that old thing?"

In many Americans' opinions, people who rely heavily on the sort of ritual interchanges that are common among Japanese and Arabs are "too shy" or "too polite," unwilling to reveal their true natures and ideas.

Americans are generally impatient with long ritual interchanges about family members' health—common among Latin Americans—or invocations of a Supreme Being's goodwill—common among Arabs—considering them a waste of time and doubting their sincerity.

Of course, people from elsewhere often doubt the sincerity of the Americans' ritual interactions: "They always ask me how I am, but they don't listen to what I say. They don't really care how I am."

A third form of interaction, one that Americans tend to avoid, is *argument*. Americans imagine that an argument with another person might end their relationship. They do not generally consider arguing a sport or a pleasurable pastime. If Americans are in a discussion in which a difference of opinion is emerging, they are likely to say, "Let's not get into an argument about this." Rather than argue, they prefer to find areas of agreement, change the topic, or even physically withdraw from the situation. Not surprisingly, people who like to argue are often labeled "pushy," "aggressive," or "opinionated."

If an argument is unavoidable, Americans believe it should be conducted in calm, moderate tones and with a minimum of gesturing. Loud voices, vigorous use of arms, more than one person talking at a time—to most Americans these are signs that a physical fight, or at least an unproductive "shouting match," might develop.

They believe people should avoid emotional expressiveness when presenting their viewpoints. They watch in astonishment when television news programs show members of the Japanese Diet (parliament) hitting each other with their fists.

This is not to say that Americans in interpersonal conversations never argue. Certainly there are those who do. Generally, though, they prefer not to. One result of their aversion to arguing is that they get little practice in verbally defending their viewpoints. And one result of that, in turn, is that they may appear less intelligent than they might actually be (see page 35 for more on this subject).

In contrast to Americans' typical avoidance of arguments in their day-to-day dealings with each other, they seem to relish arguments in their public discourse. Linguist Deborah Tannen maintains in *The Argument Culture* (1998) that media and public treatment of controversial issues is marked by oversimplified, raucous "debates" between the "two sides" of the issue. She notes that many issues have more than two sides, or perhaps only one reasonable side. Nevertheless, public-affairs television programs, talk radio, newspapers, and magazines typically engage a representative of each of the two sides who will debate each other, each trying to vanquish the other, rather than trying to illuminate the issue or find common ground. Martial metaphors such as "war," "battle," and "defeat" often frame these encounters, which can entail shouting, arm-waving, finger-pointing, name-calling, and interrupting.

A fourth and final form of interaction is *self-disclosure*. In many cases, conversations with a large amount of small talk (or of ritual interchange) produce little self-disclosure. That is, the people involved reveal little if anything about their personal lives, thoughts, or feelings. This is especially true if the people involved in the conversation do not know each other well. What Americans regard as personal in this context includes their feelings, past experiences involving illegal or otherwise imprudent behavior, and their opinions about controversial matters. In most public situations Americans reveal little that is personal. They often wait until they are in a more private setting (perhaps at home or at a bar or restaurant where fewer people are likely to know them) to discuss personal matters. Women tend to disclose more about themselves to other women than they do to men. Men tend not to disclose much about themselves to anyone. Of course, for both men and women, much more self-revelation takes place in the context of a close friendship or intimate relationship.

Americans are probably not extreme with respect to the amount of self-disclosure that takes place in interpersonal encounters. International visitors who are accustomed to more self-revelation may feel frustrated in their efforts to get to know Americans. In contrast, those accustomed to less self-disclosure may be embarrassed by some of the things Americans do talk about. As Melissa, an American college student, told me about her new friend from Korea, "Joohwan seemed so uncomfortable when I asked him to tell me more about his dating experiences. I don't understand why. I always talk about dating with my American friends, both guys and girls!"

DEPTH OF INVOLVEMENT SOUGHT

Cultural backgrounds influence the degree to which people want to become closely connected with other people outside their families. People from some cultures are looking for close, interdependent relationships. They value commitment to other people, and they want friendships in which there are virtually no limits to what the friends will do for each other.

U.S. Americans cause immense frustration for many international students and visitors with their apparent inability to become closely involved with other people. "Americans just don't know how to be friends," many people from other countries say. "You never feel that you are free to call on them at any time or that they will help you no matter what."

Many Americans do have what they call close friends, people with whom they discuss intimate personal concerns and to whom they feel special attachments and strong obligations. But as Daniel Akst argues in an article with the provocative title "America: Land of Loners?" such friendships are relatively unusual, particularly among males. Much more numerous are relationships with people who might more accurately be called *acquaintances*. With acquaintances, the degree of intimate involvement or sense of mutual obligation is much lower. Americans are likely to use the term *friend* to cover a wide range of types of relationships, much to the confusion of visitors from abroad.

Americans often relate to each other as occupants of roles rather than as whole people. Another person might be a roommate, classmate, neighbor, coworker, weekend boater, bowler, or teacher. Certain behaviors are expected of people in each of those roles. All is well among Americans if people behave according to the generally accepted notions of what is appropriate for the role in which they find themselves. Except in the case of public figures, other aspects of their behavior are not considered relevant, as they are in other societies where attention is paid to the "kind of person" one is dealing with. An accountant may be a chain-smoking, hard-drinking adulterer, but if he is a good accountant, I am likely to use his services even if I disapprove of chain-smoking, the heavy use of alcohol, and adultery. His personal life is not relevant to his ability as an accountant.

An exception—and it has become more and more of an exception in the era of the Internet—is public figures such as politicians, performers, and athletes. Former president Bill Clinton, former New York governor Eliot Spitzer, actress Lindsay Lohan, and golfer Tiger Woods are but a few examples of public figures whose careers stumbled—at least temporarily—as the result of revelations concerning sex or drugs.

In the United States the idea of "compartmentalized friendships" is accepted as natural and positive (or at least neutral). That is, instead of having friends with whom they do everything, Americans often have friends with whom they engage in specific activities. For example, they have go-out-to-dinner friends, exercise friends, and friends from whom they might ask advice. Notice that most of these friendship relationships entail doing something together. Simply being together and talking is often not enough for Americans. It seems pointless, a waste of time, as pointed out earlier.

Americans often seem to fear close involvement with other people. They will avoid becoming dependent on others, and they don't want others, with the possible exception of immediate family members, to be dependent on them. Notice that many American self-help books are targeted at people who are "too dependent" on others and who may need help achieving a proper level of self-sufficiency. (Remember, Americans have been brought up to see the ideal person as independent and self-reliant.) Americans are likely to be extremely cautious when they meet a new person who seems to want to get closely involved with them. "What does this person want?" they seem to be asking. "How much of my time will it take?" "Will I be able to withdraw from the relationship if it gets too demanding?"

International visitors will want to realize that Americans often have difficulty becoming "close friends" with each other, not just with unfamiliar people from other countries.

CHANNELS PREFERRED

Verbal Communication

Americans depend more on spoken words than on nonverbal behavior to convey their messages. They think it is important to be able to "speak up" and "say what's on your mind." They admire people who have a moderately large vocabulary and who can express themselves clearly and cleverly, but they distrust people who are, in their view, excessively articulate. A person who uses a large vocabulary is likely to be considered overeducated and perhaps snobbish. A person who is extremely skillful at presenting verbal messages is usually suspect: "Is he trying to sell me something?" "What's she up to?" "He's a smooth talker, so you'd better watch him." "Who is she trying to impress?"

This aversion to smooth talkers may be related to the general U.S. American aversion to higher education and to well-educated people. Someone who has "too much education" or "thinks too much," as President Barack Obama was accused of doing, arouses suspicion and even distaste among many Americans.

People from some other cultures, notably Arabs, Iranians, sub-Saharan Africans, and some (especially Southern) Europeans, prize verbal agility more than Americans do. People from those cultures, when they visit the United States, are likely to have two different reactions to Americans and their use of language. The first is to wonder why Americans seem suspicious of them. The second is to suppose that Americans, since they cannot carry on discussions or arguments very well, must not be very intelligent or well informed. "Americans are not as intelligent as we are," said an Iranian who had been in the States for several years. "In all the time I've been here I've never heard one of them talk about anything more important than sports and the weather. They just don't know anything about politics and they don't understand it."

A Greek diplomat in the United States commented, "It is so difficult to work with Americans. They get business degrees and they can't carry on a dinner conversation about anything but work."

It is no doubt the case that the level of knowledge and understanding of social and political matters is lower in the States than it is in many other countries. And, even though its higher-education system is supposedly based on the "liberal arts ideal" of the broadly educated person, Americans with advanced education tend to be highly specialized in what they know and can talk about. It does not necessarily follow, though, that they are less intelligent than people elsewhere. To conclude from their relatively limited verbal abilities and range of knowledge that they are unintelligent is to underestimate them.

Other people come to the United States from cultures where people generally talk less than Americans do and rely more on the context and on nonverbal means of understanding each other. Such people tend to find Americans too loud, too talkative, and not sensitive enough to understand other people without putting everything into words. "You Americans!" an exasperated Japanese woman said when she was pressed for details about an unpleasant situation involving a friend of hers. "You have to *say* everything!"

Americans' preference for verbal over nonverbal means of communicating pertains also to the written word. Words are important to Americans, and written words are often more highly regarded than words that are merely spoken. Formal agreements, contracts, and decisions are normally written down—and then reviewed by lawyers to make sure the written words have done as much as possible to forestall potential lawsuits. Official notices and advisories are written. "Put it in writing," the Americans say, if it is important and you want it to receive appropriate attention. Business-people and international students sometimes get themselves into difficulty because they have not paid enough attention (by American standards) to written contracts, notices, procedures, or deadlines.

Nonverbal Communication

"You shouldn't have your office arranged like this," a Nigerian student said to me. "You should have it so your desk is between you and the person you are talking to."

"You shouldn't have your furniture this way," a Chinese student told me. "Having your back to the door when you are at your desk brings bad luck. You should be facing the door."

"I like the way you have your office set up," a Canadian student observed. "It's nice and informal. You don't have a desk between you and the person you are talking to, so the person feels more at ease."

Furniture arrangements are just one aspect of the large topic of nonverbal communication. The types and relative positions of the furniture in an office or a home convey messages to people about such topics as degrees of formality and concern with social status. And, as the examples just shown make clear, spatial arrangements convey different messages to different people.

Facial jewelry, tattoos, volume and tone of voice, movements of eyebrows, variations in eye contact, clothing styles, and attention to punctuality are among the many other aspects of human behavior that come under the heading of nonverbal communication. The subject is large and complex. A great deal of human communication takes place on the nonverbal level and many aspects of nonverbal communication are heavily influenced by culture.

Much of the discomfort that is typical in intercultural situations stems from differences in nonverbal communication habits. People in cross-cultural interactions may feel uncomfortable for reasons they cannot specify. Something seems wrong, but they are not sure what it is. Often what is wrong is that the other person's nonverbal behavior does not fit what one expects or is accustomed to. As a result of this discomfort, one person may form negative judgments about the other person as an individual or about the group the other person represents.

Some understanding of nonverbal communication is essential, then, for people who want to get along in another culture. This section discusses several aspects of nonverbal communication and makes some observations about typical (but, remember, not universal) U.S. American nonverbal behavior.

Aspects of Nonverbal Behavior

Appearance. With respect to appearance and dress, generalizations about Americans (or any other large and diverse group) are scarcely possible. Suffice it to say that Americans, like people elsewhere, have ideas about which clothing styles are attractive and unattractive or which are appropriate and inappropriate for any given setting. These ideas change over time because they are subject to fads and fashions. So do ideas about hairstyles, cosmetics, jewelry, and body adornments, all of which are aspects of nonverbal behavior. Foreigners anywhere usually stand out because their hairstyles, clothing (including shoes), and use of cosmetics distinguish them from the natives.

Many culture groups find American dress strikingly informal. In some places in the United States, particularly away from large coastal cities, it is perfectly acceptable to wear blue jeans to church, the opera, or a wedding, occasions that in the past required much more formal clothing.

Body Movements and Gestures. Body movements are another important aspect of nonverbal communication. Many international visitors claim, for example, that there is a characteristic "American walk" in which the walker moves at a rapid pace, holds the chest forward, and swings the arms vigorously. Combined, these body movements create the impression in some foreigners' minds that Americans take up more space than they actually do, and that they are arrogant.

With respect to movements accompanying their talk, Americans consider what can be called "moderate" gesturing to be appropriate. They use hand and arm motions to add emphasis or clarity to what they are saying, but they will not generally use a gesture in which the elbows go above the level of the shoulder except, for example, when waving hello or good-bye, voting by a show of hands, or trying to get attention in a large group. People whose elbows rise above their shoulders while they are talking are considered to be "waving their arms," which may be taken as a symptom of excessive emotionalism and perhaps even anger. In Americans' eyes, Italians, Greeks, and some Latin Americans are likely to be considered "too emotional" or "hot-tempered" because of the vigorous gestures that often accompany their talk. In Asian eyes, this level of gesturing may seem childish or undisciplined.

On the other hand, Americans are likely to regard people who keep their hands and arms still or very close to their bodies while they talk as "too stiff," "too formal," or "uptight." Americans often think of Chinese and Japanese people, particularly women, in this way.

In most societies there are standard gestures for certain everyday situations: greetings (a gesture that goes with "Hello!"), leave-taking (a gesture with "Good-bye"), summoning, head movements to signify agreement or disagreement, and counting and showing numbers with the fingers. It would take more space than is available here to describe the gestures Americans typically use for each of these situations. The easiest way for international visitors to learn about them is to ask an American for a demonstration.

There are also certain gestures that are considered obscene in the sense that they refer disrespectfully to body functions, usually sexual ones. If asking for a demonstration or explanation of these gestures, international visitors had best make their request of an American of the same gender.

Foreign visitors will want to be aware that Americans are likely to overlook or misunderstand gestures that the foreigners use and Americans do not. For example, people from certain parts of India typically move their heads in a sort of figure-eight motion when they are listening to someone talk. To the Indians this gesture means "I am listening; I understand." Americans do not have a similar gesture. The Indian head movement is not the same as the one Americans use to indicate agreement (nodding the head up and down) or disagreement (shaking the head from side to side). It is something quite different. The gesture is likely to suggest to Americans that the Indian has a sore neck or a tight muscle that he is trying to loosen by moving his head around, and the Americans can even get quite annoyed with the Indian's strange behavior.

When conversing with an Indian who seems to have a sore neck, the Americans may become so preoccupied with the head movements that they lose all track of the conversation. This is one of the dangers of differences in nonverbal behavior. Unfamiliar gestures and postures can be extremely distracting.

The meaning of hand gestures can also vary. Consider a gesture made at the University of Texas at Austin, where the school mascot is the longhorn steer. The gesture is made by raising the index finger and the little finger while grasping the middle and ring finger with the thumb. To Texas students, alumni, and sports fans the gesture symbolizes the school motto, "Hook 'em, horns." In many other places, particularly in the Mediterranean, this gesture means "cuckold," a man whose wife is unfaithful. In an incident widely circulated on the Internet, former first lady Barbara Bush, a kindly woman held in affection by many Americans, flashed the Longhorn hand signal while watching a Texas football game. Not all viewers understood what she was intending to convey!

Facial Expression. Social scientists debate whether certain facial expressions mean the same thing to people everywhere. For instance, some research suggests that the emotion of happiness may be expressed similarly in many cultures. Without entering that debate, however, we can say that Americans generally permit more emotion to show on their faces than many Asians typically do, but less than Latin Americans or Southern Europeans do. International visitors who are uncertain about the meaning of an American's facial expression can ask about it. Remember, you should not assume those expressions mean the same thing they mean at home.

Smiling is a facial expression that causes particular difficulty. Americans associate smiling with politeness, happiness, cheerfulness, and amusement. They rarely realize that many Asians will smile (and even giggle or laugh softly) when they are confused or embarrassed. "I don't know why she kept smiling," an American might say. "I didn't see anything funny!"

Eye Contact. An especially complex, subtle, and important aspect of nonverbal behavior is eye contact. The issue is simple: When you are talking to another person, where do you direct your eyes? Marked cultural variations influence people's answers to that question. Americans are trained to distrust people who do not "look them in the eye" when speaking to them. The fact is that Americans themselves do not gaze continually into the eyes of people they are talking to unless they share an intense romantic relationship. Rather, they make eye contact when they begin to speak, then look away, and periodically look again into the eyes of the person they are talking to. They also typically look at the other person's eyes when they reach the end of a sentence or a point in the conversation where they are prepared to give the other person a turn to speak. When listening to another person, Americans will look for longer periods into the other person's eyes than when speaking, but they will still look away from time to time.

Foreign visitors can watch pairs of Americans who are talking and note what they do with their eyes and how long they maintain eye contact in different circumstances.

Visitors who customarily avoid looking into the eyes of a person they are talking to will be able to tell, if they are observant, that Americans are uncomfortable around them. So will those who are accustomed to looking for longer periods or to staring into the eyes of people with whom they are speaking. Americans, like any other people, feel that something is wrong when the person they are talking with does not share their eye-contact customs.

Space and Touching. Another aspect of nonverbal behavior that is strongly influenced by culture has to do with space and distance. It can be amusing to watch a conversation between an American and someone from a culture where habits concerning "conversational distance" are different. If an American is talking to a Greek, a Latin American, or an Arab, for example, the American is likely to keep backing away because the other person is likely to keep getting "too close." On the other hand, if the conversation partner is Japanese, the American may keep trying to get closer because the Japanese seems to be standing "too far away." Conversation partners in these situations might move clear across the room as one gets closer and the other backs away, each trying to maintain a "normal" conversational distance. All the while, both people are vaguely uncomfortable and are likely to be making negative judgments about each other. "They're cold and unfeeling," Latin Americans might say of North Americans who keep moving away. "They are pushy and overbearing," Japanese might say of the encroaching Americans.

International visitors are also likely to notice characteristic ways that Americans react when they feel too crowded. On elevators ("lifts") or in crowded rooms, Americans usually look down at the floor or up at the ceiling. They often draw their arms and legs in close, and they may not speak to the people around them. For many Americans these movements seem intended to communicate that they are not invading other people's personal space.

With respect to touching, the questions are these: Who touches whom? Where (that is, on what part or parts of the body)? Under what circumstances? What kind of touching (patting, rubbing, hugging)? Dean Barnlund, in his book *Public and Private Self in Japan and the United States* (1975), made an interesting comparison of touching among Japanese and among Americans. He asked his subjects, university students, to show on a diagram

41

what parts of their bodies had been touched since they were fourteen years of age by their fathers, their mothers, friends of the same sex, and friends of the opposite sex. He found striking contrasts between the two groups. The least-touched American remembered being touched more than the most-touched Japanese did. Some Japanese could not recall having been touched by anyone since age fourteen.

A comparison between Americans and Latin Americans, Arabs, or Southern Europeans, on the other hand, would no doubt show that Americans, while they touch each other more than Japanese typically do, touch less often than do people from some other cultures.

Of course, habits and preferences concerning touching vary not just by culture but by individual and by situation. Some individuals like to touch and be touched more than others do. Careful observation can reveal a particular individual's preferences in this respect. Status differences also affect this form of nonverbal behavior. In general, higher-status people are freer to touch lower-status people than vice versa.

Silence. The final aspect of nonverbal behavior to be mentioned here is silence. Except in the presence of people they know well, Americans are quite uncomfortable with periods of silence in a conversation. If conversation lapses for more than a few seconds, alert foreign visitors will notice Americans quickly devising something to say. Almost any comment, in their view, is preferable to silence. A silence of ten or fifteen seconds will make many Americans nervous.*

Suggestions for International Visitors

International visitors cannot expect to learn and employ all American nonverbal communication habits, but there are some steps that can help minimize the negative effects of differences in these habits.

- Be aware of the wide range of human actions and reactions that come under the label "nonverbal communication," and realize that such behavior is largely culturally based.

---

*For more expansive discussion of nonverbal communication, see the Knapp and Hall or the Burgoon, Guerrero, and Floyd books listed in the suggested readings.

- Learn as much as possible about American nonverbal communication habits, and practice doing things their way.
- Realize that most often, people's nonverbal behavior reinforces the intended meaning of their words. In such cases, missing or misunderstanding nonverbal behavior is not a major problem. Problems arise mainly when a speaker's nonverbal message appears to contradict the words she is speaking. Foreigners who detect such "mixed messages," if they want clarification, will need the courage to ask for it.
- Try to avoid interpreting what others mean and evaluating their behavior based on your own ideas about appropriate nonverbal behavior. For example, if you are accustomed to standing closer to conversation partners than Americans generally are, be careful not to interpret the Americans' preference for a greater space between you as a sign of coldness, dislike, or disrespect. Such an interpretation might make sense at home but not in the United States.

The more you can learn about how Americans interpret each other's nonverbal behavior, the more constructively you will be able to interact with them. You can learn about these things by watching Americans interact with each other and by asking them questions about the way they do things, particularly when you notice that you are having a strong reaction to something they've done.

LEVEL OF MEANING EMPHASIZED

Americans generally pay more attention to the factual than to the emotional content of messages. As has been mentioned, they are often uncomfortable with displays of more than moderate emotion. They are taught in school to detect—and dismiss—"emotional appeals" in other people's statements or arguments. They are taught to "look for the facts" and "weigh the evidence" when they are in the process of making a judgment or decision.

Some social scientists maintain that American women tend to be less suspicious of people whose main message is emotional rather than "logical" or "rational." Women, according to this set of ideas, will tend to pay more attention than will men to the mood of the person they are talking to. Men, by contrast, will listen for the "facts" in what the person has to say. Statements or arguments relying heavily on emotional appeals are more likely to be taken seriously by women than by men. These ideas are most closely associated with the work of linguist Deborah Tannen (1990).*

Before continuing, it is important to emphasize two points that have been raised several times already. The first is that people naturally prefer to use their own communicative style. The second is that differences in communicative style can cause serious problems in intercultural—and perhaps inter-gender—interactions. They produce uneasiness, misjudgments, and misinterpretations whose source is often not clear to the people involved. U.S. Americans, for example, believe they are acting "naturally" when they engage in small talk with a person they have just met. They do not expect their level of intelligence to be judged on the basis of such conversations. But if the person they have just met is from a culture where conversations with new acquaintances "naturally" take some form other than small talk, then the person may well be evaluating the American's intellect. The result of all this is likely to be negative feelings and judgments on both sides. The stereotypes listed at the opening of this chapter arise at least in part from judgments made on the basis of communicative-style differences.

International visitors who understand the American communicative style will be far less likely to contribute to these misunderstandings and negative feelings. As a result, their opportunities for constructive interaction will be greater.

---

* More ideas on this topic can be found in the next chapter, which discusses the closely related subject of American patterns of thinking.

CHAPTER 3

Ways of Reasoning

People in other countries who want to study in the United States must obtain a student visa from a U.S. embassy or consulate before they can enter the States. Sometimes obtaining a student visa is difficult or even impossible, as hundreds of young Chinese learned in the late 1990s and early years of the twenty-first century, when American consular officials frequently denied their applications.

To many prospective students, for whom the opportunity to study in the United States was a long-cherished dream, the denial of a student visa was devastating. In many cases they applied and reapplied, trying to figure out what to say that might persuade the consular officer to grant the visa.

Sometimes prospective students sought help from the international student adviser at the U.S. school they wanted to attend. One such person e-mailed me with a list of questions she thought the consular officer might ask her, along with her proposed answers. She asked me, "Can you tell me whether [my proposed answers are] convincing from a Western man's view?"

This prospective student realized that what might be convincing to a Chinese person might not have the same effect on a Westerner or, more specifically, a Western man. She understood that culture and gender influence the way people think about things—what they consider relevant, true, accurate, important, believable, reliable, or persuasive. How we reach conclusions varies according to many factors, including our cultural background and our gender.

The subject of cultural differences in reasoning is complex and difficult to address. Scholars writing on the topic use such terms as *Aristotelian logic*, *epistemology*, *cognitive processes*, *metacognition*, and *deductive inference*.

In this chapter we will avoid such complex terminology, at the risk of oversimplifying the topic. We will look at American ways of reasoning under five headings: The Context, The Point, The Organization, The Evidence, and The Cause. Readers will see considerable overlap in the material under these headings because, of course, the ideas under each heading reinforce each other.

First, a reminder: in the introduction we said the dominant U.S. American culture is based on the assumptions of European American males, the category of people most influential in the country's early history and development. Recently, some social scientists have argued that the idealized thinking patterns described in this chapter have been over-generalized, and that they fail to account for the differing ways that women might think about things. A book called *Women's Ways of Knowing*, by Mary Belenky and others (details are in the suggested readings), develops this point of view. However accurate that point of view may be, however, the ways of reasoning this chapter attributes to Americans represent a still-existing cultural norm.

THE CONTEXT

Psychologist Richard Nisbett reports on an experiment conducted by one of his graduate students "to test the hypothesis that Asians view the world through a wide-angle lens, whereas Westerners have tunnel vision" (2003, 89).

The experimenter presented realistic animated scenes of fish and other underwater objects to Japanese and American students and asked them to report what they had seen.

Americans and Japanese made about an equal number of references to the focal fish, but the Japanese made more than 60 percent more references to background elements, including the water, rocks, bubbles, and inert plants and animals. In addition, whereas Japanese and American participants made about equal numbers of references to movement involving active animals, the Japanese participants made almost twice as many references to relationships involving inert, background objects.

Perhaps most tellingly, the very first sentence from the Japanese participants was likely to be one referring to the environment ("there was a lake or a pond"), whereas the first sentence from Americans was three times as likely to be one referring to the focal fish ("There was a big fish, maybe a trout, moving off to the left"). (2003, 90)

In a subsequent recognition task, Japanese performance was harmed by showing the focal fish with the wrong background, indicating that the perception of the object had been "bound" to the field in which it had appeared. In contrast, American recognition of the object was unaffected by the wrong background (90–92).

In the preceding paragraph about differences between Japanese and American ways of perceiving things, the context is the background (or "field," as psychologists call it) in which something occurs—in this case the context included the water and the plants. The object is the main or focal aspect of the situation—in this scene, the fish. Nisbett and many other psychologists have noted that Americans, in their perceptions and thoughts, tend to focus on the object and pay relatively less attention to the context. By contrast, Japanese, Chinese, and other Easterners pay relatively more attention to the context.

This difference in attention to object and context also arose when I was serving as an academic adviser to undergraduate students in Malaysia. The students had to write application essays to the American universities they wanted to attend to convince the admissions committee that they ought to be admitted.

The Malay students' essays almost invariably began with the words, "I was born in 19XX in (name of city or town)." The essays went on, "My father's occupation was . . . . My mother was a housewife. I have XX brothers and XX sisters." For the Malays, this background information was necessary to convey an understanding of who they were. Without such a context, the object (their academic history and future goals) would not make sense.

For the Americans reading their applications, though, such background information was irrelevant. What mattered to the American admissions officers, in general, was not where an applicant was born, what the applicant's parents did for a living, or how many siblings the applicant had. These readers wanted to know what the applicants themselves had accomplished, the courses they had taken, the marks they had earned, the clubs they had joined, their academic goals, and so on.

We advised the Malay students to remove the background information from their application essays. "The Americans reading your application won't care about that," we told them. "Even worse," we said, "the Americans might consider you poor writers and thinkers because of your apparent inability to get to the point."

THE POINT

To understand how Americans think about things, it is necessary to understand about the *point*. Americans mention it often: "Let's get right to the point," they say. "My point is . . . ." "You're off track. What's the point of all this?"

For Americans, the point is the idea or piece of information they presume is, or should be, at the center of people's thinking, writings, and spoken comments. It is the fish, without the water or the seaweed. It is the student's academic accomplishments, not her birthplace or her father's occupation.

In general, American speakers and writers are taught to include only the ideas and information directly and obviously related to the topic at hand. They are supposed to "make their points clear," meaning that they should focus explicitly on the information they wish to convey and downplay the context.

People from many other cultures, of course, have different ideas about the point. Africans traditionally recount stories to convey their thoughts rather than stating "the point" explicitly. Japanese traditionally speak indirectly, leaving a respectful amount of room for the listener to figure out what the point is rather than, as they see it, insulting the listener's intelligence by making the point explicit. Thus, while an American might say to a friend, "I don't think that coat goes very well with the rest of your outfit," a Japanese might say, "Maybe this other coat would look even better than the one you have on." Americans value a person who "gets right to the point." Japanese and people from other countries (such as Malaysia, Thailand, and the Philippines) may consider such a person insensitive or even rude.

Some linguists argue that the Chinese and Japanese languages, for example, are characterized by vagueness and ambiguity. The precision, directness, and clarity Americans associate with the point cannot be attained, at least not gracefully, in Chinese and Japanese. Speakers of those languages are thus compelled to learn a new way of reasoning and conveying their ideas if they are going to interact satisfactorily with Americans. Such speakers often say they "feel different" when using English because their ideas come out more explicitly.

THE ORGANIZATION

It is not enough, however, to make points clear. The points must be organized in a certain way if American listeners or readers are to be expected to "follow the argument" and take it seriously.

In school many American teachers give this advice about how to organize speeches and written reports: "Tell the audience what you are going to tell them. Then tell them. Then tell them what you told them."

Sometimes teachers elaborate on this advice: "Your speech or paper should have three main parts: the introduction, the body, and the conclusion. In the introduction you do something to get your audience's attention, and then you explain what your presentation is about and how it is organized.

"In the body," the teacher would go on, "you express your points, giving the evidence for each one and showing how each point relates to the points that have come before.

"And in your conclusion," the teacher would finish, "you summarize your main points and perhaps give some implications for the future."

This linear organization of a piece of reasoning is free of what Americans label "digressions" or "tangents," that is, ideas that do not relate clearly and directly to the point of the statement, speech, paragraph, chapter, or book. Even at the level of the paragraph, this linear organization is expected.

Teachers advise their students to begin each paragraph with a topic sentence that announces what the paragraph is about. The remainder of the paragraph elaborates on the topic sentence, giving an example or presenting evidence.

THE EVIDENCE

In any system of reasoning, the *evidence* leads from some initial information, assumption, or premise to a conclusion. What constitutes evidence varies depending on the subject matter and, of course, the culture. In the general American view, a reliable speaker or writer makes clear points organized in a linear fashion, as we have seen. A responsible speaker or writer is then expected to prove that each point is true, accurate, or valid.

As they grow up, Americans learn what is and is not acceptable as proof or evidence. The most important element of a proof is the *facts*. In elementary school, children are taught to distinguish between facts (which are good things) and opinions (which might be interesting, but which prove nothing). A student might state an opinion and the teacher will ask, "What are your facts?" or "What data do you have to support that?" or "How do you know that's true?" The teacher is reminding the student that without facts to support the opinion it will not be considered legitimate or valid.

Americans assume there are facts of life, of nature, and of the universe that can be discovered by professionals (preferably "scientists") using special techniques, equipment, and ways of thinking. "Scientific facts," as Americans think of them, are assumed to exist independently of the individuals who study or talk about them. This important assumption—that facts exist independently of the people who observe them and of the field from which they are drawn—is not shared throughout the world.

The most reliable facts, in the American view, are those in the form of quantities—specific numbers, percentages, rates, rankings, or amounts. Many foreign visitors in the States are struck—if not stunned—by the abundance of numbers and statistics they encounter in the media and in daily conversations. "We've had eleven consecutive days with temperatures above 95 degrees," one small-talking Texan might say to another. "Nine out of ten doctors recommend this brand of mouthwash," says a television commercial or a magazine advertisement. (Doctors are viewed as scientists or appliers of science and are held in high esteem.) "The humidity is at 47 percent," says the TV weatherperson. "The barometric pressure is at 29.32 and rising. Yesterday's high temperature in Juneau, Alaska, was 47 degrees."

While Americans feel secure in the presence of all these numbers, international visitors often wonder what significance they really have.

Look back at the quotation from Professor Nisbett earlier in this chapter. Notice all the numbers: "60 percent more references to background elements," "equal numbers of references to movement," and so on. For many Americans, this is reliable scientific evidence from an experiment. To them it seems entirely convincing.

Citing quantifiable facts is generally considered the best way to prove a point, although facts based on personal experience can also be considered persuasive evidence. Americans accept information and ideas that arise from their own experience or that of others they know and trust. Television advertisers seek to capitalize on this aspect of American reasoning through commercials that portray presumably average people (a woman in a kitchen, for example, or two men in an auto repair shop or a bar) testifying that their experience with the product or service being advertised has been positive. Other credible testifiers are famous entertainers or athletes and people dressed to look like scientists or doctors.

Of the various ways of having personal experience, Americans regard the sense of sight as the most reliable. "I saw it with my own eyes" means that it undoubtedly happened. Not everyone in the world shares the Americans' faith in eyewitness accounts, however. Some people believe that what any person sees is influenced by that person's background and interests, and even by the quality of the person's vision. Some people believe eyewitness accounts are necessarily biased and should not be trusted.

This American trust in facts is accompanied by a general distrust of emotions, as was mentioned in chapter 2. Schoolchildren in the United States are taught (but do not always learn) to disregard the emotional aspects of an argument as they look for "the facts." In their suspicion of emotional statements, Americans differ from many others. Iranians, for example, have a tradition of eloquent, emotion-filled speech and will often quote revered poets who have captured the feeling they want to convey. They seek to move their audiences to accept them and their viewpoints not so much because of the facts they have presented but because of the human feelings they share.

A Brazilian graduate student was having difficulty in his English writing class. "It's not just a matter of verbs and nouns," he said. "My teacher tells me I'm too subjective. Too emotional. I must learn to write my points more clearly."

Female American students sometimes find themselves subject to similar criticisms, since they may be less inclined than their male counterparts to rely on objective data and more inclined to accept the validity of more emotional and holistic presentations.

In evaluating the significance of a point or a proof, Americans are likely to consider its practical usefulness. Americans are famous for their pragmatism—that is, their interest in whether a fact or an idea has practical consequences. A good idea is a practical idea. Other adjectives that Americans use to convey approval of ideas or information are *realistic*, *down-to-earth*, *hardheaded*, and *sensible*.

Americans tend to distrust theory and generalizations, which they might label "impractical," "unrealistic," "too abstract," "a lot of hot air," or "just theoretical." Remember the prospective Chinese student who wanted my Western opinion about her proposed answers to the consular officer. I suggested that she not talk to the officer about her plan to "contribute to the development of the private sector in China's rapidly changing economy." An American would be more likely to be persuaded by her statement that she could earn a specific amount of money as a chief executive officer of a Chinese business in her field.

A Latin American graduate student, to give another example, heard himself being criticized (openly and directly) by the American professor in his international organization class. The student had written a paper concerning a particular international organization and had discussed the principles of national sovereignty, self-determination, and noninterference in the internal affairs of other countries. "That's just pure Latin American bunk," the professor said to him. "That's nothing but words and theory. It has nothing to do with what really happens." The embarrassed student was told to write another paper and to ground his ideas in documentable facts.

Latin Americans and many Europeans are likely to attach more weight to ideas and theories than Americans do. Rather than compiling facts and statistics as evidence on which to base conclusions, they may generalize from one theory to another, or from a theory to facts, according to certain rules of logic. Americans believe in some theories and in certain rules of logic, of course, but in general they are suspicious of theory and generalizations unless they are associated with specific facts. Thus "French intellectuals," well known for their abstract reasoning, find only a limited audience in the United States.

In some Chinese traditions, truth and understanding come neither from accumulating facts nor generalizing from theories, but from silent meditation. In Japanese Zen, truths cannot even be expressed in language. Zen masters do not tell their students what the point is.

THE CAUSE

The final element of ways of reasoning we will mention is the matter of *cause-and-effect* relationships. Americans tend to suppose that most events have some knowable, physical cause. "Things don't just happen," they often say. "Something makes them happen." Americans tend to believe they can study individual things, place them in categories, learn how things in the category operate or behave, and devise rules for understanding them and predicting their responses.

For example, if an airplane crashes, Americans will assume that a careful study of a list of possible causes will help them to isolate the actual cause. Was it human error? A mechanical failure? The weather? Or a systemic error, which resulted from some combination of organizational or environmental factors? Very few events are considered the result of "chance," "luck," or "fate." Some religious Americans ascribe certain kinds of events (such as the otherwise inexplicable death of a child) to "God's will." But such intangible factors are not usually held responsible for what happens to people.

By contrast, people in many Eastern cultures look not to specific objects or factors to explain what happens; rather, they look at the context or the relationships among many objects when they seek to understand causes. Why did the airplane crash? Maybe the pilot simply should not have been flying on that day. Maybe it had something to do with the actions of one of the passengers. Maybe a cause cannot be ascertained.

As suggested in chapter 1, most Americans have difficulty even comprehending the notion, so prevalent in many other parts of the world, that fate determines the course of people's lives.

When people with differing ways of reasoning interact, the typical feeling they both get is that the other person "just doesn't understand," "isn't making sense," or is "on another wavelength." Each then tries harder to be more "logical," not realizing that the problem is their differing conceptions of what is logical. Foreigners in America will need to learn that Americans will consider them "not logical," "too emotional," or "fuzzy-minded" if they include seemingly irrelevant ideas in their speech or writing, if they fail to use specific facts to support or illustrate their ideas and opinions, if they speak mainly in terms of abstractions and generalizations, or if they attribute important events to nonmaterial causes.

CHAPTER 4

Differences in Customs

Four middle-aged adults, all of them immigrants to the United States, met at one of their homes to plan a conference presentation about cultural differences among their respective native countries.

Before they started working, they enjoyed a potluck dinner. Potluck meals, where everyone brings food to share, were not customary in any of their countries, but all of them had been in the United States long enough to adopt the idea. Unfortunately, it turned out, they were not familiar with all parts of the custom.

At the end of the meal there was some sushi left. When the four colleagues concluded their planning and were ready to go home, a question arose: What should be done with the leftover sushi?

A lengthy interchange ensued, but the four could not find a satisfactory way to decide what to do with the sushi.

In the end the person who brought the sushi took the leftovers back home, even though, he acknowledged later, he did not truly want them. He had offered the leftovers to others, some of whom, it turned out, did truly want them. But he had offered them only once, thinking, as an American probably would, that one offer was enough. His colleagues who wanted the leftovers had come from countries where, in such circumstances, an offer had to be made two or three times before it would be taken seriously.

Those who wanted the leftovers said later that they had thought it was inappropriate for them to openly say what they wanted and had felt they had to wait for an offer. An offer was made, they acknowledged, but only one time, meaning to them that the person who made the offer was not sincere.

So the sushi leftovers went home with a person who did not believe he was doing the proper thing. The colleagues who wanted the leftovers were disappointed that they did not have them, and they wondered whether the person who brought—and went away with—the sushi was indeed a proper gentleman.

Had the four been Americans familiar with all aspects of the potluck custom, they would have known what to do with the leftovers. (Namely: The person who brought the food would take it home or, if he wished to do so, he would offer it to the host. If the host declined, he would offer it to others at the event. The host and the others would be expected to say whether or not they actually wanted the food. Not simple!) But there was no shared potluck custom among these four people. Nor was there a custom of openly stating one's preferences. So the outcome pleased no one.

When people are planning to go to another country, they expect to encounter certain kinds of differences. They are usually prepared for differences in language, weather, and food. They expect to find differences in some of the material aspects of life, such as the availability of automobiles, electronic devices, and home-heating systems. And, without knowing the details, they expect differences in customs. Customs are the behaviors that are generally expected in specific situations, such as what to do with leftovers at the end of a potluck meal.

It would be quite impossible to catalogue all the customs international visitors might find in the United States. It would be impossible, first, because there are so many situations in which customs influence or direct people's behavior. Some examples: what you say during introductions; whether you give a tip to someone who has served you; which rooms you may enter when you visit a stranger's home; whether you relinquish your bus seat to an older person; what help you can legitimately seek from your neighbor; when you give gifts, and what gifts are appropriate; what you do if you are a student and you arrive at a classroom after the class has started; and what you do if you are a businessperson and your customer offers you an alcoholic drink your religion forbids you to take.

VARIATIONS IN CUSTOMS

Another reason it would be impossible to list all American customs here is that there is so much variation in those customs. Even among the European American middle class, whose norms still serve as the basis for our discussion of American culture, there is marked variation in customs. These variations are mainly along geographic lines. There are urban-rural differences, North-South differences, and coast-inland differences. Americans who relocate from a southern city to a western town or a New England village encounter countless customs that differ from the ones they have been familiar with. For example, they might find that New Englanders don't engage in as much small talk with people they don't know (such as salesclerks) as Southerners do.

Religious backgrounds also account for many differences in customs, not just those concerning religious practices but those concerning family life and holiday activities as well. Ethnic identities also produce differences in customs, influencing the foods that people eat and the ways in which they celebrate holidays. Mexican Americans, for instance, often eat tamales (meat seasoned with chili, rolled in cornmeal dough, wrapped in corn husks, and steamed) during the Christmas season. Other Americans from European backgrounds (Irish, German, English) traditionally celebrate Christmas with a special meal of ham or perhaps turkey.

U.S. AMERICANS AND THEIR CUSTOMS

Although it is not possible to provide a catalogue of American customs, it is possible to say a few useful things about them. We will try to do so here; later chapters contain more references to specific American customs.

Just as sojourners expect to encounter different customs when they go abroad, Americans generally expect foreigners to be unfamiliar with local ways. In general, Americans will excuse foreigners who do not follow their customs if they believe the foreigners are generally polite and are not deliberately giving offense.

Many Americans, by the way, would not apply the word *customs* to their own routine and expected behaviors. Many Americans are so convinced that their daily behavior is "natural" and "normal" that they suppose only people from other countries have customs. Customs, in this view, are arbitrary restraints on how people would behave if they were free to act naturally— that is, the way Americans act.

Some Americans might acknowledge that they have customary behaviors surrounding certain holidays. Staying up until midnight, drinking champagne, and watching fireworks displays on New Year's Eve is one example. Many holidays that were once associated with a specific religion have lost their religious significance for most Americans. For example, Valentine's Day was originally a Catholic holiday honoring Saint Valentine but is now celebrated by most Americans, regardless of their religion. Some of the major American holidays and the customs associated with them are listed here:

- Valentine's Day (February 14). Valentine's Day celebrates love. Traditionally, this is a day when men send flowers or candy to their girlfriends or wives, but now many Americans (not just men) send cards or small gifts to friends and family members. Schoolchildren also exchange cards and perhaps candy.
- Easter Sunday (March or April). Easter Sunday is a Christian holiday. For many Americans, Easter is also a time to welcome spring. Children look for colorfully painted Easter eggs and baskets filled with candy left by the "Easter bunny."
- Memorial Day (the last Monday in May). Memorial Day honors soldiers who have died in wars. Parades and patriotic speeches are common.
- Independence Day (July 4). Independence Day commemorates the 1776 signing of the United States' Declaration of Independence from England. Many cities have parades and fireworks displays, and friends and families gather for picnics or barbecues and set off sparklers and fireworks.

- Halloween (October 31). Traditionally a day to honor the deceased, Halloween evolved into a day (evening, actually) when children dress up in costumes (such as princesses, movie characters, ghosts, and monsters) and go from house to house asking for candy from their neighbors, a practice called "trick-or-treating." Concerns about children's safety have caused a reduction in trick-or-treating, in favor of costume parties. Some adults have their own Halloween costume parties.
- Thanksgiving (fourth Thursday in November). Families gather to give thanks for their abundance on Thanksgiving Day. They usually share a special dinner of turkey, dressing, cranberry sauce, and pumpkin pie.
- Christmas (December 25). Christmas is a Christian holiday commemorating the birth of Jesus. Many Americans celebrate Christmas by decorating a Christmas tree, and children wait for Santa Claus to fill their stockings or put presents under the tree on Christmas morning. Family members and friends also exchange gifts and have family dinners.

As the American media increase their attention to "diversity" within the country's population, they publish more and more material about holidays that are traditional among non-Christian and non-American groups. Examples are many: Passover and Rosh Hashanah (Jewish), Ramadan (Muslim), Cinco de Mayo (Mexico), Kwanzaa (black Americans), and Chinese New Year (many Asian countries).

CUSTOMARY BEHAVIORS

In addition to behaviors associated with holidays, Americans (like everyone else) have thousands of other behaviors that can be called customary, a few examples of which appeared on pages 56 and 57. Most customary behaviors follow from the values and assumptions discussed in chapter 1. Americans value independence and self-reliance, for example, so it is customary for them to encourage their children to speak up for themselves. They assume all people are more or less equal, so it is customary for them to talk in relatively informal ways with nearly everyone.

Other kinds of customary behaviors are more arbitrary; that is, they have no clear relationship to the basic values and worldview that underlie the culture. Table manners are an example. Americans use knives, forks, and spoons. They are taught to hold the fork in the left hand and the knife in the right while using the knife to cut their food, then to lay the knife aside and switch the fork to the right hand to eat. Europeans, by contrast, are taught to keep the knife in the right hand and the fork in the left at all times. This difference is arbitrary and unrelated to larger issues about individuality versus interdependence, equality versus hierarchical rankings, and so on.

Another example of an area where customs have no apparent relationship to fundamental cultural values is that of personal modesty. Among Americans one can find a fairly wide range of ideas and practices related to the display of the unclothed human body. Different families have different practices in this respect.

A growing number of U.S. colleges and universities have "coed floors" in their residence halls. And some are offering coed rooms. These accommodations usually have coed bathrooms as well. Some Americans are disturbed by the idea of coed bathrooms, while others find it acceptable. Controversy over this issue reflects the range of Americans' opinions about personal modesty.

Even with this range of opinions, some generalizations seem possible. Australians and some Europeans often consider Americans to be more modest about their bodies than are people at home. At least some Americans carefully try to ensure that other people, especially those of the opposite sex, do not see their naked bodies. This level of modesty is more likely to be found among older Americans; younger ones are generally less concerned about this topic.

On the other hand, some nationalities regard Americans, particularly American women, as immodest. For example, people from Muslim and some Asian countries (those categories overlap in some cases, of course) are stunned by the amount of skin visible on American campuses when spring comes and students greet the warm weather in shorts, sandals, and scant tops. Students in revealing swimsuits and bikinis will sunbathe on lawns and rooftops miles away from any body of water.

International visitors cannot be expected to learn all the customs that prevail in the United States. What they should try to learn is the relatively small number of behaviors that U.S. Americans generally consider mandatory. Violations will nearly always evoke a quick, strong, negative reaction. What follows is not a complete listing of mandatory behaviors—such a list would be impossible to compile—but a few guidelines intended to help foreign visitors avoid behaviors that are quite likely to get them into trouble with Americans.

- Be punctual. Most Americans will feel offended if you are more than ten to fifteen minutes late for a meeting, appointment, or social engagement. If you must be late, try to give notice.
- If you agree to meet someone, whether at the person's house or elsewhere, keep the appointment. It is considered particularly rude to accept an invitation to a person's home for a meal and then not appear.
- Treat women with the same respect you accord men.
- Treat clerks, restaurant servers, secretaries, taxi drivers, and other service people courteously.
- When you are standing and talking with an American, stay at least an arm's length away unless (1) you plan to hug or kiss the person, (2) the person has clearly indicated to you that he or she wants you closer, or (3) you are going to hit the person. You can stand a bit closer than arm's length if you are side-by-side rather than face-to-face. Men will want to be particularly cautious about touching other men—except when shaking hands—unless they want to convey the impression that they feel a homosexual attraction to them. (This warning may seem overstated. No doubt men from some other countries will find that American men who do not react adversely to other men who get close to them or touch them. But so many American men respond negatively to other men who get too close that foreign men are well advised to keep their distance. They can move closer—if they want to—only after it is clear that doing so would be acceptable.)
- Avoid bowing and other behavior that is intended to display deep respect for the other person. Most Americans become extremely uncomfortable if they are the object of such displays.

- In addition to politics and religion, conversation topics to avoid include a woman's age and weight, people's income and the price they paid for things, and details about one's health, especially regarding bodily functions.

Beyond these points and those that emerge from the remaining pages of this book, readers will need other sources for learning about American customs. The best source, of course, is individual Americans. Just ask them what behavior is expected in particular situations. Explain, if you want to, that you are new to the country and are not familiar with the way certain things are done. Most Americans will be happy to try to answer your questions.

Specific Aspects of American Life

In Part I we looked at some general characteristics of Americans. Here in Part II we will consider in more detail the way Americans generally think and behave in certain important and more specific areas of life, including politics, families, religion, sports, and several others.

Once again it is important to remember that what appears here are generalizations. There are exceptions to all of them. What Part II tries to capture are some distinctive features of American life that international visitors generally notice. Taking note of the ideas in Part II will help these visitors understand aspects of American life that might otherwise seem strange.

CHAPTER 5

Politics

When Juan Pablo, a graduate student in mechanical engineering from Monterrey, Mexico, first arrived in the United States, he was eager to discuss the recent U.S. presidential election with his new classmates. Juan Pablo had read many articles about the U.S. election in Mexican newspapers and had debated the relative merits of the candidates with friends and colleagues at home. Now he was interested in learning Americans' opinions about the election. In particular he had some questions about the electoral process. But Juan Pablo discovered that his American classmates had little to say about the election. Worse, they didn't seem to understand the American electoral process any better than he did and became visibly uncomfortable when he tried to engage them in debate. Juan Pablo came to the conclusion, as do many foreign visitors, that Americans do not care much about politics.

Juan Pablo would be surprised to learn that Americans are quite proud of their political system. They seem to revere their "Founding Fathers" (George Washington, Thomas Jefferson, etc.), their Constitution, and their Bill of Rights. Whether they are well informed about politics (most are not, and very many are quite apathetic about the topic) or whether they participate actively in political matters (most do not), most Americans believe their political system has advantages that many other political systems lack. They believe their system protects their individual freedom, which is a value of supreme importance to them, and that it is, or can be, responsive to their wishes in ways other political systems cannot be.

Paradoxically, most Americans have a rather negative view of politics and politicians. The system might be good, but the people who operate within it might not be. As a group, politicians are generally seen as relatively unintelligent, talkative, egotistical, self-interested, and devious. Government employees, too, are suspect. Many Americans believe that the government has too many workers, with only a few who are diligent and productive enough to deserve the pay they receive. Paradoxically, again, Americans generally expect and usually receive competent service from government employees.

Perhaps because they fear that a government can become too strong and thereby endanger citizens' freedom, Americans tolerate a political system that seems utterly inefficient to many people from other countries. The American system was, indeed, originally established in such a way as to prevent it from taking quick, concerted action in any but the most extreme circumstances. Various governmental responsibilities are divided among the national, state, and local agencies, and a "separation of powers" exists among the executive, legislative, and judicial branches of government— at both the national and state levels. The basically "two-party system" is composed of two large and ideologically ambiguous parties competing for positions in the government.

This structure results in extreme decentralization that people from many other countries have difficulty understanding. This decentralization is most evident in the domestic realm, and somewhat less so in the international-affairs area. In both realms, though, the U.S. government has more internal impediments to action than do most other governments. American citizens tend to see that as an advantage, or at least as a price worth paying for the limits it puts on the government's ability to infringe on individual citizens' lives.

The administrative side of the government does not have the built-in "checks and balances" that keep the political side from acting decisively or, some might say, impetuously. Some administrative agencies are quite efficient; others are less so. Among the least efficient, most observers would agree, is the part of the Department of Homeland Security (DHS) that deals with immigration procedures. Unfortunately, the DHS is the one federal agency with which foreign visitors inevitably have dealings.

Americans feel quite free to criticize their political leaders. The president, senators, members of congress, governors, mayors, and others are subject to public criticism so harsh that international visitors are sometimes shocked and embarrassed by it—even if they agree with it. But while they themselves feel free to criticize, Americans usually do not welcome criticism from foreign visitors. "If you don't like it here, go back to where you came from," such visitors are sometimes told when they make negative comments about American politics (as well as other aspects of American life). Moreover, as mentioned in chapter 2, politics (like religion) is considered by many Americans to be a taboo topic, to be avoided in everyday conversation. Because political discussions may lead to arguments (and many Americans are uncomfortable with arguments), most Americans discuss politics only with close friends—and then only those with whom they share similar views.

In addition to pride in their system of government and a propensity to criticize their leaders, Americans have three other general ideas about politics that international visitors will want to understand: they believe firmly in what they call the "rule of law," they idealize compromise, and they conceive of politics as something separable from other aspects of life. After some discussion of each of these matters, this chapter closes with some ideas about the fundamental political divisions among Americans.

THE RULE OF LAW

The idea behind the rule of law is that impartial laws, not human beings with their irrational and arbitrary tastes and judgments, should govern the formal aspects of social interaction. "We live under a rule of law, not of people," American teachers tell their students. The students accept the idea. They believe that "no person is above the law" and that laws apply equally to all people regardless of their wealth, personal connections, or station in life. Their faith in the rule of law explains the conviction many Americans held, which many foreigners could not understand, that President Richard Nixon should be removed from office as a result of his behavior in connection with what was called the "Watergate Scandal." Nixon had broken the law and therefore should be punished, Americans believed, even if he was the president. Similarly, many Americans believed that both presidents Bill Clinton and George W. Bush should have been removed from office—Clinton for lying under oath about his affair with Monica Lewinsky, and Bush for perceived lying to the public and the congress about the nature of the threat allegedly facing America from Iraq's Saddam Hussein.

The belief in the rule of law goes beyond the realm of politics to other areas of life that are governed by formal rules and procedures. Getting a job with a government agency, for example, or getting a government grant for a research project entails following published procedures and demonstrating that one meets the published requirements. Theoretically, personal connections do not matter under the rule of law.

In practice, personal contacts, wealth, and social influence often do matter where laws and rules are concerned. What we have said here describes the ideal to which Americans subscribe. In reality, connections sometimes do help a person get a government job. Rich people sometimes go unpunished for illegal behavior that poor people would likely be punished for. But in general the rule of law prevails, at least in comparison with many other places in the world, and Americans are proud that it does.

THE IDEAL OF COMPROMISE

A compromise is a settlement of differences in which both (or all) parties make some concessions to the other side. Both sides "give in" somewhat for the sake of reaching agreement. Americans are taught that compromise is a good thing. Mature people, in the general American view, resolve their differences through discussion and compromise. There are, of course, different ideas about what constitutes an acceptable level of compromise, but in general a political agreement that results from a compromise among contending parties is, by definition, good. One reason the U.S. Congress was held in such low public esteem in the late 1900s and into the 2000s was its failure to reach compromises and take action on such major issues as global climate change, immigration, and the U.S. Senate's own rules.

Others may not share the American assumption that compromise is good. Compromise may be seen as abandoning one's principles—one's correct viewpoint. People who see compromise in that light are likely to take a negative view of those aspects of the American system that many Americans themselves consider so positive.

POLITICS APART

Americans, perhaps more than people in any other country, believe that politics can be separated from other aspects of life. "Let's keep politics out of this," they will say, making the assumption that matters of official power do not enter into economic dealings, family structure, the efficiency of government services, and other aspects of life that do not entail the direct participation of politicians and government bodies. They will relate to other people without regard to their political opinions. They would generally rather not "talk politics." This approach seems quite naïve to most Latin Americans, Europeans, Middle Easterners, and Africans, who tend to suppose that "politics is everything, and everything is politics." Said Peruvian writer Mario Vargas Llosa, after being awarded the Nobel Prize for Literature, "It's very difficult for a Latin American writer to avoid politics. Literature is an expression of life, and you cannot eradicate politics from life."

Given their assumption that you *can* eradicate politics from life and their image of politicians as less than worthy people, it is not surprising that the portion of American citizens who actively participate in politics is rather small. Many American citizens haven't even gone through the simple procedure of registering to vote. Once they have registered, they have the right to vote in national, state, and local elections, but Americans participate in elections at a lower rate than citizens of many other democratic countries.

Beyond voting, other means of participating in politics are open to Americans. Those who have relatively strong opinions or convictions on political matters may volunteer to work in a candidate's election campaign or work on behalf of a political party. They may join organizations that seek to mobilize support for a particular candidate, law, or policy. They may even run for elective office themselves.

Americans who do not want to get involved in politics but who need some information or decision from a government body are likely to turn to their elected representatives for help. Senators and members of Congress employ staff whose job it is to respond to constituents (that is, voters or potential voters who live in their jurisdictions) who ask for assistance of some kind. Americans believe it is their right to enlist the aid of the politicians whom they have elected to represent them.

FUNDAMENTAL FAULT LINES IN AMERICAN POLITICS

Just as there are many ways to address the topic of cultural differences, there are many ways of viewing political differences. In this section we will look briefly at two approaches that might help people from other countries understand whatever political issues are dominating Americans' attention at any given time. One approach looks at two possibly incompatible ways of framing political issues, the *constitutional* versus the *cultural*. The other approach has to do with differing views of the proper *role of government*.

Constitutional versus Cultural Framework

In the summer of 2010, a Muslim organization proposed building a community center about two blocks from "ground zero," the site of the September 11, 2001 terrorist attack on the World Trade Center in New York City. The community center would include a prayer room, a gymnasium, and a number of other facilities. Whether through innocent oversimplification or intentional fearmongering, the media referred to the building as the "ground zero mosque," even though it was two blocks from ground zero and was not a mosque. The proposal set off a heated debate.

Some politicians and commentators argued that the principle of freedom of religion, enshrined in the Constitution, made it clear that the project should be approved. Opponents argued that building a "mosque" so near the site of the attacks was insensitive to the feelings of the families of those killed on 9/11 and was unwisely and inappropriately supportive of Islam, some of whose adherents were responsible for the Trade Center attack.

In a *New York Times* column called "Islam in Two Americas," Ross Douthat sought to put the issue into a larger context:

> There's an America where it doesn't matter what language you speak, what god you worship, or how deep your New World roots run. An America where allegiance to the Constitution trumps ethnic differences, language barriers and religious divides. An America where the newest arrival to our shores is no less American than the ever-so-great granddaughter of the Pilgrims [the first Europeans to settle in what became the United States of America].
>
> But there's another America as well, one that understands itself as a distinctive culture, rather than just a set of political propositions. This America speaks English, not Spanish or Chinese or Arabic. It looks back to a particular religious heritage: Protestantism originally, and then a Judeo-Christian consensus that accommodated Jews and Catholics as well. It draws its social norms from the mores of the Anglo-Saxon diaspora—and it expects new arrivals to assimilate themselves to these norms, and quickly.
>
> These two understandings of America, one constitutional and one cultural, have been in tension throughout our history. (2010, A19)

Role of Government

People in a particular country might share a set of values and assumptions that make up their culture, but they may have differing interpretations of what their shared values mean. Or they may rank their shared values differently. Americans, for example, generally value freedom, equality, and individualism. But does this mean they want the smallest possible role for government in their lives, so they can be free to pursue their individual aims? Or does it mean that the government ought to ensure that all citizens have a basic level of food, shelter, clothing, health, safety, and education, so they can be in a sound position to pursue their individual aims?

This question reflects a fundamental fault line in American politics: What is the proper role of the government? Visitors from other countries can better understand American politics if they look beneath the rhetoric of politicians and commentators for their stance on the question of the government's proper role. A few contemporary examples:

- *Abortion.* Should individuals be free to decide for themselves whether to continue a pregnancy, or should the government, for the sake of the helpless unborn, restrict access to abortion?
- *Healthcare.* Should individuals pay for their own healthcare, probably via private health-insurance corporations, or should the government ensure that everyone has basic healthcare?
- *Taxation.* Should individuals be permitted to retain as much of their income and wealth as possible, to do with as they please, or should the government exact taxes to support activities that provide a general service or benefit?
- *Homeland security.* Should individual citizens be allowed to speak, act, and move about as they wish, free of government surveillance or other limitations and discouragements, or should the government monitor and restrict people's behavior in order to protect the public from anyone who might cause them harm?
- *Reviving the economy.* Should individuals, acting in a "free market," determine how productive assets are to be allocated, or should the government enact policies intended to influence the economy's structure, scope, and activities?
- *Gun control.* Should individual citizens have an unencumbered right to own and carry firearms, or should the government, in the interest of public safety, enact some controls on gun ownership?
- *The role of corporations.* Should corporations be allowed to act according to only the perceived interest of their stockholders and to the "dictates of the free market," or should the government exert some controls over them in the name of the "public interest?"

Generally, those Americans who favor a smaller role for the government are labeled "conservatives" while those favoring a larger and more active government are labeled "liberals" or "progressives." The more conservative conservatives may be labeled "right-wing," while the more liberal liberals may be called "left-wing." Visitors ought not to make too much of these labels, though, because each covers a wide range of philosophical foundations and policy recommendations. The labels are so loose that some commentators consider them useless.

The Republican Party is usually considered the more conservative of America's two large political parties, while the Democratic Party is considered more liberal. Both parties lack the level of philosophical and policy agreement found in political parties in many other countries.

Whatever their label, politicians in the United States consistently invoke the values their prospective audiences are presumed to share—individualism, freedom (and free enterprise), equality, privacy, material achievement, and so on.

In sum, Americans tend to embody what many consider a curious combination of admiration for their political system in general and disdain for its particular operations. They criticize their leaders, but do not want foreigners to do so. They strongly believe in the value of the rule of law and of compromise. They compartmentalize politics as a separable aspect of life, one they can choose to ignore. Their low level of participation in politics, not to mention their general lack of interest in political affairs, seems inexplicable if not irresponsible to many visitors from abroad. Those who do take stands on political issues generally divide between those who are skeptical of government and those who believe the government can realize valuable goals.

SUGGESTIONS FOR INTERNATIONAL VISITORS

International visitors who wish to learn more about American politics should approach the topic carefully, keeping in mind that Americans are often uncomfortable discussing political issues.

To be in a position to discuss politics with locals, it's necessary to be informed about contemporary issues and personalities. Ways to be informed include reading the local newspaper, perhaps a national newspaper such as *The New York Times*, and newsmagazines such as *Time* and *Newsweek*. These and most other publications have websites that, at least at the time of this writing, can be accessed for free.

Many blogs offer news and commentary on political matters. When you encounter a U.S. American who seems interested in political matters, ask her what sources of information, including blogs, she relies on. Or just surf the Internet until you find sites that interest you.

Learn the names of key political figures in your area—the mayor and other top local officials, the state's governor, your area's representative at the statehouse and in Washington, D.C.

Consider attending lectures and debates on current issues, which are often sponsored by colleges, universities, and student organizations. There you are more likely to encounter Americans who have strong political opinions and who are willing to share their ideas.

If you are deeply interested in politics, you can attend political-party meetings in your area, or other meetings devoted to airing political issues.

CHAPTER 6

Family Life

When Americans use the word *family*, they are typically referring to a father, a mother, and their children. This is the so-called nuclear family. Grandparents, aunts, uncles, cousins, and others who might be thought of as family in many other countries are usually called *relatives*. These usages reflect the fact that, for most Americans, the family has traditionally been a small group of people, not an extended network.

Readers should keep three things in mind when reading this chapter's generalizations about family life. First, regional, social-class, and religious differences are associated with general differences in family life. Second, among individual families the variations are infinite. And third, key aspects of family life in the United States are undergoing significant changes. Visitors from abroad will therefore need to supplement these generalizations with their own observations.

WHAT FOREIGNERS NOTICE

Many international visitors have opportunities to visit American families and to observe their surroundings and interactions firsthand. Even those who are not invited into people's homes, however, will notice certain things about American family life, particularly aspects involving the treatment of children:

- Babies are less often carried against their parents' bodies than they are carried in backpacks or pushed about in strollers. (And strollers can sometimes reach a fearsome size. One writer said the larger strollers, with their sturdy wheels and solid construction, reminded him of the armored personnel carriers in which he had ridden as a soldier.)
- While children in public are more often accompanied by mothers than by fathers, it is increasingly common to see a man caring for children in a public place. Men's rest rooms are nearly as likely as women's to be outfitted with a diaper-changing table. "Househusbands" or "stay-at-home dads"—fathers who tend to the house and the children while the wife earns the family income—are increasingly common.
- Young children, like the boy in the Orange Julius line, will be asked for their opinions and will express opinions even without being asked.
- Children of any age may interrupt their parents, argue with them, make demands of them, or loudly express their disapproval of parental decisions they dislike.
- Children sometimes seem entirely out of their parents' control.
- Groups of teenagers, dressed nearly alike and with similar hairdos, jewelry, and in many cases tattoos, are conspicuous in shopping malls everywhere. Their parents are nowhere around.

Visitors from abroad who have visited American homes often remark on these matters:

- Typical American houses or apartments seem larger than necessary.
- Most if not all interior doors remain open.
- Babies have their own beds (called *cribs*) and do not routinely sleep with their parents.
- If the family can afford it, children have their own bedrooms, whatever their age.
- Children have many, many multicolored toys.

- If the children are more than a few years old, a schedule of family activities such as music lessons or sports practices may be posted in a conspicuous place (often on the refrigerator) where family members can readily see it and add items to it.
- The man of the house (if there is one) may be responsible for—or share responsibility for—childcare, cooking, washing clothes, or doing other household chores.
- Electric appliances and electronic entertainment devices (large-screen televisions connected to elaborate speaker systems, DVD players and recorders, CD players, computers with games, camcorders, etc.) are much in evidence. A house or an apartment may have several telephones and television sets and stereophonic sound throughout.

Comments on many of these points will appear through the remainder of this chapter.

THE CHANGING FAMILY

During the 1950s, the traditional American family included a husband, wife, and their two or more children. The man went to work every morning during the week and on the weekend relaxed or did home repairs or yard work. The woman took care of the house and the children, often socialized with other women in the neighborhood, and perhaps participated in a parent-teacher organization at the children's school or volunteered in the community. The children went to school, played with their friends after school and on weekends, and sometimes got into mischief. The family had dinner together every evening, chatting while they ate, and then watched a few TV programs. The children did their homework, and teenagers talked on the phone with their friends. On weekends the family sometimes took a drive, visited grandparents, or shared some other activity. The children grew up, finished secondary school, perhaps went on to college, got married, had children of their own, and the cycle continued.

Families of this kind were depicted in the 1950s television programs *The Adventures of Ozzie and Harriet, Father Knows Best*, and *Leave It to Beaver*, programs that are now mentioned as relics of a bygone era.

American families have changed in many ways since the 1950s:

- Families are becoming smaller. The average American household in 2009 included about 2.5 people, down from about 3.2 as recently as 1985.
- There are more single-parent families; that is, households containing only one parent—usually a woman—and one or more children.
- It is increasingly common to find unmarried couples living together; unmarried women having children; women of child-bearing age who have no children; "blended families" that are composed of a man, a woman, and their children from previous marriages; grandparent-headed households; households that include an older couple and their grown children (perhaps with young children of their own) who have moved back in on account of economic or other misfortune; gay or lesbian couples with or without children; and people living alone.

Arrangements such as these are often called "alternative families," to distinguish them from traditional families like those of the 1950s. According to Professor Geri R. Donenberg (2004), by the year 2004, alternative families outnumbered traditional families by 70 percent to 30 percent! In 2008, according to a Pew Research Center study (2008b), 41 percent of children were born to unmarried women. Visitors from abroad often comment on this great variety in living arrangements, expressing surprise at how relatively few "normal" families they hear about.

Americans are also getting married later in life. According to the Census Bureau's 2008 American Community Survey, the average age at which men married was 28, up from 27 in 2005. For women the age was 26.2, higher than ever. According to the Center for Disease Control and Prevention, the 2009 marriage rate was 7.1 per 1,000 people, the lowest since 1932. The divorce rate in 2009 was 3.5 per 1,000 people, down from 4.7 in 1980.

National averages such as those quoted here mask significant differences among regions and religious groups. For example, the average marriage age is higher in large coastal cities, and in the Northeast compared with the South. The divorce rate is higher in the South. Catholic and Mormon (Latter Day Saints) couples tend to have larger families

Observers usually attribute changes in the American family to a variety of factors:

- Following on the "women's movement," women began entering careers outside the traditional areas of teaching, nursing, and being a secretary.
- More and more women are going to college, so much so that women now earn more doctoral degrees than men. In the process women are preparing themselves for financial independence from any future husband and delaying marriage and childbirth.
- Difficult economic times have often required both parents to earn enough income to support a family, and have compelled many young people to remain in their parents' home beyond age 18 or to return to it after leaving.
- The stigma attached to divorce, cohabitation (that is, unmarried couples living together), and homosexuality has diminished but not vanished.

All these changes in living arrangements and family structure seem to reflect and reinforce cultural values that emphasize individualism and freedom. American society generally accepts the idea that young people of both genders need to "find themselves" and "develop their potential." The journey to find one's true self may entail delaying or forgoing marriage and its entanglements; delaying or forgoing parenthood and its responsibilities; divorcing a spouse from whom one has "grown apart," and living life in a way that responds to personal situations and convenience rather than to dictates of the traditional norms. When they decide what living arrangements they prefer, Americans are "doing their own thing."

These shifts in family structure and composition entail shifts in the traditional male-female division of labor, as has already been suggested. More women are working and achieving financial independence. In more and more cases, wives are earning more money than their husbands. More men have become stay-at-home parents. Children, regardless of their gender, are often expected to contribute to home maintenance by washing dishes, vacuuming carpets, cleaning their rooms, helping with yard work, or other such chores. While some children may have responsibilities that reflect more traditional, gender-based divisions of labor (such as boys taking out the trash or girls helping to prepare meals), many American parents try to encourage their children to learn a range of basic life skills so that they can be prepared to care for themselves.

PARENTING

Cultures are perpetuated by the way children are raised. Paying close attention to the way children are viewed and treated can help visitors from other countries understand how Americans turn out to be the way they are.

Parental Hopes and Expectations

In some societies the act of childrearing is highly valued. Adults want to marry and have many offspring. Some religious groups (for example, Mormons and Catholics, as mentioned earlier) and some individuals in the United States have this idea. But many Americans have a more mixed or ambivalent opinion about having children. Although they consider children important and valuable, they also know that having children is a large responsibility that entails work, inconvenience, and expense. The media frequently provide sobering reports on studies estimating the cost of raising a child in the United States. Prepared by economists, these studies estimate average costs for food, clothing, medical care, school supplies, transportation, college tuition, and so on. The conclusion of the study is a specific—and very large—dollar amount that adults should expect to spend if they have a child. Americans love their numbers!

Among educated couples, the ideal is probably a planned family, with one or two children conceived deliberately, not accidentally. Some couples might prefer at least one child of each gender. Some people choose not to have children at all, and that choice is socially acceptable—however unpopular it may be with the parents of the couple in question.

As mentioned in chapter 1, the general objective of child rearing for most American parents is to prepare their children to be independent, self-reliant individuals who will be able to manage their own lives by the time they reach age 18. Training for independence starts very early, as the Orange Julius story in chapter 1 illustrates. Infants and young children are asked to make choices and to express their opinions, and they are encouraged to do things for themselves as soon as they can. Parents will praise and encourage their children: "There—you see? You can do it all by yourself!"

Until the economic downturn of the late 2000s, American parents generally expected that their children's lives would be at least as comfortable materially as their own, if not more so. With the downturn, many parents began doubting whether their children would indeed be able to prosper in the future. When they think about their children's futures, they think about them mainly in terms of the jobs their children will get and how much income those jobs will produce. To give their children the best possible chance to have a good life, they will, if they possibly can, invest considerable time and money in a child's improvement and instruction, which may include such things as dental care (straight teeth seem extremely important); medical care for any perceived defect; a preschool (where in some cases very young children are encouraged to learn to read); lessons for learning to draw, play a sport, dance, sing, or play a musical instrument; and perhaps counseling to help overcome emotional difficulties.

American parents with the means to do so want to expose their children to as many aspects of life as possible. Parents also want their children to be "happy and healthy": free of significant physical and emotional problems, reasonably well educated, able to find employment suited to their interests and talents, and reasonably prosperous. Parents are, of course, concerned for their children's safety and will try to protect them from harm.

American children are generally not as heavily involved in schoolwork as are children in many other societies. American public schools tend to be less demanding than those in many other countries. Academic achievement gets less emphasis from the average American family than it does from families in many other, particularly Asian, countries. American parents will complain if their children are given "too much homework" when that work is seen as infringing on their extracurricular activities, friendships, or part-time jobs, which are considered as important as schoolwork in producing the ideal "well-rounded child."

While they are concerned with their children's well-being, American parents also have an interest in leading their own meaningful and productive lives. In many cases, that means both parents will have careers, and young children will be left during working hours in some form of childcare—with a babysitter or in a day-care center or nursery school. Americans generally believe that parents "need some time away from the children" and often arrange for someone to babysit so they themselves can go out.

Child-Centeredness

Very young children receive considerable attention. Many American homes are what sociologists call "child-centered." That is, the children's perceived needs, interests, and preferences strongly influence the way in which the parents spend their time and money. Parents "childproof" their homes, removing from their children's reach any heavy, sharp, or otherwise danger-ous articles as well as anything a child could damage. They play with their young children. They arrange play dates so their children can get together with others of the same age. They buy things their children want. They talk to their children as though the children were simply small adults, asking their opinions and, in some measure, taking those opinions into account when making decisions that affect the entire family. These child-centered families are often very busy, since each child has his or her own schedule of lessons, practices, and social engagements. Although the degree to which families are child-centered varies, from the viewpoint of most foreign visi-tors, American families are generally seen as more child-centered than those in their own countries.

The corporate world is well aware of the degree to which children influ-ence family decisions, and a noticeable quantity of advertising is aimed at children. Indeed, some advertising firms specialize in devising messages that will appeal to young children and adolescents. Marketers believe that if they can get a young person accustomed to using their products early on, they will have a customer for many years to come. McDonald's, Nike, Coca-Cola, and the makers of many breakfast cereals and lines of clothing are just a few of the corporations aiming to influence young people.

As the children get older, they spend less and less time with their parents. Whenever possible, older children go to and from school on their own and take care of their own basic needs. They may find themselves unsupervised between the time they get home from school and the time the parents return home from their jobs.

Even when their parents are home, older children may receive relatively little attention. The children will usually have their own bedrooms and, more and more often, their own computer, cellular telephone, and television set. And of course they have their own iPod or other device for listening privately to their own selected music. Studies have shown that the average American child spends more time watching television than attending school, and vastly more time on the Internet than engaging in any meaningful activity with his or her parents. It is no wonder that by the age of 18, most Americans are so individualistic that they are eager to leave the family home and strike out on their own—if their finances allow them to do so.

As parents become a less significant part of their growing children's lives, the children's peers become more influential. Young Americans, especially during the teenage years, are often under intense "peer pressure" to dress and act like their friends and to engage in whatever activities their friends undertake. This might involve computer games, social networking, sports, political action, or some form of voluntary service to the community. It might also involve getting tattoos or body piercings, smoking cigarettes, chewing tobacco, drinking beer, experimenting with illegal drugs, fighting with members of rival gangs, or "hanging out" at the local mall.

Another notion that underlies American family dynamics is that of the "rebellious teenager." Americans assume that adolescence is inherently a period of turmoil. Teenagers are expected to be self-centered, moody, and uncooperative while trying to "find themselves" and to establish their own identities as individuals separate from others in the family.

Punishing Children

American experts on child development and child rearing continually debate about the best means of inducing a child to behave according to the parents' wishes. Many experts emphasize "positive guidance," which means giving the child positive reinforcement when she behaves in a way that the parents like rather than punishing her when she does something the parents dislike. It also means listening patiently to the child and acknowledging how she feels while telling her what is and is not acceptable behavior. For example, an American parent might say, "I see that you are really angry at Mark for taking your toy, but you may not hit him." Another form of this idea is "positive redirection." When dealing with a child who has just marked on the walls, a parent might tell the child, "Here is some paper to write on. Walls are not for writing on."

Instead of using physical punishment such as spanking a child's buttocks or slapping a child's hand, parents are encouraged to use a "time-out" as a means of discipline. During a time-out, children who are misbehaving are required to sit, often in another room, until they can behave properly again. Many experts consider physical punishment destructive because it can teach children to hurt others who are not acting the way they want. Parents who physically harm their children, even for the purpose of discipline, can be arrested for child abuse.

In some societies, it is expected that adults other than the child's parents—other relatives, neighbors, or adults who simply happen to be present—may intervene to discourage a child from misbehaving. Americans generally do not have that expectation. A child's behavior is considered to be the business of the parents alone. There are a couple of exceptions: an unrelated adult might intervene when a child is doing something that seems physically dangerous (for example, playing with a sharp object), and an adult might intervene when one child is mistreating another. In such situations the unrelated adult would stop the threat of harm but would not administer any punishment. Punishing is usually left to parents or, in some cases, to a school or other official institution.

Preparing Children for Adulthood

International visitors are often surprised to see how many American teenagers have jobs. The teenagers earn their own money for entertainment, clothes, or a car by working in a fast-food restaurant (probably the most common form of employment for teenagers), clerking in a shop, stocking shelves in a discount store, bagging groceries in a supermarket, mowing lawns, or other such activities. Some are expected to save at least part of their income for college expenses. From the parents' viewpoint, having a job allows their children to gain valuable training in acting independently, managing their time and money, and accepting responsibility for their own decisions. Reporting regularly to a workplace and carrying out routine duties under the supervision of a boss is considered "good training" for a 16-year-old.

In the traditional "average family," the children are ready to move out of the parents' house by the age of 18—that is, when they have completed secondary school. They may "go to college" (Americans use the term *college* to refer to any postsecondary educational institution), or they may seek a job. They might stay with their parents for another year or two after graduating from high school, but after that they are expected to be "on their own."

But this traditional path, as has been suggested, is changing. Some sociologists use the term *young adulthood* to refer to a stage of life between high school and complete independence from the parents. *The Times* of London refers to these young adults as *kidults*. Young adulthood may last until age 30 or so. Before that age, the young person may not have the education, training, or opportunity to obtain employment that pays enough to make independent living possible.

These young adults may continue to live with their parents. They may live with a group of other kidults, sharing the costs of housing and food. They may live apart from their parents, even with a spouse, while the parents help them pay their bills.

Americans use the expression "empty-nest syndrome" to refer to the psychological impact on the parents, particularly the mother, of the last child's departure from home. When parents have devoted much attention to their children and the children leave, the parents often confront a sort of vacuum in their lives. What are they supposed to do with their extra time and energy? The empty-nest syndrome is a combination of boredom, loneliness, depression, and a feeling of purposelessness that afflicts parents who no longer have their children around them on a daily basis. As an antidote, many women, after their children leave, enter or reenter the workforce or pursue some new educational, social, or political interest. Surveys indicate that empty nesters, after a period of adjustment to their new circumstances, enjoy a higher level of satisfaction with their lives.

As has been said, the empty nest sometimes fills up again, at least temporarily. A child who has graduated from high school or college may be unable to find a job. A child who has gone away to college may come home for the summers. A child who has gotten a job may lose it and be left without income to support a separate household. A child who got married may encounter marital difficulties or even divorce and return, sometimes with the grandchildren, to live in the parents' house.

The next turning point in traditional American family life is the parents' retirement from the workforce. For many decades the standard retirement age was 65. For a variety of reasons associated with economic reversals and the aging of the population, the typical retirement age has been creeping upwards. Many Americans had to modify their retirement plans to compensate for the dramatic financial losses they suffered as a result of the 2008 recession. They had to delay their retirements or, if they were already retired, return to the workforce—if they could find employment.

Some retirees (the euphemism is "senior citizens") remain in the place where they are living at the time they retire. Others relocate, often to the warmer states in the southern part of the country. Those who can financially manage to do so may become "snowbirds," living in the warmer part of the country during the winter and the cooler part in the summer.

Another major turning point in family life is likely to come when the parents' parents become unable to care for themselves. Mr. Wilson's mother, from the example in chapter 1, lived in a "care facility," a fairly common situation for elderly people in the United States. Many older Americans live independently for as long as they possibly can before moving to an assisted-living or nursing home or taking up residence with one of their children. It is usually considered a difficult or awkward situation when an aged parent is living with grown children. Ideals about independence and self-sufficiency are so deeply imbued in most Americans that a situation of enforced dependency can be extremely uncomfortable for both the elderly parents and the children.

SUGGESTIONS FOR
INTERNATIONAL VISITORS

One good way to learn about American culture is by interacting with American families. Students from abroad may want to look into "host family" opportunities in the cities where they are studying. Community organizations found at some colleges and universities identify families who wish to host international students for dinner or other social activities. Host families may also offer housing or opportunities for English-language practice.

Nonstudents may find it more difficult to be invited into an American's home. Becoming involved with a church, volunteer organization, or service organization is a potential avenue to invitations into Americans' homes. Roommates or office colleagues sometimes invite foreign students and businesspeople to visit their own or their parents' homes.

Parents from abroad with small children might want to read a book or search the Internet to get more ideas about prevailing thoughts on child rearing and healthcare and to become familiar with the vocabulary that teachers, pediatricians, and other parents use.

As stressed earlier, lifestyles vary greatly among U.S. American families. International visitors interested in learning about family life in the United States should try to get to know several families.

CHAPTER 7

Education

" A nybody can get into college in the USA," Malaysians often said when I was living in their country. They were referring to the fact that at least some American postsecondary educational institutions have rather low admissions standards. Applicants who had no possibility of entering a Malaysian university could often get into one in the States. Malaysians who remarked on the accessibility of American colleges and universities were comparing the American system unfavorably with that of the British, who once ruled Malaysia and provided the model for Malaysia's educational system. Under the traditional British approach, difficult school-leaving examinations were used to limit the number of people given places in postsecondary institutions and to ensure that the people who got those places were well qualified.

On the other hand, these Malaysians would also observe, "You [Americans] put men on the moon. So there must be something right about your system."

Many people interested in education get trapped into trying to answer the question, "Which is the better educational system, the American, the British, or some other?" That question cannot be answered. A more appropriate question is this: "What are the advantages and disadvantages of the

American educational system?" We will return to that question after considering a number of issues related to it.

This chapter does not focus on the structure of the U.S. educational system. Many other publications do that. One is Alan Margolis' 1994 article, "Key Concepts of U.S. Education." A more comprehensive explanation is in the online (and unofficial) encyclopedia called *Wikipedia*, at http://en.wikipedia.org/wiki/Education_in_the_United_States.

To understand any discussion of American education, one must be familiar with the basic concepts and terms in the glossary on the next page.

This chapter offers an overview of the ideals that guide the American educational system. It then discusses some social forces that influence American educational institutions, and some contemporary issues those institutions face. All this will help international visitors understand what they hear about American schools and will lead into some comments about the system's advantages and disadvantages.

GUIDING IDEALS

Access to Education

The American educational system is based on the idea that as many people as possible should have access to as much education as possible. All fifty U.S. states have "compulsory attendance" laws requiring young people to attend school or to be homeschooled. According to the National Conference of State Legislatures, twenty-six states require students to continue attending school at least until the age of sixteen. Other states set the age at seventeen or eighteen, or else they require completion of a specified grade.

Most states, under the influence of a controversial 2001 federal law known as No Child Left Behind, have developed examinations intended to prevent students from graduating from secondary school without attaining prescribed test scores.

The U.S. system has no standardized examinations whose results systematically prevent secondary-school graduates from going on to higher levels of study, as is the case in the traditional British and many other

Glossary of Terms Related to the American Educational System

Note: *While most glossaries are organized alphabetically, this one is organized according to the sequence students in the American educational system follow.*

School: For Americans, the term *school* can refer to any institution offering education at any level, from preschool through post-doctoral programs.

Public versus private school: A public school, at any level, is supported by the pertinent local or state government. At the K–12 levels (see entry), nearly all support for public schools comes from the government. Public colleges and universities receive a smaller portion of their total income from government sources. Private schools, at any level, derive most of their income from students' tuition. A **proprietary school**, whatever curriculum it offers, is a profit-making business.

Preschool: A private organization offering childcare and perhaps some educational activity for children below the age of five.

K–12: Kindergarten through grade 12, which is considered the basic education for all U.S. Americans. Children enter kindergarten at age five and, unless things go amiss, complete 12 more years of school and receive a high school diploma at or around the age of 18.

Elementary school or primary school: Typically, grades 1–6.

Middle or junior high school: Sometimes grades 6, 7, and 8; sometimes grades 7 and 8; sometimes grades 7, 8, and 9.

High school or secondary school: Grades 9–12 or 10–12.

Postsecondary: Any formal education beyond the 12th grade.

Community college or two-year college: A postsecondary institution offering associate degrees.

College: (1) any postsecondary educational institution; (2) a four-year, postsecondary institution that offers a bachelor's degree; (3) a component of a university, such as a "college of law" or a "college of liberal arts."

University: A postsecondary institution offering bachelors, masters, and, usually, doctoral degrees.

Post-graduate study: Any formal education beyond the bachelor's level.

Professional school: An institution offering a degree needed to practice a profession, such as medicine, law, dentistry, or architecture.

Technical, trade, or **vocational school:** Post-secondary, non-academic institution offering training for trades or crafts.

systems. (There are some well-known standardized tests, such as the SAT, ACT, TOEFL, GRE, and GMAT, but results on these tests are just one among several factors considered in college and university admissions decisions.)

Through secondary school and sometimes in postsecondary institutions as well, the American system tries to accommodate students even if their academic aspirations and aptitudes are not high, even if they have a physical and in some cases mental limitation, and even if their native language is not English.

The idea that as many people as possible should have as much education as possible is, of course, an outcome of Americans' assumptions (discussed in chapter 1) about equality among people. These assumptions do not mean, however, that everyone has an equal opportunity to enter Harvard, Stanford, or other highly competitive postsecondary institutions. Admission to such institutions is generally restricted to those with the most impressive academic—and co-curricular—records. Others can usually matriculate in some postsecondary institution, as the Malaysians observed, but one perceived to be of lower quality.

As of 2008, according to the U.S. Census Bureau, more than 93 percent of all Americans aged 25 or older had completed at least nine years of schooling. More than 84 percent of those aged 25 or older had completed four years of high school or gone beyond that, and 27 percent had completed a bachelor's degree or more. According to data from the Organization for Economic Cooperation and Development, the number of tertiary (that is, postsecondary) students per 100,000 inhabitants in 1996 was 5,840. Only Greece, South Korea, and New Zealand had more.

Naturally, an educational system that retains as many people as the American system does is likely to enroll a broader range of students than a system that seeks to educate only the few who seem especially suited for academic work. In the American system, academic rigor tends to come later than in most other systems. In many instances American students do not face truly demanding educational requirements until they seek a graduate (that is, post-baccalaureate) degree. In contrast, many other systems place heavy demands on students as early as their primary years—though college may be far less demanding, as is the case in Japan.

Universal Literacy

A second ideal underlying the U.S. educational system is that of producing a society that is 100 percent literate. All American states, as has been mentioned, have compulsory attendance laws, which, if students stayed in school as required and teaching methods were effective, would mean that everyone who passed through the system could read and write. The goal of 100 percent literacy has yet to be achieved, and may never be achieved, but it remains the stated goal.

Equal Opportunity

A third ideal, again in keeping with American assumptions about equality, is that of providing comparable educational programs to everyone, regardless of gender, race, income level, social class, or physical or mental disability. Equal opportunity is another ideal that has yet to be achieved, although assorted factors have transformed the character of student bodies at American schools over the years. At the K–12 level, for example, special programs have resulted in the enrollment of more and more students with physical or cognitive limitations. Before World War II, U.S. tertiary institutions enrolled mainly European American, upper- or middle-class, English-speaking males in their late teens or early twenties. By the turn of the twenty-first century, however, more females than males were enrolled at the tertiary level, and looking in on classrooms at colleges and universities, one will see countless people who are different from the "traditional" college student—people of many ethnic and racial backgrounds, people in wheelchairs or using aids for vision or hearing impairments, and "returning students" who are middle-aged or older.

Local Control

Fourth, the American educational system is based on the ideal of local control. The United States has no national ministry of education. (There is a U.S. Department of Education, but it has no direct authority over individual schools.) State departments of education have considerable influence over the curriculum of primary and secondary schools, whether they are public (that is, supported by taxes) or private (supported by tuition and other non-governmental sources). Local bodies, however, bear the main responsibility for guiding educational institutions. Public primary and secondary schools are under the general direction of bodies that are usually called boards of education or school boards. Those boards hire and fire superintendents and sometimes principals, oversee the curriculum of the schools in their jurisdiction, select textbooks, and review teacher performance. Each school district has a separate board of education, usually elected by the public. A school district may be no larger than one city or county; each state has many, many school districts.

The level of decentralization is higher at the postsecondary level. Most colleges and universities, whether public or private, have their own board of regents or some such body that hires and fires the president (or chancellor, or whatever the chief executive officer is called) and provides general guidance for the institution. Sometimes all the public colleges and universities in a given state will be guided by a single board. The more specific policies that govern colleges and universities are determined not by these boards but by faculty and administrators at each separate institution. Faculty groups set curriculum and graduation requirements. Individual professors decide what they will include in their courses and how they will evaluate their students.

At all levels of education, standards are set and (arguably) maintained by regional accrediting associations that the schools subscribe to, not by the government.

Few if any countries have educational systems as thoroughly decentralized as that in the United States. Many foreign visitors have difficulty comprehending the fact that so much control over educational matters rests at the local level and that there is no national body empowered to override local decisions.

Parental Involvement

Fifth, many primary and secondary schools idealize parental involvement in children's education. Schools encourage parents to become acquainted with the facilities and with their children's teachers, to talk to their children about what happens in school, and to confer and work together with the teachers if a child encounters any academic or social difficulty.

Schools often have "back-to-school nights" near the beginning of the school year to allow parents to visit the school, meet the teachers, and learn about the curriculum. Throughout the year schools send information to parents to inform them about school activities. Periodic parent-teacher conferences are intended to encourage parents to talk with their children's teachers.

Parents are normally expected to help their children with homework, keep track of their children's assignments and important school-related deadlines, and attend the athletic competitions, music performances, and theatrical productions in which they participate. They may even be asked to chaperone their children's field trips or volunteer in some other way. This call for parental involvement may seem odd to parents from countries where education is considered the teachers' business, not a process in which parents have such an active role.

More and more often, parents are maintaining their involvement with their children's education even when the "children" have graduated from secondary school and enrolled in a post-secondary institution. Called "helicopter parents" because they hover nearby and can swoop down at any moment to intervene in their children's lives, these parents do such things as question professors about grades they've given, or ask a residence hall official to find their children more suitable roommates. These days, conferences of academic and academic-support personnel are likely to include sessions on how to deal with helicopter parents.

Analysis and Synthesis

A sixth ideal has to do with the assumptions Americans make about the basic nature of knowledge and learning. The assumption is that only a certain part of all that is potentially knowable is already known. Scholars and students—mainly advanced scholars and graduate students—work at the "frontiers of knowledge" to discover new information or to conceive new ways of understanding or interpreting what is already known. Learning at all levels is thus considered not just a process of memorizing a fixed body of knowledge that already exists in books and in teachers' minds. Learning is viewed as an enterprise of active exploration, experimentation, analysis, and synthesis—processes that students engage in along with their teachers and professors. The ideal educational situation is, therefore, one in which students are actively involved in the process, learning the skills of analysis and synthesis and applying those skills to discovering new knowledge or taking a new view of established knowledge.

The widespread popularity of e-learning reflects a system in which students are expected to have enough self-discipline and motivation to pursue their studies with only limited reliance on teachers.

Students who come to the United States from educational systems that rely on memorization and reverent acceptance of teachers' words often face academic difficulty until they learn the intellectual attitudes and skills that go along with analyzing and synthesizing the material they study. Another way to say this is that Americans tend to view education as a *productive* activity, while people educated in many other systems conceive of the educational process as a *receptive* activity. (Thanks to L. Robert Kohls for this idea.)

This view of the educational process is an outgrowth of the value Americans place on individualism and equality, namely, the propensity to "question authority." Students at all levels are encouraged to think for themselves, which can entail questioning or even challenging a teacher. For U.S. Americans, questioning a teacher or other authority figure is normally viewed as a good thing, showing that the student is developing "a mind of her own." For people from many other societies, however, this behavior may be viewed negatively and seen as disrespectful of teachers, older people, people in authority, or tradition.

Well-Rounded People

Finally, the American educational system seeks to turn out "well-rounded people." Such people might have specialized knowledge in one area, but they are also expected to have a general acquaintance with many disciplines. Having passed through a system that requires them to study some mathematics, some English, some humanities, some science, and some social science (and perhaps a foreign language), students presumably have an array of interests and can understand information from many fields of study. Thus, again, specialization in the American system comes later than it does in many other educational systems. Students are required to take courses that they might not be particularly interested in and that appear to have little relationship to their career aspirations.

Being well-rounded also means participating in nonacademic "co-curricular" activities in and out of school. Secondary students are continuously reminded that they will be more attractive to college and graduate admissions officers and to prospective employers if they take part in school clubs, sports, or community activities. Many secondary and tertiary institutions have developed "service learning" programs, in which students receive academic credit for community-service work such as volunteering in a library, homeless shelter, or home-construction program. In some schools, participation in service learning is required for graduating.

SOCIAL FORCES AFFECTING AMERICAN EDUCATION

A few aspects of the social context surrounding the American educational system are worth mentioning. These include the social status of people in the education field, financial support, politics, and anti-intellectualism.

Social Status of Educators and Students

Many American teachers (that term usually applies to people who teach in kindergarten through grade twelve, the final grade in secondary school) would say that they do not enjoy a particularly high status in society. They are not especially well paid, and their working conditions are usually less comfortable than those of workers in many other occupations. Survey results published by the *New York Times* in 2005 showed that secondary-school teachers ranked 34th among other occupations, while elementary and middle-school teachers ranked 45th and kindergarten and preschool teachers 100th. (The top-ranked occupation was "physicians and surgeons.")

Similarly, U.S. college and university professors are not generally held in the high regard enjoyed by those in many other countries. The *New York Times* survey ranked the status of postsecondary teachers at 25. Even within that category there is a status ranking. At the top is the chairperson of the surgery department, very much an applied, rather than a theoretical, discipline. Professors are sometimes viewed as people who teach because they are not capable of doing anything else. The stereotype of the professor living in an "ivory tower," detached from the real world of things that matter, reflects this view.

In some societies students also enjoy considerable respect, since being a student is relatively unusual and requires special effort. Not so in the United States. Nearly everyone under the age of eighteen is a student, as are many who are older. Under these circumstances students, even graduate students, with the possible exception of students in doctoral programs, are rarely accorded special respect.

Finally, there is the matter of teacher education. In most colleges and universities, people who teach prospective teachers are at or near the bottom of the status hierarchy, looked down upon by most others within academia.

Financial Support

Another factor affecting education—here we are referring to public education—is the amount of money devoted to its support. Public education competes with other public enterprises that need money. Some states consistently devote a higher percentage of their budgets to education than others do, but (despite much talk by politicians about its value) none consistently give education highest priority. Public education at all levels suffered significant reductions in governmental support as a result of the late-2000s depression. In my home state of Colorado, for example, funding for higher education was reduced by 60 percent in 2009–2010.

Most educators believe their institutions are always underfunded. For many years pro-education groups have complained that states spending more money on prisons than on schools.

Politics

A third social factor influencing education is politics. In some states and communities, contemporary political conflicts are directly reflected in the administration of primary and secondary institutions. School boards may debate the value of "sex education," "drug education," or "multicultural education." State legislators who view government negatively argue that state support for education should be in the form of vouchers given to parents so they can choose which school, public or private, they want their children to attend. This view conflicts with that of legislators who support public education.

State governors may appoint their political supporters to positions on the board of regents that governs the state's major public university, and the political beliefs of those supporters may influence university policies. The degree to which political conflicts are manifested in educational institutions in America, however, is probably minimal. National political conflicts, as opposed to local ones, rarely have a direct influence on the staffing, governance, or policies of American educational institutions at any level. Except during times of national crisis (for example, the war in Viet Nam), American students are generally nonpolitical, though small, vocal groups of students periodically engage in attention-getting activities to support their views on major social and political questions such as world trade, human rights, gay rights, and environmental preservation.

Anti-Intellectualism

A final social force affecting the American educational system is anti-intellectualism. As chapter 3 sought to make clear, most Americans are suspicious of theorizing and "intellectualizing." They want to see practical results from the time and money they spend. Secondary school and university graduates are expected to be well educated, but not to the extent that they cannot do anything "useful." Many Americans are unimpressed by most learning that is undertaken purely for the sake of learning, and they place a high value on professional fields of study such as engineering, medicine, computer science, and business, which they see as leading to high-paying and available jobs.

In contrast, Americans place a relatively low value on fields such as literature, philosophy, history, and art, which many consider a "waste of time." Compared with people from many other countries, Americans have little general reverence for students who excel or pursue advanced studies in one exclusive field (particularly, it seems, if that field is mathematics: a person who seems excessively interested in mathematics—or computers—is labeled a "geek" or a "nerd"). Nor do they necessarily show any particular respect for well-educated political candidates, a fact that mystifies many international visitors.

ISSUES FACING AMERICAN SCHOOLS

Like other social institutions, educational institutions are the subject of continuing controversy about one issue or another. Some of these issues concern just primary or secondary schools; some concern just postsecondary institutions. Some touch institutions at all levels.

Schools at all levels face the issue of *accountability*. How does one determine whether a particular teacher is doing a good job? A particular school? These questions cannot be answered in the quantifiable terms Americans prefer (see chapter 3), so they continue to vex educational administrators, politicians, and the American public.

At the primary and secondary level, there is often heated debate about the content and quality of textbooks. Are they biased? Have they been made too simple? Have controversial issues been avoided so that potential textbook buyers are less likely to be offended by a book's contents? Have "facts" been distorted to make them more palatable to potential consumers?

Some other recurrent controversial issues are these:

- Should primary and secondary schools allow students to pray to a Supreme Being during the school day? (See the discussion about the separation of church and state in chapter 8.)
- Should particular books (usually famous novels) that contain profane or sexually explicit language, "adult themes," or violence be assigned in classes or be available in secondary school libraries?
- Can religious symbols be used in school activities related to national holidays, especially Christmas and Easter, which have religious origins?
- What should students be taught about the origin of humankind; specifically, should they be taught the theory that humankind evolved from "lower animals" or the theory that humankind was created by a Supreme Being (the theory called *creationism*)?
- What should students be taught about American history; specifically, how should people of color, women, and homosexuals be portrayed in

the story of the country's past? This conflict comes under the rubric of *multicultural education.*

- What measures can appropriately be taken to ensure that schools in poorer school districts offer facilities and opportunities reasonably similar to those offered in wealthier areas?
- What measures, if any, should be taken to accommodate students who are not native speakers of English and who may not be able to use English well or at all?
- What is the proper balance between general (or "liberal") education and education or specialized training intended to prepare students to work in particular fields?
- Should female secondary school students be allowed to participate on athletic teams (such as football and wrestling) that are traditionally all male?
- What is the proper balance between providing special assistance for students with special needs (for example, students with learning disabilities, physical limitations, or English-language limitations) and "mainstreaming" them (that is, incorporating them into regular classrooms and school activities)?
- How can colleges and universities prevent faculty members from having "conflicts of interest" between their research and the terms of financial support they may receive from corporations or other organizations with vested interests in the outcome of the research?

The issue of religious garb—veils, etc.—that has excited so much attention in some European countries has yet to receive much attention in the United States.

American elementary and secondary schools are often called upon to add one topic or another to their curriculum in order to remedy perceived social problems. Thus, schools may be asked to address matters such as values and ethics, conflict resolution, racial integration, environmental preservation, world peace, sex education, and health and fitness. In most other countries such issues would more likely be placed in the domain of the family, religious organizations, political parties, or some other social institution.

Because the American educational system is so decentralized, it is possible for these issues to come up again and again in place after place. Different solutions evolve in different localities. There is no uniform, authoritative answer to them, as there might be in a country with a more centralized educational system.

ADVANTAGES AND DISADVANTAGES

From what has been said here, many of the American educational system's advantages and disadvantages become clear.

The system provides formal education for a relatively large portion of the population, but the quality of that education is not as high as it might be in a more selective system. (Most experts agree that people who earn Ph.D. degrees in the United States are as well prepared to work in their disciplines as are people who earn Ph.D.s in other systems. Below the Ph.D. level, though, many other systems offer more depth in students' chosen disciplines.)

The system's decentralization serves to insulate educational institutions from national political entanglements and to give citizens some voice in what happens in their local schools. Schools can modify their curricula to accommodate needs and conditions that pertain to their own areas. On the other hand, this decentralization makes it relatively easy for an outspoken and committed minority in a given community to embroil local schools in controversy and also makes it possible for particular schools to maintain low standards if they wish or feel compelled to do so.

The well-rounded people that the American system hopes to produce stand a better chance of becoming "good citizens" (as Americans use that term) because they have a general familiarity with many topics and can keep themselves informed about matters of public policy. Well-rounded people, however, may not be so well equipped to begin working in specific occupations because they might not have learned as much in school about specific fields as have students whose systems encourage earlier and more intensive specialization.

The American educational system, like any other, is integrally related to the values and assumptions of the surrounding society. American ideas about equality, individualism, and freedom underlie the U.S. educational system. Whatever its advantages and disadvantages, the system will retain its current general characteristics as long as the values and assumptions that predominate in the surrounding society prevail.

SUGGESTIONS FOR INTERNATIONAL VISITORS

Many readers of this book will be enrolled in an English-language, undergraduate or graduate program at a U.S. college or university. These readers will have the opportunity to experience the American educational system firsthand, and can explore all of the educational resources available at their institution.

Other readers will be parents of children enrolled in American elementary or secondary schools. Such parents can readily get to know their children's teachers and some of their children's classmates' parents. One of the best ways to do this is to get involved in the school's parent-teacher association or to volunteer to help with a school-related activity.

All foreigners—whether they are students, parents, businesspeople, or visitors—can talk with individual Americans about their educational experiences. Although there are always exceptions, most Americans will be happy to discuss their own experiences and to give their opinions on topics such as the quality of the local public school system as well as on current social and political issues related to education.

Talking to teachers can also be illuminating. Ask teachers or professors you meet about their duties, the satisfactions and dissatisfactions of their jobs, and their views of changes that are taking place in their student bodies and at their schools.

Many people from abroad find it interesting to visit a primary or secondary school to see the facilities and observe student-teacher interactions. Many colleges and universities have programs through which their foreign students can visit public schools to make presentations about life in their own countries. Participating in such programs gives international students the opportunity to see a vital aspect of American life that would otherwise remain outside their view.

CHAPTER 8

Religion

"In my country," said a Syrian physician in the United States on an exchange program, "religion is a part of everyday life, like it is in other Middle Eastern countries. Even if a person is not particularly religious, Islam still affects that person's life because it is an important part of our culture. Religion is not just praying like it is here in America."

Most Americans do indeed tend to separate religion from other parts of their personal lives in a way that many people from other countries have difficulty understanding. We will return to the topic of religion in Americans' daily lives after considering some general information about religion in the United States. This chapter also specifies some exceptions to our generalizations about Americans and religion and offers some suggestions for international businesspeople, students, and other visitors who want to learn more about religion in the U.S. or who wish to practice their own religion while here.

THE GENERAL CONTEXT

Americans learn in their history classes that many of the Europeans who originally settled here were escaping religious persecution. Adherents of religions that were out of favor with their governments were seeking a place where they could practice their religions without governmental interference. What evolved from this concern, when the government of the United States was established, was the doctrine of "separation of church and state," meaning that the government is not to give official support to any particular religion, or to prevent individuals from practicing their chosen religion.

Although the doctrine of separation of church and state is one of the foundations of America's legal framework, it has not resolved all the issues arising from the relationship between religion and the state. Far from it. There are varying interpretations of what constitutes a religion and varying ideas about what constitutes governmental support for or opposition to a religion. Many fundamentalist Christians disapprove of separating church and state, believing the government should actively support their own views and oppose those of others. Therefore, there are recurrent public controversies about aspects of the church–state relationship. Controversial issues that have arisen in the recent past, and in many cases persist, include these:

- Should prayer be allowed in public schools?
- Should public schools teach "creationism," the belief that the earth and life on the earth were created by a supernatural being, and not through a process of evolution?
- Is prayer a proper part of school-sponsored activities such as sporting events and graduation ceremonies?
- Should faith-based organizations that administer social programs such as job training and feeding the hungry receive federal financial support?
- Can municipal governments properly mount Christian-related displays on public property at Christmastime? Can they display other religious symbols or icons?
- Can corporations permit spiritual affinity groups among their employees?

- Can public educational institutions offer any kind of support for faith-based student organizations that require members to have certain beliefs?
- Can Moslems wear headscarves or veils for photo identification documents?
- Should evangelical religious organizations be allowed to recruit new members at college- or university-sponsored events?

For a vocal minority of Americans, issues such as these are extremely important. Whether on one side of the debate or the other, they see these church-state issues as closely related to their country's ultimate destiny. Some believe their country's basic ideals are threatened by violations of the doctrine of separation of church and state. Others believe that the United States is threatened by a severe decline in adherence to Judeo-Christian values.

Although they may disagree about the details of church-state separation, Americans generally take pride in the religious freedom their government provides. The most prevalent religious values are the Judeo-Christian ones brought by early European colonists. At the start of the twenty-first century, the principal religions were Christianity (Catholicism and Protestantism, which has numerous denominations), Islam, and Judaism. The largest Christian churches are Catholic, Southern Baptist, and Southern Methodist.

The United States is regarded as the world's most religiously diverse country. Non-Christian religions represented, in addition to Judaism, include Islam, Hinduism, Baha'i, Unitarian Universalism, Sikhism, Jehovah's Witnesses, and assorted Native American practices.

Although the American constitution prohibits the government from officially lending its authority to any particular religion, Christian traditions and holidays do enjoy special standing. For example, the winter vacation period in most school systems typically falls during the week between Christmas and New Year's Day. Non-Christians sometimes complain that their traditions and viewpoints receive inadequate recognition and respect.

What came to be known as the "Christian right," a label that was applied to a set of fundamentalist Christian churches and organizations that promoted what they called "pro-family" and "pro-life" values and practices, gained both prominence and power in the late 1990s and maintained its strength into the 2000s. Several fundamentalist televangelists (evangelists using the medium of television rather than personal appearances to convey their message) gained large national followings and raised millions of dollars for their causes. Fundamentalist Christians in many communities established Christian schools as alternatives to public schools they believed inadequately supported proper values. The number of parents who home-schooled their children (that is, kept them out of public schools and instructed them at home instead) increased significantly, for the same reason. In several states the Christian right engaged in grassroots political organizing and gained considerable influence in local and state elections and in policy making.

Many Americans are not affiliated with any formal religion. Such people may be atheists—that is, people who do not believe any higher power exists. Or they may be agnostics, meaning that they are uncertain as to the existence of a deity. Many Americans also hold spiritual beliefs but do not subscribe to any of the denominations that make up what is called "organized religion."

To further complicate this already complex picture of religious practices among Americans, consider this finding from a Pew Research Center survey:

> Roughly one-quarter of adults express belief in tenets of certain Eastern religions; 24 percent say they believe in reincarnation (that people will be reborn in this world again and again), and a similar number (23 percent) believe in yoga not just as exercise but as a spiritual practice. Similar numbers profess belief in elements of New Age spirituality, with 26 percent saying they believe in spiritual energy located in physical things such as mountains, trees or crystals, and 25 percent professing belief in astrology (that the position of the stars and planets can affect people's lives). (2009a)

Adherents of the various religions practiced in the United States are not distributed randomly in the population. There are groupings by geographic area, ethnic heritage, and social class. For example, Lutherans dominate in much of the state of Minnesota, the ultimate destination of many early

European American settlers from the Lutheran countries of Scandinavia. Eastern urban areas have concentrations of Catholics and Jews. The southern and southwestern parts of the United States are sometimes called the "Bible Belt" in recognition of the fact that fundamentalist Protestants are especially prominent there, and the states of Utah and Idaho have large Mormon populations.

Americans of Irish, Italian, and Latin American descent are likely to be Catholics, if they subscribe to a religion. African Americans who are affiliated with a church are likely to be Baptists. According to another Pew study, "African-Americans stand out as the most religiously committed racial or ethnic group in the nation." (2009b)

Different religious affiliations are also associated with different levels of income and education. Adherents of Judaism are heavily represented in the wealthier stratum of society, and Unitarians generally have a higher level of education than the average among churchgoers.

Despite the variety of religions in the United States, relationships among religious groups are normally peaceful and are sometimes even quite harmonious. Some religious officials actively support "ecumenical" policies and practices, seeking cooperative arrangements with officials of other religions.

While it may be instructive for international visitors to know something about the doctrine of separation of church and state, the variety of religions practiced in the United States, the numbers of people who subscribe to each denomination, and the nature of the relationships among various religious groups, it is probably more helpful to understand the role religion plays in Americans' daily lives.

RELIGION AND INDIVIDUAL AMERICANS

To be religious in America means different things to different people. Generally, religion is seen as providing spiritual guidance, helping people lead a life according to the tenets of their faith. For Christians, this means following the principles of brotherly love, forgiveness, charity, righteousness, and humility. In a 2008 survey, the Pew Forum used four indicators of religiosity:

- Level of importance of religion in people's lives
- Frequency of attending religious services
- Frequency of praying
- Absolute certainty of belief in God (2008a)

The survey uncovered wide geographic variations. Mississippi and three other Southern states were found to be the most religious. Three New England states, along with Alaska, were the least religious. Seventy-seven percent of Mississippian respondents said they prayed at least once daily, for example, while only 41 percent of respondents in the New England state of Massachusetts said they did so.

Two other Pew studies cast light on the complexity of religious life in the United States:

- Younger people belong to a particular faith less often than older people (Pew Research Center, 2010b).
- An increasing number of people attend religious services not just of their own faith, but of other faiths as well (Pew Research Center, 2009a).

The media sometimes report on practitioners of "me-ism," Americans who have devised their own set of religious beliefs and practices outside any formal religious institution.

Individual Americans have been known to decide which church or synagogue to attend based on such factors as the presiding official's level of charisma, the quality of the building in which the congregation meets, the quality of the organ or organist that provides music in a church, the church's location, or the quality of a church choir.

Many people who consider themselves religious do not attend religious services regularly, if at all. They may attend as infrequently as once or twice a year, such as on Easter Sunday and Christmas Eve—two special days on the Christian calendar.

Whether or not they consider themselves religious, Americans are likely to turn to a religious official to perform the ceremonies associated with marriage and death.

As was suggested in chapter 2, most Americans consider their religious beliefs and activities private matters. They do not readily discuss religion with other people whom they do not know well or who are not known to share their religious views. Americans do not usually ask each other, "What is your religion?" or "Do you go to church?" Discussion and debate about theological issues is not common outside the setting of co-religionists meeting together.

EXCEPTIONS

There are important exceptions to some of what has been said so far. First, there are certain religious groups, mainly fundamentalist or evangelical Christians, whose members consider it their duty to try to convert others to their own faiths. Members of these groups will readily bring up the subject of religion and will try to induce people who do not belong to their group to become members. It is not unusual for such people to single out foreign students, attracting them with offers of help and support and then persuading them to attend Bible-study groups or other activities intended to gain their adherence to Christian beliefs and practices.

Second, as has been mentioned already, there are some communities— Lutherans in Minnesota, Mormons in Utah, and Hasidic Jews in certain sections of New York City are a few examples—where virtually everyone belongs to the same religious denomination. In such communities people's religious views are likely to be known by many people and talked about rather freely.

Third, even though the American Constitution calls for separation of church and state, there are conspicuous examples of religious symbols and activities in public life. American coins bear the words "In God we trust." The pledge of allegiance Americans say to their flag refers to the United States as a nation "under God." Each session of the U.S. Congress, Supreme Court, and some other official bodies opens with an invocation (that is, a prayer for divine guidance). Some people are concerned about the apparent contradiction between the church–state separation doctrine and these official uses of religious symbols and activities, though most Americans accept them as harmless rituals.

Fourth, candidates for and holders of elective office at the national and sometimes the state level often make their religious views and activities quite public. They announce what religious tradition they belong to, and they have themselves photographed attending religious services, usually in the company of their families. All this is usually regarded as part of an effort to portray themselves as wholesome, right-minded people who deserve the public's trust.

SUGGESTIONS FOR INTERNATIONAL VISITORS

If they are interested in Americans and religion, international visitors may want to attend various religious services. Newspapers list the times that services begin, and most churches and other places of worship (except Mormon temples) welcome people who simply stop in to observe or join in.

Students will find campus ministries on almost all U.S. college and university campuses. Campus ministries are affiliated with particular churches or religions (although they often regard themselves as ecumenical and cooperate with each other in carrying out large-scale activities). They sponsor meetings, activities, and services intended specifically for young adults. Campus ministries are often a recognized part of a campus community and may even have official roles in school activities such as orientation, counseling, and guidance.

Of course, attending services and witnessing rituals is not enough to convey a comprehensive understanding of religion in the United States. Visitors will want to talk to individual Americans about their ideas concerning religion. This can be difficult, as has been said, but it can be done. Once they have established a reasonably secure relationship with an American, or for whatever reason feel confident that it is safe to do so, foreign visitors can bring up the topic of religion with particular Americans. Taking care not to generalize too much, they can then reach their own conclusions about what religion and being religious mean to Americans. Some questions to ask:

- What are the main religions in your community?
- Do you consider yourself a religious person? If so, what are your religious beliefs and practices?
- Do you have the same religious ideas and practices as your parents?

- Do your children have the same religious ideas and practices as you do?
- How does your religion affect what you do?
- In your mind, what are the most important beliefs of your faith?
- Do you have family members or friends whose religion is different from yours?

CHAPTER 9

The Media

"When I was growing up," said Clarisse, a biology researcher from Paris now living outside of Boston, "my friends and I loved watching American movies and listening to American music. We especially enjoyed going to see old movies like *Casablanca* and *Gone with the Wind*, and we dreamed of visiting Hollywood some day. Now that I'm older, though, I see things a little differently. When I go home to visit my family in France, it bothers me that my nieces and nephews and their friends only seem to talk about American movie stars and American music. Why can't they be more interested in French culture?"

In some ways it seems pointless to talk here about the American media. American television programs, motion pictures, DVDs, and CDs, along with downloads of many if not all of these media, are available in all but the most remote parts of the world. American actors, actresses, and singers are familiar figures almost everywhere. The American public's appetite for glamorous and exciting movies and TV shows seems to be widely shared, even though the pervasive influence of American culture in other countries is often viewed with alarm.

But there are some points about the American media (referring mainly to mainstream television and film industries, the press, and some Internet sites) that might help international visitors have a more accurate understanding of them. Three general topics are discussed here: the question of what makes the American media "American," Americans' own views of their media, and misconceptions about America that the media promote in other countries.

WHAT IS AMERICAN ABOUT THE AMERICAN MEDIA?

Different people will have different opinions about what makes the American media distinctively American. A few brief opinions and observations are offered here.

The Content of the Media

The U.S. America media mirror the values and assumptions of most Americans. Among them:

- Admiration for the individual who disregards other people's opinions and does what he or she wants to do
- Admiration for the individual who somehow outwits or bests the establishment or the authorities
- A faith that good will triumph over evil
- Glorification of people who are young and physically attractive
- Glorification of people who earn large amounts of money or who have acquired impressive quantities of material goods
- A fixation on the action-filled life, as opposed to the contemplative one
- A bias toward the concrete (for example, "reality TV") over the abstract or analytical
- A need for what may seem like speed and efficiency, with fast-moving advertisements and dialogue, text "crawling" across the bottom of a screen, and several things happening on the screen at once

Characteristics of contemporary American life that many foreigners find frustrating or even objectionable are also conveyed—perhaps in an exaggerated form—through most of the media: a lack of intellectual depth; a greater concern for appearance than for substance; a fixation on sex; a strong interest in violence; superficial and parochial news and commentary, with little in-depth analysis of developments in other countries; and a fascination with computer-generated special effects and with "gadgets" or new technological devices that enable people to do things with less effort.

Some media outlets and personalities have become openly partisan. At the time of this writing, those expressing rightist views (such as Fox News and the *Washington Post*) outnumber those expressing leftist views (such as some MSNBC programs).

The Structure of the Media

Like many Americans and American businesses in general, the American media are driven by competition for money. In that sense, the media epitomize the American economic system and the American view of success as largely material in nature. A diminishing number of ever-larger corporations have taken over all parts of the entertainment industry, from controlling individual performer's contracts to producing movies, TV programs, and CDs to distributing and advertising those products worldwide. Corporate efforts to prevent free downloading of products that are intended for sale (songs, television programs, movies) continue.

Media executives are always looking for new ways to attract audiences and buyers. These same executives are frequently fired when their products fail to attract large enough audiences, even if they have had successes in the past and even if the movies, TV programs, music, or publications in question have received critical acclaim. The executives experiment, trying new ideas and dropping old ones. Trends and fads in television programs and motion pictures come and go with striking rapidity. Stars are in heavy demand one day and forgotten the next. Likewise, the press often covers some sensational news stories in great detail while overlooking other seemingly more noteworthy developments.

One manifestation of media competition has been a segmentation of the market. Cable and satellite television have made it possible to devise not just programs but entire networks aimed at specific subsets of the population. One survey found that the average American household received nearly 120 television channels. There are channels directed toward children, teenagers, women, families (meaning households with young children), African Americans, and Latinos. There are channels aimed at people with specific interests, such as cooking, history, literature, current affairs, romance, movies, and, of course, sports.

Radio stations normally target specific audiences as defined by age, race, language, and, in effect, level of education.

Music producers also target specific groups when they select and promote different artists. The availability of personal music-storage devices makes it possible for each individual to listen to his or her favorite kind of music in virtually any setting.

The print media also play to a segmented market. In addition to many well-known national magazines and national or regional newspapers, the print media include a thriving alternative press comprising magazines (some published on the Web, where they may be called "webzines") aimed at people in specific categories—butterfly collectors, square dancers, nudists, followers of Eastern spiritual disciplines, and on and on.

The Web also thrives on Americans' devotion to individuality. People establish their own—often very idiosyncratic—home pages. They visit chat rooms where they can express their views anonymously. They join "social networks" where they can be in electronic contact with "friends" all over the world. They seek out information on arcane topics and shop for virtually anything without having to interact with anyone.

As the Web has grown in scale and scope, it has partially replaced traditional print media as Americans' main source of news and opinion. Indeed, the future of these traditional media remains quite uncertain. The traditional media have lost audiences and thus have lost the advertising revenue that once supported them. Traditional news sources—network radio and television stations, newspapers, and magazines—have dramatically reduced their staffs, particularly their staffs for covering overseas news. Some long-established newspapers and magazines have gone out of business.

Some commentators have suggested that the government subsidize selected news outlets, on the theory that good citizenship requires access to current and sophisticated information about current events and issues. But in the context of Americans' general distrust of government, these suggestions are considered quite radical and receive little if any consideration from people who might be in a position to enact them.

AMERICANS' VIEWS OF THEIR MEDIA

In America, as in other countries, consumers vote with their dollars. If a motion-picture producer makes a science-fiction movie featuring creatures that visit the earth from outer space and the movie attracts large audiences, then there will be more movies with a similar theme. If a newspaper sells larger numbers of copies when it begins carrying more articles about politicians' sex lives and fewer articles about separatist tendencies in Indonesia (or even the American state of Texas), the newspaper will carry more of the former and less of the latter.

American consumers also vote by responding to surveys. Media outlets regularly poll audiences to find out what people are watching, reading, or listening to so they can determine what potential audiences want. As stated previously, a program with a low audience rating, no matter how critically acclaimed, soon disappears.

Thus, American audiences can be said to get what they want from their media. That American movies, television programs, and performers are so popular elsewhere suggests that what the American public wants does not differ dramatically from what audiences elsewhere want. In fact, some media analysts believe that one of the reasons American film studios make so many sexually explicit and violent, action-oriented movies is because these movies appeal to the widest possible audience (or the "lowest common denominator," as some critics put it), both in the United States and abroad.

This is not to say that all Americans are satisfied with the quality of their television, radio, and newspapers. They are not. Some Americans criticize their media, especially television, for being racist and classist (by showing only middle- and upper-middle-class European American people as responsible, important individuals), sexist (by portraying women as sex objects rather than as whole human beings), and violent.

Members of the American public have organized to protest what they consider to be objectionable aspects of the media, including the amount of violence and sex portrayed on television during the evening hours, the practice of directing advertising toward children (a topic discussed in chapter 6), and the allegedly racist, misogynist, and anarchic lyrics of some rock and rap musicians.

Some Americans (including some media executives) praise radio and television for providing huge amounts of free or inexpensive entertainment for the American people and for giving Americans common experiences that create bonds of understanding among them. This argument has lost virtually all its force in the face of the audience segmentation mentioned earlier. Before cable and satellite television became available, and before the Web's explosive growth, generations of Americans listened to the same songs, watched the same television programs, and went to the same movies. They did indeed have common experiences to respond to and discuss. Now, though, the media may do as much to divide as to unite the population.

Professional critics in the quality media argue that there is a larger audience for quality programming than the media decision makers, especially those in television and newspapers, recognize or admit. Such critics believe that television and many newspapers pander to uninformed opinion and unsophisticated tastes and should try to elevate the intellectual level of their products. They criticize the media for providing only superficial treatment of complex topics and events and for distracting Americans from important issues. For example, during times of national crisis, such as the wars in Iraq and Afghanistan or the decline in value of the U.S. dollar, some Americans feel the need to turn to the independent or foreign press for more thoughtful coverage of international developments.

On the other hand, there are those who argue that many high-quality programs do in fact appear on television, even if they are difficult to find amidst the more trivial broadcasts. They applaud noncommercial public radio and television networks (NPR and PBS, respectively), which are supported primarily by corporate sponsorships and individual donations rather than by advertising revenue (or the government), for at least attempting to provide "serious" entertainment programs and in-depth analysis of current issues.

They also recognize that some news sources (for example, the *New York Times* and the *Christian Science Monitor*) provide substantive coverage and commentary on current and international affairs. So do some magazines. The so-called "serious magazines" often have their own political stances, from conservative (*National Review, The New Republic*) to liberal (*The Nation, Mother Jones*).

These and other magazines, like the country's major newspapers, have websites that have increasingly become important sources of news and commentary, as have several websites that are independent of any print publication. Examples of the latter are the *Huffington Post* (liberal) and the *Drudge Report* (conservative).

MISCONCEPTIONS THE MEDIA PROMOTE

A foreign graduate student at the University of Pittsburgh was unhappy about his housing arrangements. He had come to Pittsburgh with the hope that he would be able to live in an apartment like the one he had seen portrayed in a popular American movie. In that movie the main male actor had taken a job as the manager of a small apartment complex. The apartments were modest, clean, and attractive. There was a swimming pool on the grounds. Most of the tenants were beautiful, single women, who frequently sat around the pool after work in skimpy bathing suits and who were free with their sexual favors.

The student did not find such a place to live in Pittsburgh. Nor would he have likely found one anywhere else in the States. The movie had encouraged some false expectations about people and their lifestyles in this country. Modest, clean, and attractive apartments are indeed available (although not usually near universities), and many have swimming pools. But the addition of the many beautiful, available women (who spend most of their free time socializing with the apartment manager!) took the story into the land of fantasy.

The movie was not intended to mislead foreigners, of course. Its purpose was to earn money, which means it had to attract audiences in America and possibly in other countries as well. American audiences are drawn to novelty, glamour (as they themselves define it), and action. They view their movies and television programs in the context of their own real-life experiences, so they have information on the basis of which to interpret them more or less accurately. Most Americans will know, for example, that apartment complexes like the one the graduate student sought exist "only in the movies."

People abroad who see American films and television programs and who read American publications do not have the same context for understanding what they see and read. They inevitably relate American media products to their own experiences in their own countries, and the result is often misunderstanding and misconception.

One of the main misconceptions TV and movies unintentionally convey abroad is that many American women are readily available for sexual activity. Others:

- The United States comprises New York City, Los Angeles (or Hollywood), San Francisco, Chicago, Las Vegas, Disneyland, and Texas.
- Most American women are beautiful (according to contemporary Western standards), and most American men are handsome (according to the same standards). Those who are not beautiful or handsome are criminals, deceitful people, or members of the lower class.
- Average Americans are rich and usually do not have to work (or do not have to work very hard) to earn money.
- Average Americans live in large, modern houses or apartments.
- Most things in America are large, modern, and shiny.
- There is a stratum of American society in which most people are nonwhite, physically unattractive, uneducated, and dedicated to violence.
- Violent crime is an ever-present threat in all parts of the country.
- Most Americans have guns.
- High-speed automobile chases frequently occur on American streets.
- Non–European American people are inferior to European American people.

International visitors who come to the United States with open minds will see for themselves that these images are inaccurate. Such visitors are well advised to take stock of the ideas they have about America from TV shows and movies they have seen, and then to consider carefully how well those ideas fit with what they actually see and hear in this country.

International visitors sometimes comment on the American media's treatment of international news. One visitor from India was particularly dismayed by what he perceived as a lack of coverage about his country on American television networks. "How will Americans ever learn about the world outside the United States when all they ever see on television are stories about Americans?" This criticism is often echoed by international observers and was borne out following the World Trade Center and Pentagon attacks and the wars in Iraq and Afghanistan, when it became clear how little most Americans knew about their country's behavior in other countries, about the Islamic faith, about the Arab world, and about conditions in Central Asia. It also became clear how little Americans knew about others' perceptions of them.

In recent years, the widespread availability of the Internet and cable television has afforded access to a wide variety of media. Foreign visitors frequently use these sources to learn about developments in their own countries.

SUGGESTIONS FOR
INTERNATIONAL VISITORS

Foreigners visiting the United States for any length of time are encouraged to explore the many types of music, movies, television programs, and periodicals available in the communities where they live. Finding out which songs, movies, TV programs, websites, newspapers, and magazines are popular in a particular city or region can provide valuable insights into the prevailing social or political viewpoints. Many cities have annual film festivals featuring small, independent films and documentaries that offer different views of American life from those presented in Hollywood movies. Local and regional music festivals are also common.

International visitors with a more general interest in the American entertainment industry can find ratings and commentary on many Internet sites. They can talk with Americans they meet about their viewpoints and preferences. They will find that most Americans enjoy discussing their favorite music, movies, television shows, and performers.

Sophisticated analysis and commentary about the media's performance are available from several sources, including:

- *Columbia Journalism Review* (*www.columbiajournalismreview.com*)
- Pew Research Center's Project for Excellence in Journalism (*www.journalism.org*)
- Fairness and Accuracy in Reporting (*www.fair.org/index.php?page=4*), which, in addition to its website, publishes a magazine called *Extra!*

International visitors wanting assistance in identifying television programs that might interest them can refer to the television review pages of major newspapers (especially the Sunday editions) and to the magazine called *TV Guide*.

CHAPTER 10

Social Relationships

Writing about "Why I Love America," the late British journalist Henry Fairlie recounted this memory:

One spring day, shortly after my arrival [in the United States], I was walking down the long, broad street of a suburb, with its sweeping front lawns (all that space), its tall trees (all that sky), and its clumps of azaleas (all that color). The only other person on the street was a small boy on a tricycle. As I passed him, he said "Hi!" just like that. No four-year-old boy had ever addressed me without an introduction before. Yet here was this one, with his cheerful "Hi!" Recovering from the culture shock, I tried to look down stonily at his flaxen head, but instead, involuntarily, I found myself saying in return: "Well—hi!" He pedaled off, apparently satisfied. He had begun my Americanization.

The word *Hi!* Fairlie goes on to say,

is a democracy. (I come from a country where one can tell someone's class by how they say "Hallo!" or "Hello!" or "Hullo," or whether they say it at all.) But [in America] anyone can say "Hi!" Anyone does. (1983, 12)

Like many people from other countries, Fairlie was struck, even stunned, by the degree of informality and egalitarianism that prevails among Americans. Anyone can say "Hi!" to anyone. First names are used almost immediately. People (most of them) seem warm and friendly from the very start. Fairlie remembers his first meetings with the Suffragan Bishop of Washington and with President Lyndon B. Johnson. Both greeted him with "Hi, Henry!" In most countries, such a thing simply would not happen.

There is a difference, however, between friendliness and friendship. While Americans may seem relatively warm and approachable upon first encounter, they may later seem remote and unreachable. *Superficial* is the word many longer-term international visitors use to describe Americans' relationships with other people. Some of them believe that it is only with foreigners that Americans tend to make friends slowly, if they make them at all. More observant visitors notice that Americans tend to be remote and unreachable even among themselves. They are very private, keeping their personal thoughts and feelings to themselves. They are difficult to get to know on a deeper level.

So far we have been generalizing about Americans' behavior toward people they have just met and about some aspects of their behavior in social interactions. The points made so far are the ones international visitors most commonly make when they discuss their experiences with Americans. What follows is more information and ideas about meeting new people, friendship, relationships prescribed by roles, courtesy, schedules, and gifts. The chapter closes with suggestions for foreign visitors who want to meet and develop relationships with Americans.

MEETING NEW PEOPLE

Fairlie indicated that in his native country, one person does not usually talk to another until the two have been introduced to each other by a mutual friend or colleague. So it is in many countries, but not in the United States. Of course, such acquaintanceships may well begin when people are introduced to each other, but they may also begin when one person simply starts a conversation with another. There is no need, Americans will say, to "stand on formality."

Why do people pursue relationships with others in the first place? Cultural differences in this respect can lead to misunderstanding and disappointment. When I was working at a binational cultural center in Peru, some of the people I met through my work showed an interest in spending more time with me. They stayed after a class or meeting to talk with me. They invited me to accompany them here or there. Sooner or later, they would get around to asking me if I could help them get a scholarship to study in the United States.

Americans who have lived in China report similar experiences. Some Chinese would go out of their way to be friendly or helpful, and a personal relationship seemed to be developing. Sooner or later, though, came a request for an intercession to get admitted to a university in the United States, for a letter of recommendation, for help providing a document about financial support, or for some other type of assistance.

In personal relationships, Americans tend to feel they are being taken advantage of when they believe someone is being friendly to them just because they have (or are perceived to have) connections or abilities that can help the other person. Americans have not been raised to see other people as potential links to still other people whose favorable attention they might sometime wish to gain. Their motivation in pursuing social relationships is generally not to make connections that might be helpful in other aspects of life, but to find companionship based on shared personal interests.

In the business world, of course, the idea of pursuing acquaintance-ship on the basis of connections—or "networking"—is widely accepted. People who are building their careers are advised to "develop a network" of people who might be able to help them. Some 65 million business and professional people now use a multilingual website called "LinkedIn" for just this purpose. Employees might even be evaluated in part on the basis of their "networking skills." Notice, though, that such relationships are not considered friendships, in which people develop close, personal ties. They are explicitly for potential benefit in a career or business enterprise, and all parties involved have that same idea in mind.

How do Americans get to know the people who might possibly become their friends? They meet each other at school, in offices, in religious and volunteer organizations, at sports facilities, through mutual acquaintances, in bars, over the Internet, and, as Fairlie learned, on the sidewalk. Anyone can say "Hi!" to anyone and can stop to ask a question. (Asking a question is a more common way of opening a conversation than is making a statement.) A tone of friendly informality is nearly always appropriate. Those people who do not wish to be engaged in a conversation with someone to whom they have not been introduced will make that fact clear by their response.

The small talk topics discussed in chapter 2 are common among Americans and are appropriate for interactions with new people. Foreigners meeting Americans will want to keep in mind the other aspects of communicative style addressed in chapter 2—the favorite mode of interaction, the depth of involvement sought, and so on. Remember that Americans, like everyone else, prefer to employ their accustomed communicative style. In their country, their style prevails.

More ideas about initiating interactions with Americans appear in the final section of this chapter.

THE AMERICAN CONCEPT OF FRIENDSHIP

International visitors sometimes feel betrayed by Americans whom they meet and who seem so kind and interested at first but who later fail to allow new acquaintances to really get to know them as individuals. That initial friendly "Hi!" may come to seem dishonest or misleading as the small talk continues and Americans' ideas about important topics remain hidden. "They seem cold, not really human," one Brazilian woman said. "Americans just can't let themselves go."

The Nature of Friendship

Many Americans seem unavailable for the close friendships that many foreigners have had (and taken for granted) at home and assume they will find in the United States. Sometimes people simply lack the time required to get to know another person well. Many have moved from one place to another in the past, assume they will do so again, and thus may prefer not to establish intimate friendships that will be painful to leave. Americans have also been taught, as was discussed in chapter 1, to become independent, self-reliant individuals. Although such individuals may have a large circle of friends, they are likely to avoid becoming too dependent on other people or allowing others to become dependent on them. With the exception of their immediate families, they often remain apart from others, because they most likely have not learned to do otherwise.

This is not to say that Americans never have close friendships. They do. Such relationships are relatively rare, however, and can take years to develop. Moreover, the close friendships Americans form often differ from those to which many foreigners are accustomed. Because Americans are so busy with school, their careers, and other activities, it is not uncommon for them to go weeks, months, or even longer without seeing their close friends, especially if they live in different cities. They might or might not be in regular contact with their friends by telephone, e-mail, Twitter, Facebook, a blog, or even, in ever fewer instances, a letter written on paper and sent through the mail. The most important characteristics of a close friendship, for many Americans, are the freedom to discuss private, personal matters as well as the persistence of the relationship over time and distance.

It is important to remember that there are exceptions to these generalizations. Some Americans are indeed willing to devote the time that is necessary to get to know new acquaintances well and to develop close friendships with them. They will talk openly about personal thoughts and feelings that other Americans rarely reveal.

Compartmentalized Friendships

Americans typically assume that when people gather to socialize, they will undertake some activity together. They may go to a restaurant for lunch or dinner, go to a movie, play cards, engage in or watch sports, or "have a few drinks." Americans do not usually assume that it can be pleasant or rewarding to sit and talk with other people for extended periods. (Americans would probably say "just sit" and "just talk.") Their discomfort with such a lack of structured activity is often evident if they are forced to sit and interact with people they do not know fairly well.

In some ways teenagers are an exception to what has just been said. They often "hang out" (or just "hang") with other teens—at a mall, in someone's car, or at one of their homes. Even so, the sense they often convey is not that they are enjoying each other's idle company but that they are looking for something to do or waiting for something to happen.

When they are apart from their peers, many teenagers—and not only teenagers, as things are evolving—use electronic social networks or other electronic means to "keep in touch" with their "friends" or "followers" and possibly arrange to get together in person.

Perhaps because of their emphasis on "doing things" with friends, Americans typically develop what have been called *compartmentalized friendships*. That is, they tend to have different friends with whom they engage in different activities. For example, Americans might have friends with whom they study, others with whom they go to the gym, and still others with whom they go shopping or dancing on Saturday nights. Likewise, coworkers who eat lunch together every day and occasionally go out for drinks after work may never set foot in one another's homes or meet members of one another's families.

Gender Roles and Friendship

In many countries, a friend must be a person of one's own gender. Most Americans, though, believe it is possible to have friends of the opposite sex, and they do not generally assume that a male and female will participate in sexual activity if they are alone together. This is not to say that Americans see no sexual component in a male-female friendship; they believe the people involved are capable of showing the restraint and maturity necessary to avoid sexual interaction if it is inappropriate for the situation. Thus, male and female business colleagues might travel to a conference together without anyone's assuming their relationship entails sexual contact.*

Staying in Touch with Friends

How people stay in contact with their friends is influenced by technology and age. I remember an almost-stereotypical scene at an outdoor café on a

---

* Chapter 12, "Male-Female Relationships," explores the issue of male-female relationships more fully.

Greek island. As I had expected, there was the bright sunshine, the white buildings and blue tile, a patio for the diners, and, at the table adjacent to mine, four young men with their drinks and their cigarettes. They were talking animatedly. But they were not talking to each other. Each had a cell phone and was talking to someone somewhere else.

So it is with younger Americans, among whom cell phone ownership is more and more common. Talking on a cell phone, though, is becoming less common than using one to send and receive text messages.

Older Americans are more likely to talk than text on their cell phones, if they own one. U.S. Americans in the "senior citizen" category are less likely to own cell phones than are younger people, and they rarely use them for texting.

Letters are also fading in popularity. With the continuing advances in communications technology and the increasing preference among young people for "instant gratification," ever fewer people write letters on paper and mail them to their friends.

RELATIONSHIPS PRESCRIBED
BY ROLES

The anthropologist Edward T. Hall, in a famous book called *The Silent Language* (1959), has described the United States as a "low-context culture." In such a culture, the meaning in a message is conveyed mainly by the words in the message itself. The "sender" of the message is expected to make meanings explicit and clear. In a "high-context culture," by contrast, meanings may be conveyed more by the context. A "receiver" is expected to understand a sender's indirect message. Japan, China, and Saudi Arabia are examples of high-context cultures. Some argue that U.S. American females among themselves are more high-context in their behavior than are their male counterparts.

In a high-context culture, rules—normally unspoken, but still known to all who share the culture—are built into many situations. For example, a proper young Latin American woman does not allow herself to be in the company of a man unless some responsible third party is present. That is the rule, and everyone knows it. In Japan, rules govern who sits where in a meeting, who speaks first, and which specific words are to be voiced in specific circumstances. Cathy Davidson, writing about her experience as a visiting professor in Japan, recounts an instructive incident that took place when she and her husband were eating in an elegant restaurant. Seated near them was a Japanese couple who would soon be traveling to the United States. The couple was intensely watching Professor Davidson and her husband, studying their table manners. Eventually, the Japanese woman asked them the correct angle for tipping one's soup bowl when one is taking the last spoonful of soup from the bowl (Davidson, 2006, 25–27). Americans have no rule for such a detail as this, and would typically be stunned by the idea that anyone else would have a rule about it.

In a high-context culture such as Japan's there are rules for countless situations. There are even rules governing when usual rules can be broken! (Davidson, 2006, 148).

In the United States, however, there are far fewer situations in which people's behavior is governed by widely agreed-upon rules. Still, some roles generally entail certain expected behaviors. Such roles include customer, tenant, neighbor, and coworker. While it is possible to observe regional and institutional variations in the behaviors described here, a few generalizations seem warranted.

Customer. When shopping, dining out, or otherwise using the services of clerks, servers, or other service people, Americans tend to show their respect for the ideals of equality and individual dignity. They treat clerks and others as more or less equal to themselves, not as people they consider inferior. Treating a service person rudely or dismissively is highly frowned upon.

Tenant. A tenant's responsibilities are normally made explicit in the lease, or rental contract, the tenant signs. These responsibilities—paying a specified amount of rent by a specified date and properly caring for whatever appliances and furnishings the landlord provides—are the only ones that the tenant owes the landlord. In effect, the landlord-tenant relationship is governed by the rule of law that is discussed in chapter 5. The law in this case is the lease.

Particular tenants and landlords sometimes develop more personal relationships, of course.

Neighbor. A general rule among neighbors is to "mind your own business"—that is, don't intrude in one another's lives. Some neighborhoods are more friendly than others, meaning that more people in the neighborhood know each other and that the neighbors socialize with each other.

In a 2010 study of "Neighbors Online," the Pew Research center found that 19 percent of respondents "said that they knew the names of all of their neighbors," while 24 percent knew most of them. Twenty-eight percent didn't know any of their neighbors by name (2010a).

Residents of friendlier neighborhoods may have neighborhood "block parties," where neighbors get together for food, drink, and conversation. However friendly the neighborhood, there is generally an expectation among Americans that neighbors will assist each other in times of emergency or very pressing need. For example, they may take food to the home of a neighbor just home from a hospital stay or in grief over the loss of a family member. It is considered reasonable to ask a neighbor to "keep an eye" on a house or an apartment that will be vacant temporarily, as during a vacation. Newcomers to a neighborhood may take the initiative in inviting neighbors for coffee, a pastry, and a get-acquainted conversation. Or they may themselves be invited by neighbors for such a visit. In contrast, neighbors in an apartment building may have virtually no interaction with each other.

Coworker. In general, coworkers treat each other politely and with respect, regardless of their status in relationship to the others. The boss says "Good morning" in a pleasant voice to the receptionist and the file clerk; the latter smile and say "Good morning" back. Coworkers help each other with job-related matters, and they try to avoid open expressions of displeasure or other negative feelings toward each other. Although coworkers do not feel obligated to develop close relationships, they generally do feel they should contribute to keeping the emotional tone of the workplace pleasant for all who spend the day (or night) there. Many Americans believe that the workplace should have a kind of family atmosphere, even while this general atmosphere of polite friendliness can mask what might be a very hierarchical method of operating.

COURTESY, SCHEDULES, GIFTS

Courtesy

Among Americans, being courteous has a number of elements:

- Acknowledging another person's presence or arrival, either verbally (if not with "hi!" then with "hello," "good morning," or some such greeting) or nonverbally, with a direct look, a nod, or a brief smile (By contrast, someone's departure from a group or gathering does not necessarily require explicit acknowledgement—as does a German's departure from a group of Germans, for example—except that a guest leaving a social event is expected to say thank-you and goodbye to the host.)
- Participating in at least a bit of small talk with people when one expects to be in their presence for more than a few minutes
- Using vocabulary, tone of voice, and vocal volume no less respectful than those used with peers; never "talking down" to others, issuing commands in an officious way, or in any way treating others as though they were inferior
- Saying "please" when making requests and "thank you" when requests are granted by anyone, including service people such as servers, taxi drivers, and hotel desk clerks and maids
- Saying "you're welcome" in response to a "thank you"
- Taking a place at the end of the line (what people in much of the world call a *queue*) and waiting patiently when a group of people have lined up for service or attention

Schedules

Considerate people will be mindful of other people's domestic schedules and will not telephone too early, too late, or during mealtimes. Most Americans

take breakfast between 7:00 and 9:00 A.M., lunch at noon or shortly there-
after, and an evening meal (called *dinner* in some parts of the country and
supper in others) between 6:00 and 7:00 P.M. On Sundays, all meals may be
taken somewhat later.

It is generally a good idea to make telephone calls to a person's home
between the hours of 9:00 A.M. and 9:00 P.M. (except at mealtimes), unless
there is reason to believe that everyone in the family will be awake before
or after those hours.

Gifts

Comparatively speaking, Americans give gifts on a relatively small number
of occasions and to a relatively small circle of people. Since offering gifts to
people who do not expect them can be mutually embarrassing and can even
lead to the suspicion that the gift-giver is seeking to influence the recipient
inappropriately, international visitors will want to be mindful of Americans'
practices concerning gifts.

Generally, Americans give gifts to relatives and close friends. Frequently they give gifts to hosts or hostesses (flowers, wine, or candy are
common). They do not normally give gifts to teachers (except perhaps
elementary-school teachers, who sometimes receive gifts from children in
their classes), business colleagues, or other people who might be in a position
to grant or withhold favorable treatment (such as a good grade in a class or
a contract for a sale). In fact, giving gifts to people who are in a position to
grant or withhold favors can be construed as an improper attempt to gain
favor. Many states have laws strictly limiting the value of gifts that public
employees can accept.

Christmas comes close to being a national gift-giving day in the United
States. Except for adherents of non-Christian religions, Americans exchange
Christmas gifts with relatives, close friends, and sometimes schoolmates and
business associates. Other typical gift-giving occasions include birthdays,
graduations, weddings, and childbirths. Some people give gifts on Mother's
Day, Father's Day, and Valentine's Day. A "housewarming" gift is sometimes
given to people who have moved into a new home.

Americans try to select a gift they believe the recipient could use or
would enjoy. People are not expected to give expensive gifts unless they can

readily afford them. "It's the thought that counts," Americans say, not the amount of money the gift cost. Increasing numbers of Americans give gift cards or gift certificates, which allow their recipients to choose whatever merchandise or service they prefer.

Internet gift registries take the guesswork out of deciding what gift to buy for the registrant. Such registries are most often used in relation to weddings, where the bride and groom indicate which of a store's items of merchandise they would like to have. Gift-givers then log on to the store's website and select from the items so identified. In some cases the store will send the gift, with a card, to its intended recipient.

Many Americans send Christmas cards to their friends, acquaintances, distant family members, and, in some instances, business colleagues. Those who follow a non-Christian religion may send a holiday card to convey "season's greetings" or some such nonsectarian message. Along with cards, many people send a "Christmas letter" or "holiday letter" that summarizes their family's activities of the past year—normally emphasizing the positive and minimizing the negative. The advent of e-mail and economic hardship has caused many Americans to shorten their list of recipients for Christmas cards. They may send e-mails (which, of course, are free) instead, or simply fall out of touch.

SUGGESTIONS FOR INTERNATIONAL VISITORS

The preceding paragraphs offer a number of specific suggestions for visitors. This chapter closes with some general ideas for those who want or are compelled to become involved in relationships with Americans.

The general advice is simple: take the initiative, but go slowly.

Take the initiative, because most Americans already have their lives organized and their time occupied before you come on the scene. For them it is easier to interact with other people who share their own language and culture than it is to interact with international visitors. Like most people in most countries, Americans will not usually seek out international visitors. Thus, those people here from abroad who want to get to know Americans will have to take the initiative in meeting people, starting conversations, and setting up opportunities for subsequent interactions. By closely watching how Americans interact with each other in various settings, you can learn how they greet each other, start conversations, keep them going, and end them.

Go slowly, because it takes time, in the United States as anywhere else, to develop interpersonal relationships in which people know and trust each other and feel at ease in each other's company. Some foreign visitors become so lonely and make their need for companionship so plain to the people they meet that Americans are frightened away. "He seemed absolutely desperate for someone to talk to," Americans might say after meeting a lonely foreign visitor. "I was afraid to get involved." Remember that Americans do not value dependent relationships the way many other people do. Rather, they fear them. Go slowly.

Have some conversation topics ready, so as not to be at a loss for something to say. (Remember, even brief lapses in conversation can make Americans uneasy.) Most Americans are interested in topics or questions that have to do with cultural differences and with language. Make note of idiomatic terms or slang you hear and do not understand, and ask Americans what they mean. Keep in mind things you see Americans do that you are not sure you understand, and ask Americans about them. Tell them about amusing or mildly embarrassing experiences you have had in their country. Ask them about themselves, their families, their jobs, their travels, their interests. (But don't ask them questions about money!) If other topics fail, talk about what to talk about. Explain what two people in your current situation would normally talk about if they were in your country, and ask what two Americans would normally talk about here.

Find people or groups who share your interests. Millions of Americans belong to clubs or organizations centered on various hobbies, sports, and other avocational activities.

Finally, be persistent. Patient, but persistent. Not all of your efforts to establish rewarding social relationships with Americans will succeed. You are likely to have to try again and again until you meet a person or a group of people in whose company you find mutual enjoyment. When you do discover such people, you will not only enjoy their companionship but also have the best possible window on American culture.

CHAPTER 11

Racial and Ethnic Diversity

Joohwan Park, a young advertising executive at a Korean company, traveled to Chicago on a business trip from Seoul, South Korea. Park knew that he would be in the Chicago area for only a short time and that he would be interacting primarily with other team members from his company. So he was pleased when his supervisor told him that Bill Young, an advertising representative at the Chicago office, had volunteered to show him around Chicago on the Saturday before he returned to Seoul. Park was looking forward to meeting an American, practicing his English, and learning more about American culture.

When Park met Young in the hotel lobby on Saturday morning, he was surprised to see a Korean face. Young told Park that he was Korean American; his parents had moved to the United States from Korea before he was born. Though glad to have Young's companionship, Park was also somewhat disappointed. He had hoped to meet a "real" American—someone more like the European Americans he had seen in television programs and movies.

A Word about Terms

Some scientists argue that race is not a scientifically valid notion. The differences commonly ascribed to race, they say, are in fact results of social consensus rather than objective, measurable fact. This chapter uses the term *race* anyway, because Americans commonly use it to refer to people with different physical characteristics, notably color of skin, type of hair, and shape of eyes, nose, and lips.

This chapter uses the term *ethnic* to refer to differences associated not with physical characteristics but with values and customs. Mexicans, for example, may appear to be of the same race as many Caribbean Islanders, but they have their own version of the Spanish language and their own cuisines, holidays, music, and so on. For purposes of this chapter, these are *ethnic differences.*

WHAT INTERNATIONAL VISITORS SEE

The racial and ethnic diversity that international visitors experience in the United States depends very much on the part or parts of the country they visit. According to the 2008 and 2009 estimates from the U.S. Census, people of European ancestry make up approximately 66 percent of the U.S. population. Such people are commonly referred to as *white* or *Caucasian.* Despite the increasing diversity that is discussed here, then, most of the people in the U.S. are white. In some parts of the U.S., particularly the middle of the country and the northern reaches of New England, nearly everyone is white. For example, Maine's population is 96 percent white; Iowa's 94 percent; Nebraska's and North Dakota's, 91 percent. Although the situation is changing, corporate boards of directors, evening television programs on major networks, lists of wealthy people, and governmental bodies at virtually all levels are dominated by European American people, usually males.

Hispanic Americans, who trace their ancestry to Mexico, Central and South America, Spain, and Portugal, constitute approximately 15 percent of the American population, but that percentage is climbing rapidly.

Blacks and African Americans, whose ancestors come mainly from central and southern Africa, make up about 13 percent of the population. Asians, including Hawaiians and Pacific Islanders, are about 5 percent, and Native Americans, once the proud nations that spanned the continent, constitute less than 1 percent. The remaining 2 percent identify themselves as "mixed race" or of some other ancestry.

Such culturally and racially diverse people are not randomly distributed around the country, however. For example, people visiting the West Coast, including the states of Washington, Oregon, and California, will notice the strong influence of East Asian culture in cuisine and the arts. Residents in large cities such as San Francisco shop in open-air markets offering produce and specialty items from many parts of Asia.

It is no accident that the first major-league baseball teams to give prominent roles to Japanese and Korean players were those representing the West Coast cities of Los Angeles and Seattle.

Visitors to southwestern states such as Arizona, California, New Mexico, and Texas will experience the many ways in which Latino, most prominently Mexican, culture has influenced the region. Mexican food is very popular, and regional varieties have developed in different parts of the Southwest. Mexican music (or Tejano music, as it is called in Texas) is also popular, especially in the border region, and Mexican holidays such as Cinco de Mayo (May 5), which recognizes a Mexican military victory over France in 1862, are widely celebrated.

In southern states such as Alabama, Louisiana, Mississippi, and Georgia, the black and African American influence is particularly noticeable. In fact African American culture has had a strong, if often unremarked, influence on mainstream American culture for a very long time. For example, many foreigners (and many Americans, for that matter) are surprised to learn that most of the styles of music that are considered in other parts of the world to be "typically American," such as jazz, blues, rock 'n roll, rap, and hip-hop, originated in the African American community.

In the Midwest, where the influence of other ethnic groups might not be as pervasive as it is along the coasts, the presence of such groups cannot be overlooked. Detroit has a large population of Arab Americans. Minneapolis is home to more Hmong refugees than any other American city and also to thousands of refugees from Somalia. Many small midwestern towns that have meat-packing plants are home to noticeable numbers of Hispanics, Somalis, or other ethnic groups.

Finally, the East Coast is known for its many different cultures, particularly in large cities such as New York, Boston, and Philadelphia. Visitors frequently remark that it is almost impossible to find a native-born American driving any of the thousands of taxicabs that serve Washington, D.C. or New York.

Joohwan Park and Bill Young spent the day touring Chicago and talking together. Young pointed out several of the city's ethnic neighborhoods. Like many large U.S. cities, Chicago has a Chinatown. There is also a Greektown, a Little Italy, an Indiatown, and a Ukrainian Village. Mexicans constitute the largest of Chicago's ethnic populations; Poles are the second largest. There are also concentrations of people from Vietnam, Thailand, Russia, Puerto Rico, and the Dominican Republic. Park saw cafes and other businesses with signs in assorted languages that he did not recognize. He also noticed that most of the ethnic neighborhoods were in poorer-looking parts of town, with buildings in obvious need of paint and repairs and streets in need of attention.

Young explained that people from many countries had come to the Chicago area over the years, often from economically poor backgrounds. They tended to settle in proximity to each other and to establish businesses that catered to the tastes of people "from home." Those who did well economically sometimes left these neighborhoods and moved to other parts of town where the housing was more attractive and where the neighborhood lacked or had already lost a particular ethnic identity. Young and his wife lived in such an area.

Some parts of Chicago, Young told Park, were considered too dangerous to pass through, even in daylight. They were usually dominated by one or another nonwhite group, he said, and were home to many young, unemployed males, gang members, drug dealers and users, and others considered to be potentially violent. Unlike Chinatown or Greektown, Young explained, the parts of a city dominated by black or Hispanic people do not usually have names that clearly reflect their ethnic character. Instead, their names often reflect their location or some topographic or historical feature. Examples include Cabrini Green (Chicago), The Hill District (Pittsburgh), Five Points (Denver), or simply the West Side or the East Side (many cities).

From their conversation, Park learned that Young's wife was also a Korean American, as were most of the people with whom Young and his wife socialized. Despite all of America's ethnic diversity, it seemed to Park that the amount of interaction among members of different groups was limited. Young described incidents in which he and his wife had encountered racial prejudice and stereotypes and reported that European Americans often asked him and his wife if they were Chinese. Many appeared to have one image of people from East Asia, labeled "Chinese" or "Orientals," Young said, and they seemed not to know that Koreans, Japanese, Malays, Thais, and Chinese represent different ethnic groups, languages, religions, and cultures. Some even spoke to Young and his wife in a sort of baby talk, apparently assuming that they could not speak English (their native language) very well.

Young's own boss had thought Young would be best qualified to host Park, not realizing that Young had never been to Korea, barely remembered the language his parents had spoken when he was a child, and ate Korean food (except kimchi, a ubiquitous Korean dish) only on special occasions.

Park realized that Young held his own stereotypes about groups different from his. His distrust of and dislike for black Americans was evident from his tone when he talked about them during the tour of Chicago. Since Park had already understood from news reports in Korea that animosity between blacks and Koreans in large American cities was common, he was not surprised by Young's words.

Had Park stayed longer in the United States, he might have learned that members of American minority groups are far from constituting a single community. Prejudice and stereotypes are as common within and among minority groups as they are between the majority of European Americans and members of other groups. Lighter-skinned blacks versus darker-skinned blacks, blacks versus "browns" (as Hispanics are sometimes called), Cubans versus Puerto Ricans versus Mexicans, Hindus from India versus Sikhs from India, Vietnamese with higher education versus Vietnamese with little or no formal education—these are but a few of the divisions within and among groups of "people of color" in the United States.

Like many international visitors, Joohwan Park had arrived with an image of the people of the United States that was in some ways quite different from the reality. Although the U.S. has often been called a "melting pot" (or, more recently, a "salad bowl," a "mosaic," or a "stir-fry") of many different cultural and religious groups, the dominant image of the U.S. portrayed by media is that of a relatively homogeneous society. The "typical" American is often portrayed as young, European American, and middle class. And, as stated in the Introduction, the predominant values and ideas that have historically shaped American culture have been those of the European American, Protestant male. Although racial and ethnic minorities have long played a role in shaping American society, their cultural values have not always been recognized or valued. Their influence on mainstream U.S. culture has grown considerably over the past few decades, however, and continues to increase, even as the second or third generations of immigrant families typically become assimilated into the mainstream culture. They learn English better than they learn their parents' or grandparents' language; their command of their parents' native language is limited; they adopt the clothing styles, interests, and customs of the dominant culture. (The resulting intergenerational conflicts provide material for many popular books and movies.)

Many foreign students, businesspeople, and visitors remark on the racial and ethnic diversity they observe, not only in large cities but increasingly in smaller towns as well. And, like Joohwan Park, they may also see indications of a rather stratified society, with different minority groups concentrated in particular geographic areas and with darker-skinned people more often occupying lower-level positions while lighter-skinned people enjoy more prestigious and better-paying ones. It is evident that the United States is not only a racially and ethnically diverse society but a nation divided by class as well.

HOW AMERICANS VIEW RACE AND ETHNIC RELATIONS

Of course, the way Americans think about race and ethnic relationships is deeply influenced by their cultural assumptions and values. Generally, European Americans view the topic through the lens of individualism. People of color, though, may view it through a lens of collectivism, see-ing themselves as a group with shared characteristics and concerns. Both European Americans and people of color, Americans all, are likely to seek numerical data to help them understand the topic and to support their opinions about it.

American newspapers and magazines sometimes draw on the results of public-opinion surveys when they report on the state of race relations in the country. These surveys seem to represent an effort to discover the "truth" about race relations by determining what portion of the population holds this or that opinion on the matter. If a survey finds that 55 percent of respon-dents strongly agreed with the statement that "conditions for nonwhites in the United States have improved significantly in the past ten years," many Americans take this to mean that the conditions have in fact improved.

Governmental and nonprofit agencies seeking to understand race rela-tions are likely to do studies, collecting statistical information on a wide array of topics. Some examples:

- the percentage of black males aged 21 to 25 who are unemployed, as compared with the unemployment rate among European Americans in the same age range
- the average college-entrance examination scores of members of differ-ent racial or ethnic groups

- the frequency with which various diseases (such as AIDS, tuberculosis, and diabetes) occur among blacks, Hispanics, and Native Americans in a certain age range compared with the frequency among European Americans in the same age group
- the rate at which members of different nonwhite groups drop out of secondary school compared with the dropout rate of European Americans
- the rates at which young people in various racial or ethnic groups complete secondary school, enter a college or university, graduate from a college or university, undertake graduate-level studies, or earn advanced degrees
- the portion of managers or executives in a business who are not European American
- the frequency with which unmarried teenage girls in various racial or ethnic groups become pregnant
- the frequency with which people of color appear in television programs broadcast during weekday evenings and the nature of the roles they play
- the per capita income of individuals in various groups
- the net worth of families in various groups
- the frequency with which police stop nonwhite versus European American motorists
- the disparate effects of economic hard times on European Americans versus other groups

Two often incompatible conclusions appear to emerge from all these surveys and studies. On the one hand, some people conclude that race relations in the United States are indeed improving. They cite statistics showing (they say) improved health, higher levels of educational attainment, and improved incomes, especially among blacks. They point to the increased presence of people of color in the media. They cite individuals such as the late Michael Jackson, Oprah Winfrey, and Michael Jordan, who are among the best-known Americans in the world. And of course they cite the case of Barack Obama, the black man elected to the U.S. presidency in 2008. With his election, many people thought, the issue of racism in America had passed a historic threshold. Americans, some commentators said, had shown that they were past the point of responding only to a person's race—that they could consider, as the civil rights leader Martin Luther King famously said, the "content of their character."

On the other hand, there are those, more often nonwhite than European American, who believe that Americans of color continue to suffer huge disadvantages. Such critics cite studies showing (they say) that nonwhites often earn lower incomes, have less wealth, live in lower-quality housing, suffer more often from more illnesses, fail to enter or complete school, and so on. They point to the portion of black males who are underemployed, unemployed, or, worse, in prison—or dead at an early age.

In a forum on inequality in the United States, sociologist Orlando Patterson explains these apparently contradictory viewpoints this way:

> The civil rights movement . . . succeeded wonderfully in the public sphere of American life. From being virtual outcasts in nearly every area of public life as late as the 1950s, black Americans are now an integral part of the political, cultural and civic fabric. They are a critical component of one of the nation's major political parties; they are fully integrated into the military . . . ; they exercise disproportionate influence in popular culture—in music, sports, theater, dance, film, and TV—and they have been incorporated into elite public and corporate positions to a degree unparalleled in any other white-majority nation in the world . . . .
>
> However, accompanying this historic public achievement has been a stunning failure: the persisting exclusion of blacks from the private sphere of American life. Outside elite circles, blacks are as segregated today from the private domain of white lives—their neighborhoods, schools, churches, clubs and other associations, friendship networks, marriage markets and families—as they were fifty years ago. (2010, 21)

Americans, or at least European Americans, are so influenced by the value of individualism that they often have trouble seeing the race-relations situation in terms of groups in the way Professor Patterson does. If Barack Obama can succeed in life (which means, for many Americans, becoming rich and famous or achieving high office), then so can other individuals. Look how hard Obama worked to overcome his humble background. See

147

how intelligent he is, how well he has learned to express himself and to present himself to the public. Other nonwhites could succeed too, according to this view, if they just worked hard enough and behaved appropriately.

Yet Obama's election did not seem to move America past its race-relations troubles. Authorities reported an unprecedented number of assassination threats aimed at the black president; hate crimes aimed at blacks increased, while those targeting other minority groups declined. Seemingly invigorated right-wing extremists challenged Obama's patriotism and even the legitimacy of his presidency. Sales of guns and ammunition increased dramatically after his election victory. Public-opinion surveys taken well after Obama assumed office showed far more blacks than others approving of his performance.

Whether one takes the view that things are getting better or worse, it is certainly the case that the United States still faces major issues regarding the relationship between the traditional European American population and people with other backgrounds. Even the language used to discuss the topic is open to emotional debate. For example, by the year 1970 it was no longer acceptable to refer to someone with African ancestry as *colored*, which had long been considered a polite term. *Colored* was supplanted by *Negro*, which in turn gave way to *black* (sometimes capitalized, sometimes not) and then, at least in some circles, to *African American*. (The word *nigger* is virtually always considered highly insulting and degrading—unless used among African Americans themselves. International visitors will certainly want to avoid the word entirely—as they will words that convey disrespect for members of other ethnic or cultural groups.)

Indeed, the matter of terminology regarding non–European American groups became so sensitive that, around 2010, some well-known media personalities were forced to retire after using "racial slurs" or other demeaning language in public settings. In private, international visitors may well hear U.S. Americans using racial slurs or other derisive language when talking about racial or ethnic groups other than their own,

Foreign visitors are probably safe if they refer to America's various racial or ethnic groups with a term that relates to the group's regional or cultural background: African American, Asian American, Arab American, Japanese American, European American, and so on. This terminology conveys the idea that all such groups are fundamentally equal—that none is to be looked down upon. *People of color, non-majority groups,* and *non-dominant groups* are acceptable terms for referring to non-Caucasian groups in general.

Wariness about terminology, coupled with an aversion to verbal confrontation and inconclusive statistical information, leads many Americans to avoid the controversial topic of race relations. Many of them just don't talk about it unless they are angry, frustrated, intoxicated, or in the presence of people who they know share their opinions on the topic.

Like people in other countries with heterogeneous populations, people in the United States are continuing to confront ethnic and racial tensions resulting from factors such as discrimination and the negative stereotypes that different groups hold about one another. Most Americans firmly believe in the idea of equality, at least in theory. Since the U.S. Supreme Court's famous 1954 decision in the case of *Brown v. Board of Education of Topeka, Kansas,* a decision that outlawed racial segregation in public schools, many court decisions and laws have been aimed at producing more racial equality within the society.

In another key case, the Supreme Court ruled in 1967 that state laws banning interracial marriage were unconstitutional. At the time, such laws still existed in sixteen states, many of which did not officially change their laws to allow interracial marriage until well into the 1970s. The last state to officially remove the law, Alabama, did not do so until 2000. The Census Bureau found in 2008 that 8 percent of marriages were interracial, up from 7 percent in 2000. Interracial marriages, which were most common between blacks and European Americans, were gradually gaining public acceptance.

Another issue that has been widely debated in recent years, particularly on college campuses, is affirmative action. *Affirmative action* refers to policies or programs that try to reduce the effects of current and historical discrimination by giving minority-group members and women greater access to opportunities in education and employment. For example, many universities and professional schools (such as law and business schools) instituted programs designed to increase the enrollment of minority students and females. These programs included outreach to high school students, special admissions criteria, remedial educational programs for students deemed unprepared for college-level work, and admissions plans that call for a certain level of minority enrollment in a student body.

Americans continue to be divided on the issue of affirmative action. Many see affirmative action programs as positive and even necessary, because they allow minorities greater access to businesses and educational opportunities that are still largely dominated by European American males. Others believe that affirmative action programs are unnecessary or undesirable, because they give an advantage to minorities based not on their merit as individuals but on their membership in groups defined by color, gender, or national origin. As stated in chapter 1, Americans are taught that the ideal person is self-reliant and should advance on the basis of his or her own accomplishments, not because of special treatment given as a result of membership in a particular group.

The issue of affirmative action is complex and evokes people's strong feelings, whatever their points of view on the matter. It is not likely to be resolved in the foreseeable future. One possibility seems to be that *socioeconomic status* will replace race as an indicator of disadvantage. If that happened, and it does seem to be happening, then such factors as parents' level of wealth and education, rather than skin color, would be taken into account in making employment and college admissions decisions.

SUGGESTIONS FOR INTERNATIONAL VISITORS

First, think about your own ideas concerning whatever ethnic minority groups are present in the part of the United States you are visiting. What are your stereotypes of them? Do you assume they are kind and hardworking? Intelligent? Ignorant? Dangerous? Consider what your stereotype is based on. Do you have any personal experience on which to base your stereotype?

Think also about your own experience as a member of a "minority group," which is what you are while in the United States. Do people here notice that you are not an American? Do they treat you differently from the way they seem to treat Americans? In your own experience, what is it like to be part of the minority?

And think about the state of "race relations" in your own country. What are the minority groups there? What stereotypes prevail? How, in general, are members of minority groups treated? (If you yourself are a member of a minority group in your country, you may be an expert on this.)

Thinking about questions such as these gives you some context for the remainder of these suggestions.

How often do you see members of different racial or ethnic groups interacting with each other? In what settings? Do you see many mixed-race couples?

If you see people playing sports in public places, are they doing so in mixed groups?

What seating patterns do you see in public places such as buses, cafeterias, parks, and classrooms? Are there clusters of people who appear to share an ethnic background, or are groups intermixed?

Do you notice any apparent correlation between skin color and the kinds of jobs you see people doing?

What housing patterns do you observe? Do you see neighborhoods dominated by one ethnic group or another? Particular apartment buildings? Do you see mixed-race roommates in college housing?

After thinking and observing, seek out opportunities to learn more. Ask a librarian or bookstore employee to suggest a book or two that would help you learn more about whatever minority groups live in the area where you are. Seek out movies made by members of minority groups. Attend performances or festivals mounted by members of minority groups, such as a Cinco de Mayo event in a Mexican community, Oktoberfest among Germans, or Kwaanza among African Americans. Go to performances by members of minority groups; eat in restaurants with cuisines representing different ethnic groups.

Finally, find ways to talk to non-majority people. This can be delicate; it will require some intercultural sensitivity on your part. Have ready some questions about people's backgrounds, experiences, and perceptions. Remember that you can always introduce your questions by saying you are new in the United States and are trying to learn more about the country. If you approach members of minority groups, you can ask them what name they prefer you to use for their group. Then ask your questions. Expect a wide variety of responses, given the complexity of the topic.

It may be easier if you approach members of mixed groups or couples. The fact that they are with others who are different from themselves probably means they will be more open to your questions.

You could also approach professional people who are likely to know something about racial or interethnic relations in your area—teachers, police officers, ministers, journalists. Again, just explain that you are new in the United States, want to learn more about racial and ethnic relations here, and would like to hear what they know and think about that topic.

CHAPTER 12

Male-Female Relationships

Sanjeev Balakrishnan astonished his American friends when, just after completing the first year of a Ph.D. program in mechanical engineering, he told them he was going home to India to get married.

"We didn't know you had a fiancée," they said to him.

"I don't," he replied. He explained that his parents had selected thirteen possible brides for him. As soon as he got home he would begin interviewing them, spending an hour with each and selecting one of the thirteen to marry. After the wedding his bride would get an American visa and come back to the States with him.

At the start of the next semester, Balakrishnan returned to the United States with his new wife. He told his American friends that this woman had attracted him the most during the interviews. She was intelligent, lively, and had an engaging sense of humor. Furthermore, she seemed to have a spirit of adventure; the idea of going to another country to begin her married life greatly appealed to her.

Balakrishnan also said that the three-day wedding ceremony had gone off with no problems. Relatives on both sides seemed to get on well. The couple's future looked bright.

In the minds of Balakrishnan's American friends, the idea of choosing a marital partner from a group of strangers on the basis of a one-hour interview was simply incredible. We will look at American ideas about romantic and other male-female relationships shortly, but first we will consider some of the factors that influence Americans' views of those relationships.

INFLUENCES ON
MALE-FEMALE RELATIONSHIPS

Cultural Values

As discussed in chapter 1 and mentioned elsewhere in this book, Americans fervently embrace the idea that people should be treated as individuals. In male-female relationships, this ideal means that men and women can interact with each other as individual human beings rather than as representatives of a gender. It is not always assumed that a man and a woman are romantically involved if they spend time together. Many men have women whom they consider to be "just friends" and vice versa.

Nor are women viewed as representatives of their families, representatives whose behavior helps determine the family's social or moral standing. Americans did not seem troubled by the fact that 2008 vice presidential candidate Sarah Palin's unmarried teenage daughter, Bristol, was pregnant. Indeed, two years later and still unmarried, Bristol was invited to be a contestant on the popular television program, *Dancing with the Stars*.

Americans are generally shocked by the "honor killings" that sometimes occur in certain immigrant communities, where a female family member is killed for having behaved in a way deemed to have "dishonored the family."

The general American idea that males and females can interact with each other in a manner that appears to ignore gender differences seems unrealistic and even bizarre to many international visitors, especially to those who come from places where male-female differences dictate aspects of the social order. A group of French exchange students in the United States for a summer academic program commented on the way that Americans seemed to disregard gender. "It is natural that there should be differences in the way that men and women behave," said one woman. "Why can't Americans accept this biological fact?"

Another important influence on male-female relationships in the United States arises from the value placed on equality. Both men and women in America generally believe (at least in theory) that all people, regardless of gender, should be treated as equals. Neither gender, according to this view, should have built-in advantages in social or economic worlds due simply to their gender. This, of course, is the ideal, not the reality.

Women's Liberation and Feminism

The belief in equality of the sexes gained strength as a result of the women's liberation movement of the 1960s and 1970s and has continued to grow as feminist ideas have gained a stronger hold in society.

Representatives of women's movements have pointed out discrepancies between the professed ideals of individualism, freedom, and equality, on the one hand, and the actual practices of gender discrimination, stereotyping, and inequality, on the other.

Women's liberation refers to a collection of opinions and developments that, in general, seeks to end discrimination against women—at least, discrimination that is based on the notion that women are somehow inferior to men. "Equal rights for women" is one of the movement's stated goals. "Equal pay for equal work" is another, although that goal has yet to be met, as women still earn only about 80 cents on each dollar earned by men.

Before the women's movement, women in the United States were generally expected to spend their lives preparing to be wives and mothers. Young women in school took "home economics" courses, which taught them how to cook, sew, manage household finances, and care for children. In light of the unfortunate possibility that they might not marry or might someday have to earn an income, women were also encouraged to take other courses that presumably prepared them for one of the three occupations that were deemed appropriate for women at that time—teacher, nurse, or secretary. Most women did not attend college, and those who did were not normally expected to pursue a career outside the home after graduating. Most women married at a relatively young age, after which they were expected to stay at home with their children while their husbands went to work.

Since the 1960s, supporters of the feminist movement have sought to change the role of women in the United States. Parents are more likely to try to convey the idea to their daughters that their prospects in life depend more on their personality, intelligence, and ambition than on their gender. School textbooks and teachers now acknowledge women's contributions to literature, politics, science, and other fields. Feminists argue for an end to what they see as stereotyping of women on television and in other media. They call for female representation on committees or other bodies whose decisions affect women's lives. In general they seek to raise the consciousness of all Americans concerning what they consider to be pervasive, unfair, and unwarranted anti-female attitudes.

The feminist movement has changed certain expectations for women. Many American women no longer see marriage and family life as their main goals and have broader ideas about the prospects life holds for them. Women wait longer to get married, as mentioned in chapter 6, and they also wait longer to have children so they will have time to develop their careers.

More females than males are attending postsecondary educational institutions; by 2009, more women than men were earning doctorates. Movies and television programs featuring women have become more numerous. Women's athletics have achieved significant stature in schools at all levels and in professional leagues.

Women are now found in many lines of work formerly considered male domains, including law enforcement, construction, and truck driving. There are many female doctors, lawyers, and professionals in the business world. Female political figures prominent in the early years of the twenty-first century include Secretary of State Hillary Rodham Clinton, Former House of Representatives Speaker Nancy Pelosi, and 2008 vice-presidential candidate Sarah Palin. Several major American universities now have female presidents, and some major corporations have female CEOs.

According to the AFL-CIO, an American labor union, the number of women who work outside the home has grown noticeably over the years. In 2008, according to the Bureau of Labor Statistics, women comprised 59.5 percent of the labor force. In comparison, only 29.6 percent of women worked in 1950. The U.S. Labor Department estimates that 99 percent of American women will work for pay at some point in their lives.

The feminist movement; along with the 1960s introduction of the birth control pill, no doubt has had something to do with the increasing equality that women enjoy. Difficult economic times have also contributed to the increase in female participation in the labor force. Indeed, more males than females lost their jobs in the late 2000s recession, increasing the rate of female participation in the labor force and increasing the number of households in which the female earned more money than the male.

The increased presence of women in the workplace has implications for male-female relationships. More women are earning money and are therefore in a position to assert their independence. Traditional female responsibilities in the areas of child care and household maintenance are being reallocated, as has been mentioned. Certain tasks that were once considered "women's work," such as childcare, cooking, grocery shopping, and cleaning the house, are no longer performed solely by women. In fact, some couples have decided, for whatever reason, that the woman will be the one whose work supports the family financially and that the man will take care of the house and the children. As mentioned earlier, such men are popularly called "househusbands" or "stay-at-home dads," and there are more and more of them.

The themes underlying the feminist movement are the same themes—individualism, independence, and equality—that underlie American society in general. Even so, support for the movement has not been universal, even among women. The women's movement has shaken a traditional social order in ways that some people of both genders welcome and that others find disturbing. Visitors from abroad will see many indications of continuing flux in male-female relationships in America, including vigorous debates about the morality and legality of abortion, lawsuits alleging sexual discrimination, and, among individuals, widely varying views about women's roles in family life and about social values.

One's Upbringing

Aside from cultural values and the women's movement, people's own upbringings also influence the way they think about and interact with members of the opposite sex. Children notice the patterns of interaction between their parents and between each of their parents and people outside the family who are members of the opposite sex. They notice the ways their parents speak to each other, the way they divide household labor, and the amount of respect they show one another.

Some American children grow up in homes that limit the amount of interaction between males and females. In these homes parents may not allow their children to go out on dates with members of the opposite sex before the age of sixteen or so. They may be less open to discussing sex in their homes, and they may not let children watch sexually explicit movies until they reach what the parents consider to be an appropriate age. More conservative families may also send their children to private schools that separate girls from boys or that promote "conservative" values.

On the other hand, some American families are less restrictive about their children's interactions with members of the opposite sex. These parents may encourage their children to go out on dates, or they may let their teenage children host or attend mixed-gender parties.

Foreign visitors, then, are likely to encounter a wide range of views about male-female relationships.

MALE-FEMALE RELATIONSHIPS IN VARIOUS SETTINGS

Informal Relationships

Strict segregation of the sexes is not the norm in the United States except in increasingly rare male- or female-only educational institutions. In most settings males and females interact freely. In shops, for example, male and female customers and employees behave in ways that tend to ignore gender differences. Strangers of both sexes will speak with each other on sidewalks or buses, in classrooms, or in other public places. At receptions and parties, males and females may readily mingle with each other. Granted, the men may often gather in one area where they discuss sports and other "men's topics" while the women collect elsewhere and discuss "women's topics." This segregation is attributed more to differences in interests than to differences in gender as such.

In schools male and female students may study together or participate jointly in recreational activities. Coed (that is, combined male and female) sports teams are common in communities, colleges, and universities. In a few noteworthy cases, young women have joined wrestling, baseball, and (American) football teams, which are traditionally male. Coworkers in companies often meet for "happy hour" after work in a bar or restaurant. Both men and women are likely to be included in such gatherings.

The characteristics of conversation in what is called "mixed company" are likely to differ from those in single-sex groups. Males are more likely than females to initiate conversation when strangers of different sexes interact. Both males and females are likely to be more willing to discuss "personal" topics among themselves than in mixed company. Americans are advised to "watch their language" when in mixed groups and typically refrain from using profanity or sex-related terminology, particularly in "bar talk" or at parties where heavy drinking occurs and inhibitions are lowered. These restraints are less salient than they were in the past, but they still have their effect, and international visitors will want to monitor their own language accordingly.

Workplace Relationships

The issue of sexual harassment provides a useful way to view the matter of male-female workplace relationships in contemporary America. This issue lies at the intersection of several cultural values and a tradition of male dominance, and complaints and even lawsuits are the outcome of what is perceived as sexual harassment. Here are some examples:

- A worker is disciplined for sexual harassment because he posted a photograph of his bikini-clad girlfriend at his workstation in full view of fellow workers, some of whom were women.
- A department head is disciplined because a female supervisee reported to him that a male colleague persistently touched her hair or shoulders when he walked past her desk, and the department head took no action to stop the behavior.
- A company's treasurer is fired after two of his female staff members reported that he threatened to prevent them from being promoted if they refused to engage in sexual activity with him.

- A university professor is charged with sexual harassment after a female student reported that he had offered to raise her grade in his class if she would allow him to see her breasts.
- A female high-school teacher is accused of inappropriately touching a male student in one of her classes.
- A committee of college professors and administrators spends months debating whether their institution's policy on sexual harassment should proscribe romantic relationships between teachers and students.

Many cultural values and assumptions underlie the Americans' concern with sexual harassment. They include individualism, equality, a belief that conditions of life can be changed and improved through conscious effort, and a belief that laws and rules can help bring about those changes. These values and assumptions have led to a search for "gender-neutral" policies, procedures, and behaviors in the workplace.

What this means in general is that hiring policies, training and supervisory procedures, salary schedules, and day-to-day workplace behavior are to be free of distinctions between men and women. Again, this may seem strange to people from societies where males and females are expected to behave and be treated differently, as was illustrated when a visiting Frenchman went to his host organization's office and asked to see the organization's sexual harassment policy. He had not had any problem related to sexual harassment, he said. He explained why he wanted to see the policy: "I teach English in France, and it's hard to keep the students engaged. But they find American issues about sexual harassment so amusing that they pay attention!"

In the United States, governments at all levels have passed laws—and many employers have policies—concerning sexual harassment. Even though there is still disagreement about the appropriateness of those laws and policies, and although there are various interpretations of them, international visitors who spend time in an American workplace will need to try to understand and abide by them. Failure to do so can lead to disciplinary action or even dismissal from a place of employment.

Many organizations require employees to have "training" concerning sexual harassment, so they presumably know what behaviors they should avoid. Generally speaking, sexual harassment policies are intended to exclude from the workplace any behavior that entails discomfort for or mistreatment of employees that is based on the employees' gender. One definition of sexual harassment is "unwelcome behavior" of a sexual nature that makes someone feel uncomfortable or unwelcome in the workplace by focusing attention on her (or, less commonly, his) gender. Sexual harassment may be directed toward men or women, although stories about women who feel that they have been sexually harassed are much more numerous. Examples of sexual harassment in the workplace, in addition to the six instances given above, include unnecessary touching; telling jokes of a sexual nature that may make someone feel uncomfortable; placing sexually explicit posters or photographs in view of others; or asking a person for sexual favors in exchange for a promotion, pay increase, or favorable treatment of any kind.

As was said at the beginning of this section, the issue of sexual harassment provides a useful lens for looking at male-female workplace relationships in the United States. This does not mean that sexual harassment is an all-consuming topic in almost every workplace, but it does mean that, in general, males and females in a workplace are expected to treat each other as individual human beings with personalities and employment-related qualifications that have nothing to do with their gender. As has been stressed, behaving in accordance with this general idea can be difficult for people from societies where males and females customarily occupy separate realms and treat each other in ways that expressly acknowledge gender differences.

"My boss here is a lady," said a visiting scientist from Korea. "In Korea, my boss will not be a lady." The scientist had to make a number of adjustments in his ideas and behavior in order to become an accepted member of his American workplace.

Romantic Relationships

Americans believe that the selection of a marital partner should be left entirely to the two individuals concerned. An "arranged marriage" such as Sanjeev Balakrishnan's is incompatible with the independence, freedom, and equality that Americans value so highly and is virtually unheard of in the United States, except in some immigrant communities.

This does not mean, however, that marital partners are selected at random. In fact, most Americans marry people of their own ethnic background, religion, and geographical origin—the same factors Balakrishnan's parents no doubt considered when choosing potential partners for their son. Traditionally, Americans meet their future mates through mutual friends or family, at a bar or restaurant, at their place of work, or in secondary school or college.

Those who marry (or remarry) later in life can have difficulty finding mates in the traditional ways. An increasing number of such people turn to Internet matching services that attempt, for a fee, to help people who are seeking romantic partners.

Marriages between adherents of different religions (usually called "interfaith marriages") or of different racial or ethnic groups are increasingly common, although they still constitute only a small minority of marital unions.

Traditionally, romantic relationships began with a date. Dating once meant that a man asked a woman out for dinner and a movie (or some similar activity) so the two could get to know each other. The couple would arrange a time to meet, the man would pick the woman up in his car, and they would "go out." The man would pay for the meal and the movie tickets, and sometimes, if everything went well, the woman would give the man a goodnight kiss at the end of the evening.

This concept of dating may still prevail among older Americans who find themselves single later in their lives. But for younger people, dating in this way is not so common. Instead they may go out in groups rather than in pairs. "Meeting up" or "hooking up" may be arranged spontaneously, perhaps by telephone but more often by some other form of electronic communication. Women might take the initiative in making arrangements to get together, and it is increasingly common for a woman to pay her own way, thus emphasizing her independence and equality and reducing her sense of obligation to her male companion.

Some reports indicate that, at least in some circles, dating in the traditional sense no longer takes place at all. "People here don't date," wrote a columnist for the Cornell University *Daily Sun*. "They either couple up and act married [that is, they live together like husband and wife] or do the random, one-night hook-up thing" (that is, they get together once for commitment-free sexual activity) (Reimold, 2010).

As recently as a few generations ago, Americans generally disapproved of cohabitation—that is, of unmarried males and females living together. By now such arrangements are quite common and in many circles are entirely acceptable and even expected. The decline in the marriage rate—it was 11 per thousand in 1980 and 7.1 per thousand in 2008, according to the U.S. Census Bureau—can be attributed in part to the increasing numbers of couples who live together without getting married. In fact, cohabitation has become so acceptable that a growing number of colleges and universities were reported in 2010 to be offering coed rooms in their student residence halls.

Couples may date or otherwise spend time together for any length of time before they discuss marriage. International visitors should be aware that most Americans do not consider going out on one or even several dates to be indicative of a serious relationship. In fact, many Americans go out on first dates and decide that they never want to see the other person again. For couples that "hit it off" or decide they would like to see more of one another, dating can last a short time—several weeks—or extend over many years before they discuss marriage, if indeed they ever do.

Usually, Americans introduce their romantic partners to their parents only after they think the relationship is becoming more serious or when they think marriage is likely.

When Americans do decide to marry (usually at about twenty-eight years of age for men and twenty-six for women), some traditional rituals are usually observed. Often, the man asks the woman to marry him, although that is certainly not always true. Sometimes, the man will even ask his fiancée's family if he may marry her. This ritual, however, is considered a formality.

Many couples choose to have their wedding ceremony in a church or synagogue even if they do not consider themselves particularly religious. Other couples choose to get married by a judge at a courthouse. This type of wedding is called a "civil ceremony," as opposed to a religious one. In either case, it is usually important to the couple to have at least some friends or family members attend their wedding ceremony.

Although an American wedding is far shorter than the three days of

Balakrishnan's experience, it may still be an elaborately planned event that follows a year or more of planning and costs many thousands of dollars.

This chapter has focused on romantic relationships between heterosexual couples, but it should be noted that homosexual romantic relationships are increasingly open and are becoming more accepted in American society. Many American cities have visible and vocal gay, lesbian, bisexual, and transgender communities. Polls consistently show that the younger generation is generally much more accepting of gay people than are their elders. More and more movies and television programs depict gay and lesbian people, including some in romantic relationships. Contentious debate has occurred in many states over proposals to allow same-sex couples to marry. At the time of this writing, same-sex marriages are legal in six states, while thirty states have constitutional amendments banning them. In some states these amendments are being challenged in court.

SUGGESTIONS FOR INTERNATIONAL VISITORS

To learn more about the many ways that males and females interact in American society, foreign visitors may want to observe female-male interactions as portrayed in movies and TV programs, then ask Americans how the movie and TV portrayals relate to reality.

Many Americans will be happy to speak about their own experiences in choosing a mate, their family's views on the subject, their notion about an ideal partner, or their views on feminism.

Discussing the topics of "interfaith" and "interethnic" marriages with people who are in such relationships can be particularly illuminating, because those involved in them have been forced to give more thought to the topic than those in marriages not involving major social, cultural, or religious differences.

Of course, international visitors who have these conversations will want to compare what they have learned with what they are accustomed to in their own countries. Rather than evaluating which system is better, international visitors can look for similarities and differences between the cultures.

CHAPTER 13

Sports and Recreation

L egend has it that Adolf Hitler got the idea for his mass rallies from observing the behavior of spectators at American college football games. Orchestrated by uniformed cheerleaders and roused by martial music, those spectators engaged in exuberant and emotional displays of support for their teams. Hitler used similar devices to rouse support for the country he came to dominate.

Sports and recreation absorb a huge amount of Americans' emotion, time, and, in many cases, money. *Sports* here refers to spectator sports, in which people watch others—mainly high school, college, and professional athletes—engage in competitive games. *Recreation* refers to leisure-time participation in athletics or other avocational activities.

SPORTS

Americans' interest in spectator sports seems excessive and even obsessive to many international visitors. Not all Americans are interested in sports, of course, but very many are. Some seem interested in little else. Television networks spend millions of dollars arranging telecasts of sports events and constantly search for new ways (such as using ever-evolving computer graphics and hiring famous or glamorous announcers and commentators) to make their coverage more appealing. Three television networks broadcast sports news and commentary twenty-four hours. Some channels are devoted entirely to specific sports, such as golf and professional football. Superbowl Sunday, the day of the National Football League's championship game, has become almost a national holiday. Talk shows focused on sports are prominent on many radio stations.

Americans bet millions of dollars on the outcome of sports contests. Publications about sports sell widely. Fans may display not just ardent support for their favored teams, but ardent dislike of their teams' rivals. Professional athletes often become national heroes. Sports stars such as Michael Jordan and Tiger Woods became more widely recognized than any national leader other than the president. Many professional athletes—and their coaches—receive yearly salaries in the millions of dollars.

The Internet has made it possible for uncounted sports fans—usually males—to live vicariously through *fantasy sports leagues*. Participants in these leagues select groups of professional athletes to form imaginary teams and then compete against each other based on the statistics each (real) athlete generates in live competitions. These leagues can be recreational, or they can involve gambling with significant amounts of money.

What seems distinctive about the American interest in sports is that it is not confined to particular social classes. People in all walks of life are represented among devoted sports fans, and the collective audience for sports events is enormous.

In the United States sports are associated with educational institutions in a way that is unique. High school faculties include coaches, and school athletic teams compete with each other in an array of sports. Each team's entourage may have a marching band (especially associated with football, as Americans and Canadians call the game played with the oblong-shaped ball) and a group of cheerleaders. In some American communities, high school athletics are a focal point of the townspeople's activities and conversations. *Friday Night Lights*, a bestselling book about a high school football team in a Texas community, became the basis for a major motion picture and then a long-running television series.

College sports, especially football and basketball, are conducted in an atmosphere of intense excitement and pageantry. Games between teams classified as "major football powers" attract nationwide television audiences numbering in the millions. An entire industry has been built on the manufacture and sale of badges, pennants, T-shirts, blankets, hats, underwear, and countless other items bearing the mascots and colors of various university athletic teams. Football and basketball coaches at major universities are paid higher salaries than the presidents of their institutions, and athletic department budgets are in the millions of dollars.

Said a recently arrived foreign student in Iowa City, after seeing legions of black-and-gold-clad fans swarming the town on a game-day morning, "It looks like the most important part of the University [of Iowa] is the football team. Maybe the team *is* the most important thing in the whole town."

Sports are a very frequent topic of conversation, especially (as noted earlier) among males. Small talk about sports is safe—interesting but not too personal. Participants can display their knowledge of athletes and statistics without revealing anything considered private.

In some social circles, associating with athletes is a way to achieve social recognition. A person who knows a local sports hero personally or who attends events where famous athletes are present is considered by some people to have accomplished something worthwhile.

Expressions from sports are extraordinarily common in everyday U.S. American speech. Baseball is probably the source of more idiomatic expressions (examples: *get to first base, touch base with, cover all the bases, throw a curve, strike out*) than any other sport. That fact can disadvantage international visitors trying to communicate with Americans, because most of them come from countries where baseball is not played, and even if baseball is a national sport in their country, they still may not understand these American idioms.

For reasons too complex to examine here, African Americans are heavily overrepresented in football, basketball, and track. While African Americans constitute about 12 percent of the country's total population, they make up well over half of most college and professional football and basketball teams. It is not unusual to see a basketball game in which all the players on the floor are black. (Arguably reflecting continuing racial discrimination, blacks make up only a small minority of coaches, managers, and executives, even in the sports where black players are so prominent.)

The women's movement can be credited with bringing increasing attention to women's athletics in the United States. Female athletes and their teams get more attention in the States than in many other countries. The attention given to women's sports in the United States is no doubt due in large part to a 1972 law that outlawed gender discrimination in schools. The law mandated equal opportunity and treatment for men and women in athletic as well as in academic programs. Although female professional athletes and coaches are still paid less than their male counterparts, American women's participation in sports has grown significantly over the past few decades. Beginning in the late 1990s, women's professional basketball was regularly televised on national networks, and female professional basketball players began to appear in television advertisements—the ultimate sign of social acceptance and respect.

The most popular sport in much of the world—soccer—is becoming increasingly popular in the United States as well. Nevertheless, the most popular sports here are still American football, baseball, basketball, and in some states, hockey—games that are not played in large numbers of countries.

Sports play such an important role in American life that the sociology of sports, sports medicine, sports psychology, and even sports marketing have become respectable academic specializations.

RECREATION

The word *recreation* brings to mind relaxing and enjoyable activities. An evening walk around the neighborhood, a Sunday picnic with the family, and playing ball in the yard with the children all seem relatively spontaneous and relaxing pastimes.

Much American recreational activity, however, seems to international visitors to be approached with a high degree of seriousness, planning, organization, and expense. Spontaneity and fun are often absent, as far as the visitor can tell. "These crazy Americans!" a South American exclaimed after seeing yet another jogger go past her house in subzero winter weather. Many

Americans jog every day, or play tennis, handball, racquetball, or bridge two or three times a week; some do aerobic exercises three times weekly, work out in gyms up to six days a week, or engage in other regularly scheduled recreation, whether alone, with a partner or small group of acquaintances, or a members of some team or league. They go on vacations, ski or canoe, or go on hiking trips, and hunting or fishing expeditions that require weeks of planning and organizing. In the American's view, all these activities are generally fun and relaxing, or are worth the discomfort they may cause because they contribute to health and physical fitness and may also offer opportunities to socialize.

Much American recreation is highly organized. Classes, clubs, leagues, newsletters, contests, exhibitions, and conventions are centered on hundreds of different recreational activities. People interested in astronomy, bird watching, cooking, dancing, ecology, fencing, gardening, hiking—and on and on—can find a group of like-minded people with whom to meet, learn, and practice or perform. Even if the level of participation in group recreational activities is declining, as political scientist Robert Putnam argues in his often-quoted and somewhat controversial book called *Bowling Alone* (2000), foreign visitors are frequently struck by the extent of Americans' involvement in recreational and avocational associations.

Recreation is big business in America. Many common recreational activities require clothing, supplies, and equipment that can be quite costly. Recreational vehicles (RVs) that are used for traveling usually include provisions for sleeping, cooking, and showering and can cost more than half a million dollars. Running shoes, hiking boots, fishing and camping supplies, skiing equipment, cameras, telescopes, gourmet cookware, and bowling balls are not inexpensive items. Beyond equipment, there is clothing. The fashion industry has successfully persuaded many Americans that they must be properly dressed for jogging, playing tennis, skiing, swimming, yoga, biking, and so on. Fashionable outfits for these and other recreational activities can be surprisingly expensive.

A final point that astute international observers notice is the relationship between social class and certain recreational activities. This relationship is by no means invariable, and the element of geography complicates it. (For example, a relatively poor person who happens to live in the Colorado mountains may be able to afford skiing, while an equally poor resident of a Plains state could not afford to get to the mountains and pay for lodging there.) In general, though, golf and yachting are associated with wealthier people, tennis with better-educated people, and outdoor sports such as camping, hiking, fishing, hunting, and boating with middle-class people. Those who bowl or square dance regularly are likely to be members of the middle or lower-middle class, as are the legion of fans attracted to automobile racing. Foreign observers will be able to find other examples of these relationships between social class and recreational activities in whatever part of the United States they come to know. (Wherever they are in the country, though, Americans themselves are likely to deny the existence of social classes.)

SUGGESTIONS FOR INTERNATIONAL VISITORS

International visitors—especially males—who plan to be in the United States for an extended period will enhance their ability to interact constructively with Americans if they take the trouble to learn about local sports teams. Knowing something about the games and players and about their importance in the natives' minds improves a foreign visitor's chance of getting to know "average" Americans.

Realize that it is fruitless to interest most Americans in soccer or, particularly, cricket.

Long-term visitors who are interested in getting to know Americans are also encouraged to take a class, join a club, or participate on a recreational sports team. Most Americans enjoy meeting new people with whom they share a common interest.

Physical fitness can be a good thing, unless it is taken to the obsessive extremes shown by some Americans. Take advantage of your time in the United States to make use of the walking trails, running tracks, bicycle paths, swimming pools, and gymnasiums that are relatively accessible in many localities.

CHAPTER 14

Driving

"You can always tell when a car is being driven by a foreigner," said a Midwestern chief of police. "You don't have to be able to see the driver. They just don't drive the same way we do."

Foreigners' driving is noticeable in any country. Driving entails not just the mechanical manipulations of the car—starting the engine, shifting gears, steering—but customary styles of driving as well. Because such customs vary from place to place, foreigners' driving is often different from that of the locals.

Driving customs within the United States also differ from one part of the country to another. In Pittsburgh, for example, a driver waiting at a red traffic light and wanting to turn left may race into the intersection and execute the left turn in front of oncoming cars just as the light turns green. Denver drivers seem less likely to do that; instead, they will wait until the oncoming traffic has passed and then make the turn. In Boston there seem to be almost no traffic rules, and drivers may seem quite aggressive to non-Bostonians.

While there are marked regional differences in the driving behavior of Americans, there are some commonalities that international visitors who drive in the States will want to know about. After discussing some general information about cars and driving in the United States, we will consider traffic laws, attitudes toward driving, and suggestions that may help drivers from other countries.

GENERAL INFORMATION

The United States has the highest ratio of motor vehicles to people in the world. With a few exceptions, mainly large Eastern cities such as Boston, New York, Washington D.C., and Philadelphia, public transportation is generally not as accessible as it is in many other countries, and Americans tend to be too independent-minded to use it anyway. As a result, there are many motor vehicles. In 2007, more than 250,000,000 of them were licensed to operate in the country. In some places the number of registered vehicles exceeded the number of licensed drivers!

Concerned about the rising cost of gasoline and seeking to be "green" (that is, interested in the quality of the air and water), increasing numbers of Americans are trying to reduce their reliance on private automobiles and trucks.

Most Americans who have reached the age at which they can legally drive (16 in most states) have a driver's license. Females are as likely to drive as males.

Automobile accidents are not the grave social problem that they are in some other countries, but they are still considered serious. Between 1994 and 2008, the number of fatal auto accidents in the United States declined from 1.73 to 1.27 per 100 million vehicle miles driven. A significant percentage of U.S. auto accidents involves drivers who have consumed enough alcohol to impair their judgment and reflexes. Drunk driving is considered a serious highway safety problem, although not so serious that American states have adopted the stiff legal penalties faced by drunk drivers in some other countries.

The U.S. road system is quite complex. State, county, and municipal authorities are responsible for building, maintaining, and patrolling (with police) different highways and roads. Although traffic laws may vary slightly from one jurisdiction to another, there is general uniformity regarding road signs, traffic lights, and the basic aspects of traffic engineering. (Some road

signs are uniquely American; international signs are slowly being introduced.) Highways are kept as straight as possible. Except in old, East Coast
cities, streets are generally laid out in a grid pattern unless geographical
features such as rivers or hills make that arrangement difficult or impossible. Systems for naming and numbering streets vary. So it is not just
international visitors, but also Americans who relocate, who need to learn
the street name and numbering systems in their new location.

Road conditions vary, depending mainly on the local weather. Cycles of
freezing and thawing, typical in the northern part of the country, damage
road surfaces. The financial condition of the pertinent road-maintenance
agency also affects road quality, and sometimes political considerations
do too.

TRAFFIC LAWS

Generally, American traffic laws cover the same subjects as traffic laws
elsewhere: the legal driving age, minimum and maximum speeds, turning,
parking, entering moving traffic, responding to emergency vehicles, vehicle
maintenance, and so on. Driver's licenses are issued by the separate states,
often through offices housed in county government buildings.

Traffic laws are enforced by state police on some roads, county sheriff's officers on others, and municipal police on still others. Police devote a
significant portion of their time and effort to enforcing traffic laws, issuing
what are called *traffic tickets* (or simply *tickets*) to violators. Drivers who get
tickets must normally pay a fine, although it is sometimes possible to dispute
a ticket in traffic court. In addition, most states have a point system whereby
drivers are given points for each traffic offense. Drivers who accumulate
a specified number of points will lose their driving privileges for a certain
period of time and may be required to undertake counseling or attend a
course about driving safety. Serious or repeated traffic violations can result
in loss of license and even incarceration.

Reflecting their belief that laws can produce improved human behavior,
Americans have passed a variety of laws aimed at decreasing the likelihood
of accidents and ensuring the safety of drivers and passengers. In addition
to laws against drunk driving, many states have passed laws requiring the

use of seat belts for drivers and passengers, and child-safety seats (which must meet specified standards) for infants and young children. Federal law requires that automobiles have air bags to cushion the impact of collisions. A few states have passed laws permitting authorities to photograph and ticket drivers who fail to stop for red traffic lights, exceed posted speed limits, or enter an intersection against a yellow traffic signal.

Some jurisdictions have enacted laws against using cell phones or texting devices while driving. These "driving distractions" have become more and more commonplace and are widely regarded as threats to traffic safety.

Laws also prescribe what drivers must do when they are involved in a traffic accident. These laws require such drivers to report to the police within a specified period of time, particularly if the accident causes injury to a person or property damage above a specified dollar amount.

Trucks, motorcycles, and bicycles—all of which are wheeled vehicles that use the roads—are subject to traffic laws just as automobiles are.

It is not at all customary for drivers apprehended for traffic violations to offer money or any other kind of payoff to the law officer who has stopped them. Indeed, offering a bribe could lead to more serious legal problems. The usual advice for drivers who have been stopped is to be calm and respectful.

ATTITUDES ABOUT DRIVING

Drivers' attitudes probably explain more of their behavior on the road than do the traffic laws. International visitors driving in the United States, of course, need to know the traffic laws, but they will also want to understand the attitudes that govern American drivers' behavior.

Attitudes Toward Traffic Laws

Generally, Americans expect traffic laws to be enforced and operate on the assumption that a police officer might apprehend them at any time if they violate the law. In general, American drivers take traffic laws seriously. A Southeast Asian high school teacher visiting the States for advanced studies learned just how seriously when he tried to obtain an American driver's license. He failed the driving test twice before finally passing it. "They're so picky," he said of the driver's license examiners. "They kept saying I was breaking the laws." He had rolled through some stop signs and failed to signal his intention to turn. In his own country such behavior was routine and acceptable.

Attitudes Toward Other Drivers

Except for those who are considered "aggressive" or "discourteous"—and there are many, as discussed next—American drivers tend to cooperate with each other. They are not likely to constantly compete with each other to see who can get the farthest the fastest, although there are some locations where such competition seems to be taking place. If they observe another driver trying to enter the flow of traffic, for example, U.S. American drivers are likely to move over (if there is a lane for doing so) or even slow down (if they are not going too fast) to allow the other driver to enter. If they see that another driver wishes to change lanes in front of them, they are likely to allow it.

At the same time, American drivers do observe the concept of "right-of-way." Traffic laws try to specify which driver has the right-of-way in every possible driving situation. For example, drivers going straight have the right-of-way over those heading in the opposite direction who wish to turn left. Drivers without the right-of-way are expected to yield to those who have it.

The ideal in the United States is the courteous driver who pays attention to other drivers and cooperates with them in what is considered a joint effort to keep the roads safe for everyone. Like other ideals, this one is violated. But it is the ideal nonetheless.

Despite the common goal of cooperative, respectful driving, many Americans consider "road rage" to be a growing problem. According to some commentators, the apparent increase in rude, aggressive drivers on U.S. highways is a result of factors including increased traffic congestion, lengthy commuting times, and a perceived increase in the stress of daily life. Drivers who want to get where they are going as quickly as possible are becoming increasingly frustrated and even dangerous when they are not able to do so, and they sometimes resort to violence directed at other drivers.

Attitudes Toward Driving Safety

Americans generally assume that individual drivers are responsible for their own safety and that of other drivers around them. Traffic accidents are usually considered the result of carelessness, irresponsibility (for example, driving while under the influence of alcohol or drugs, or using a cell phone while driving), or mechanical failures, not the result of "fate," "God's will," or other forces beyond human control. But "accidents happen," Americans will say, referring to the fact that an accident can occur through a random configuration of circumstances or as a result of factors that drivers could not reasonably be expected to foresee.

Attitudes Toward Pedestrians

Driver attitudes toward pedestrians vary from place to place. In some localities pedestrians are viewed as competitors for space on the roadway, and the burden is on the pedestrians to be wary. In other localities pedestrians are viewed as people whose wishes and apparent intentions deserve attention and respect. Pedestrians normally have the legal right-of-way when crossing a street within a designated crosswalk (which may be indicated by a traffic sign, painted lines on the pavement, or both).

One need only stand at an intersection and observe for a few minutes to see how local drivers and pedestrians respond to each other.

Attitudes Toward Bicyclists

For a variety of reasons, including a desire to be physically fit, save money on parking fees, or reduce the quantity of carbon emissions going into the atmosphere, a noticeable number of Americans use bicycles to get from place to place. Many cities have created special bicycle lanes on their streets. In areas where bicycles are particularly numerous, as they tend to be around colleges and universities, relationships between bicyclists and automobile drivers may be less than harmonious. The bicyclists think the motorists are careless; the motorists think the bicyclists are arrogant and provocative.

SUGGESTIONS FOR
INTERNATIONAL VISITORS

Many international visitors find it difficult to live in the United States without a car, unless they live in a large city with relatively good public transportation. Foreign students and businesspeople who will be in the United States for an extended period may therefore wish to obtain a driver's license from the state in which they are living. They may find it convenient to obtain an International Driving Permit before leaving home, so they can legally drive in the United States. But IDPs, or their underlying national driver's licenses, expire, after which obtaining a state license is essential. Obtaining a state license as promptly as possible is a good idea in any case, since doing so requires learning local traffic laws.

Before attempting to drive in the United States, spend some time watching local drivers. Notice such things as how fast they drive under various conditions; how they respond to traffic signals, other drivers, pedestrians, and bicyclists; where and how they park their cars; how they go about entering a stream of traffic; how much distance they keep between vehicles when traffic is moving; the degree to which they remain within specified traffic lanes; when they use their headlights; and how frequently they honk their horns.

Ask some local people how they are expected to act if a police officer stops them when they are driving. Behaving improperly when stopped by a police officer can make an unpleasant situation worse.

CHAPTER 15

Shopping

"Things are so inexpensive here," a Latin American's visiting mother-in-law exclaimed. "I've bought a TV, a DVD player, some dresses and sweaters, perfume, and two hair dryers." She had also bought several pairs of pantyhose, her son-in-law confided, but she was too shy to mention that.

Whether planning a short or a long stay, visitors to other countries often spend considerable time shopping. Short-term visitors such as the mother-in-law with the pantyhose are often looking for souvenirs or products that cost more in their country or aren't available there. Long-term visitors are shopping for daily necessities.

Visitors from at least some other countries are astonished when they see the variety and quantity of goods that are routinely available to American consumers. A Nepali woman, for example, was visiting a medium-sized U.S. city. Her host took her to what the Americans call a "big box" store, a large store with a grocery department and many other departments. Amazed, she asked her host, "Is this where they keep all the food for the whole city?"

Of course, she was seeing only one of the city's many grocery stores.

International visitors who shop in the United States will find that Americans are eager shoppers, although the 2008 recession certainly slowed them down. Materialism and consumerism represent a significant part of American life. Giant shopping malls are open seven days a week. "Superstores" that offer an enormous array of goods at discount prices are open twenty-four hours a day. The Internet makes it possible to shop for nearly anything at nearly any time. For many people, a trip to the outlet mall (where name-brand merchandise sells at reduced prices) is a satisfying way to spend part of a weekend.

When the American economy went into a slump after the September 11, 2001 terrorist attacks, leaders urged citizens to return to their normal daily lives. What this meant, according to then-president George W. Bush, was that citizens should go shopping. Experts generally agree that the health of the American economy depends on a high volume of consumer spending.

Shopping has common elements wherever it takes place. A buyer looks for a seller who is offering something the buyer wants or needs at a price the buyer can afford to pay. Sellers often advertise their wares in newspapers, on the radio or television, on posters, on the Internet, on billboards, or elsewhere. Sellers use a variety of tactics to induce buyers to purchase products from them at a price that leaves some profit. Among the aspects of shopping in the United States that international visitors may find unique are features of advertising, the pricing system, customer-clerk relationships, some sales tactics, the procedures for returning and exchanging merchandise, and private sales. This chapter touches on each of these matters before closing with some precautions for shoppers from abroad.

ADVERTISING

In the United States, advertising itself is a huge business. Companies of all sizes spend billions of dollars on television, radio, Internet, and printed messages to prospective consumers. Advertising firms do market research for their clients, testing out various sales pitches in the quest for ones that promise to influence differing age, income, gender, ethnic, and other groups. Advertising is visible nearly everywhere—not just in the media but on billboards and computerized, illuminated signs along streets and highways, inside taxicabs, inside and outside buses, in restaurant bathrooms, public schools, sports arenas, and even (at least before September 11) trailing behind private aircraft circling crowded sports stadiums. The recordings that telephone callers hear when placed on hold while trying to speak to someone at a business normally tout the business's products.

In the United States, advertising seems inescapable.

From the viewpoint of American consumers, advertising informs them about available products and services while encouraging them to buy. From the viewpoint of visitors from abroad, though, advertising can serve an additional purpose: it affords countless insights into American values, tastes, and standards. From examining American advertising, foreign visitors can gain some understanding of these and other aspects of American society:

- Ideas about youthfulness and physical attractiveness in males and females
- Ideals concerning personal hygiene
- The emphasis on sex, speed, and technical sophistication
- The faith in numbers and (perceived) facts
- Materialism
- Male-female relationships, both pre- and post-marital
- The attention paid to the words of celebrities
- The characteristics of people Americans consider "authorities" whose ideas or recommendations are persuasive
- The sorts of things Americans find humorous
- The kinds of messages deemed persuasive
- The ethnic, age, and gender categories advertisers assume exist in the society

By comparing the advertising they see in the States with what they have seen at home, international visitors can gain a deeper understanding not just of American society but of their own as well.

PRICING

With a few exceptions, Americans are accustomed to fixed prices on the merchandise they buy and sell. Typical exceptions include houses, automobiles, and sometimes major appliances such as refrigerators and washing machines. In addition, some online Internet companies allow customers to bid for low prices on items such as airline tickets and hotel rooms. Private sales, which are discussed in this section, are another exception. In general, though, Americans are not accustomed to bargaining over prices, and in fact usually feel uncomfortable with the idea. People who try to bargain for a lower price in a shop or store are likely to be considered either odd or inappropriately aggressive.

International visitors should realize that the price marked on an item does not include the sales tax that is added on as part of the payment. Sales tax rates vary from one jurisdiction to another. Five states—Alaska, Montana, Delaware, New Hampshire, and Oregon—have no sales tax at all. This variation in state financial systems reflects the "federal system" of government, with certain powers reserved for the states and not allowed to the central government. The federal system manifests the typical American suspicion of government.

CUSTOMER-CLERK RELATIONSHIPS

Some points about customer-clerk relationships have already been made. One is that clerks or salespeople are generally treated with courtesy and not considered less worthy than people in higher-status occupations. In fact, foreign visitors are often startled by the degree of informality with which some salespeople and restaurant staff treat their customers.

Unlike people from many other cultures, Americans do not generally assume that commercial transactions will include particular attention to the human relationships involved. Customers look for the item they want, decide whether they can afford the price marked on it, and, if they want to buy it, find a clerk or salesperson who is available to take their payment.

Both parties are considered to have a role to play, and they play them without necessarily making an effort to learn about each other's personal viewpoints or lives. This fact is quite plain to a customer who notices the mechanical smiles of clerks in many stores and who hears again and again the refrains "Have a nice day" and "Thank you for shopping at [name of store]." To clerks, the customer-clerk relationship may seem utterly dehumanized.

There are some exceptions. Experienced sellers of automobiles, houses, major appliances, and other so-called "big-ticket items" are likely to pay much attention to the buyer as an individual human being. People selling these products will assume that they must become acquainted with their clients and their individual tastes and preferences in order to help them select a product that will suit them and, at the same time, in order to ascertain what "pitches" will be most effective. For example, an automobile salesperson is likely to try to determine whether a particular customer will be more attracted to a high-performance sports car or to a "sensible," more conservative automobile. A person selling clothing may try to determine whether a particular customer is the type who will prefer an outfit that is more unusual or one that is popular. All this is intended to increase sales, which in turn increases the salesperson's income.

Another exception: in smaller specialty shops and in smaller towns, clerks are more likely to pay attention to the human-relations aspect of a sales transaction.

International visitors will notice striking differences in the degree to which clerks and salespeople are able to be helpful. Some, particularly in specialty shops, are well informed about their products and can readily answer questions about them and about their employer's policies and procedures. Others, particularly in big-box stores where employees cover many areas, appear to know little other than the location of the restrooms. This lack of knowledge is partly because retail sales jobs do not normally pay well, resulting in a lack of commitment to the work and a high turnover among employees.

SALES TACTICS

Sales tactics, like advertising, reflect the basic assumptions and values that prevail in a country. By carefully listening to salespeople who are trying to sell them something, foreign visitors can more clearly understand the way Americans interpret and think about things. Here are some common sales tactics:

- Trying to make the buyer feel sympathetic toward the seller
- Trying to make a male buyer feel that he will be less manly if he does not make the purchase

- Trying to make a female buyer believe that a particular purchase will enhance her attractiveness to males
- Placing a premium on a rapid decision to buy
- Suggesting that the opportunity to make the purchase will soon be gone
- Implying that the purchase is necessary for the purchaser to "keep up with the Joneses," which means to avoid being outshone by one's neighbors or people in other reference groups
- Trying to make the buyer believe that a particular purchase would be "wise," an example of the buyer's cleverness and foresight
- Trying to induce a commitment to buy by asking something like, "Would you prefer the green one or the blue one?"

Such tactics, of course, are used in other countries, but the subtleties with which they are employed in the United States are likely to be distinctive.

One sales tactic that startles some international visitors is that of the telephone solicitor. Salespeople—whether real-life salespeople or their recorded voices—will telephone a person's home and attempt to sell the person something. Such calls frequently come during the dinner hour. International visitors should know that they are not obligated to be particularly courteous or attentive to such callers. They can interrupt the salesperson, state that they are not interested in the product, and hang up the telephone.

Americans became so disturbed by the frequency of unsolicited sales calls that they prevailed upon Congress to legislate a "do-not-call" list. Getting onto that list, which can be done via the Internet or a telephone call, eliminates most unsolicited calls. In arguing for the creation of this list, Americans stressed that their privacy was being invaded by unwanted interruptions.

PROCEDURES FOR RETURNING
AND EXCHANGING

As was noted in chapter 2, Americans consider it essential to have a written record of any important transaction. Sellers routinely give—or will give if asked—receipts for purchases that serve as evidence of a sale. Many sellers will not honor a request to return or exchange an item if the buyer cannot present the receipt for the original sale.

Most businesses will exchange a buyer's purchases for alternative items if the original items prove unsatisfactory. Some businesses will give cash refunds; others will give "store credit," which the buyer can use to purchase a different item in the same store. Without a receipt, though, some businesses may neither exchange goods nor provide cash refunds or store credit.

Many products, including electronics, appliances, and automobiles, come with guarantees and warranties. Buyers are expected to present these documents if they want to get replacements or services that the guarantee or warranty covers.

PRIVATE SALES

Americans who want to sell a used car, furniture, or other major items often advertise such items in the newspaper or online and try to conduct a sale themselves, rather than going through a dealer.

Many foreign visitors are struck by the phenomenon of "garage sales" and "yard sales" (also called "tag sales" in some parts of the country). At such events, Americans sell used items such as furniture, bicycles, pots and pans, clothing, tools, outgrown children's clothes, toys, and books. They will go through their houses and collect items they no longer use, sorting and marking the items they want to sell and setting them out for display in the garage or yard. They will advertise the sale in the newspaper or by tacking up signs and then wait hopefully for large numbers of people to come to their house and buy the items offered.

Sometimes the residents of a given neighborhood will band together and mount a "community garage sale," where buyers can find items contributed by an array of households.

Internet sites called *eBay* and *Craig's List* offer electronic versions of private sales. The popularity of these two sites reflects Americans' interest in efficiency.

International visitors who are living temporarily in the United States often find that they can purchase many of the household items they need at garage sales or yard sales, where the prices are likely to be quite low and where bargaining over prices is acceptable. Likewise, searching for wanted items on eBay and Craig's List can yield bargains.

PRECAUTIONS FOR SHOPPERS
FROM ABROAD

Americans often quote the Latin axiom *caveat emptor* ("let the buyer beware") to convey their general conviction that people who buy things do so at some peril and must be vigilant against unwise use of their money. One axiom Americans use is "You get what you pay for." This suggests that purchases that seem like unbelievable bargains are usually not the bargains they appear to be.

These precautions are as valuable for international visitors as they are for Americans. So are the following suggestions:

- Keep receipts for any purchases that might need to be returned or exchanged. Keep the written guarantees and warranties that come with many products.
- Be careful when making purchases over the telephone or the Internet. Do not give out your credit card number or other personal information (such as your address, birth date, or social security number) unless you know the company you are dealing with is reputable.
- Do not allow yourself to be rushed or pressured into making a purchase. Take your time and think your decision through. Ask questions. Talk with other people who have bought the product or service you are considering and ask whether they were satisfied.
- Before making a significant purchase, check prices on a few Internet sites to be sure the price you are considering paying is not unnecessarily high.
- When considering a large purchase, take an American friend with you to help you make sure you are getting a reasonable deal.
- Be aware that many salespeople may have some reaction to you because you are from another country, especially in areas where few foreign visitors live or pass through. Some salespeople will have a beneficent

attitude toward international visitors and will want to be particularly fair and helpful. Others will have a negative attitude and will see their interaction with a foreign customer as a chance to take advantage of someone's presumed ignorance.

- Remember that most businesses with merchandise displayed on shelves employ people, cameras, mirrors, and other devices designed to protect against shoplifting. People who believe it is easy to remove some item from a shelf, put it into a pocket, and leave the store without paying for it might quickly find themselves in trouble with the police. Shoplifting is illegal and unwise. Most shoplifters are caught, and businesses generally do whatever they can to see that shoplifters are punished.
- Finally, guard against identity theft. To prevent anyone else from making purchases in your name and using your money, take care never to give your social security number or bank account numbers to anyone you do not know to be honest and reliable.

CHAPTER 16

Personal Hygiene

Anne, an American graduate student in the chemistry department, telephoned her school's international student adviser. Anne told the adviser that she shared a small office with an international student and that she was bothered because the international student had what Anne considered an offensive body odor. She wanted advice on handling the matter. After a long talk with the adviser, Anne decided that rather than talking directly to her office mate about the issue, she would ask her department chair if she could switch to a different office. The prospect of talking to her office mate about her body odor was simply too daunting.

As noted in chapter 1, most Americans consider the subjects of body and breath odors too sensitive for discussion. They are "embarrassing." So most Americans will avoid telling other people that they have offensive breath or body smells. Sometimes, as in the example of Anne, Americans will consult others for advice on how to handle the situation. At universities, for instance, American students or staff members may call upon an international student adviser to address such matters.

Although they may be unwilling to discuss the offending behavior, Americans, like people anywhere, will respond nonverbally to what they perceive as unpleasant smells. In the presence of a person whose odors they dislike, Americans will avert their faces, sit or stand further away from the person than they normally would, and draw the interaction to a close as quickly as possible so they can move away. Like Anne, they may even remove themselves completely from interaction with the person.

Too much of a presumably good smell will elicit the same reactions as an unpleasant smell. "Too much" perfume, cologne, or aftershave lotion will drive most Americans away.*

People's notions about proper personal hygiene are deeply held. When encountering a person who violates those notions, they are likely to respond quickly and negatively. Foreign visitors who want to interact constructively with Americans will therefore want to know what personal hygiene habits Americans are likely to consider appropriate—or offensive. The information in this chapter is intended to give international visitors a basic understanding of typical Americans' mindset and practices related to personal hygiene.

THE BASICS

American television commercials make clear what Americans consider ideal personal hygiene habits. Advertisers claim that their products give users a "shower-fresh" feeling or "squeaky-clean" skin. Commercials for personal hygiene products suggest that people who use such products are happier and more attractive than those who do not. From commercials and elsewhere, Americans are taught that the odors a human body naturally produces—those of perspiration, oily hair, and breath—are unpleasant or even offensive. A person who follows what Americans consider to be good hygiene practices seeks to control such odors.

The popular conception in American culture is that people should bathe or shower at least once daily, using soap (some varieties of which supposedly

---

* There seems to be a growing incidence of allergic reactions to these scented products, which can make breathing difficult for some people. Organizers of public events sometimes request participants not to wear scented products to an event, so as to avoid causing problems for people with such allergies.

contain "deodorant"). People should also brush their teeth with toothpaste at least twice a day, if not more frequently, and should use an underarm deodorant to control perspiration odor. They should also wash their hair as often as necessary to keep it from becoming oily.

American drugstores and supermarkets have entire aisles filled with personal hygiene products designed to meet these needs. There are countless deodorants made especially for men and for women. Toothpaste comes in many varieties, not only to combat cavities but also to whiten teeth and freshen breath. Breath sprays, mints, mouthwashes, and chewing gums are available to supplement the freshening effects of toothpaste. Some products claim to eliminate foot odor, and others are designed to hide odors associated with menstruation. In fact, an entire industry has grown up around personal care products. Shops devoted exclusively to "bath and body" products are multiplying.

In addition, people often use perfume, cologne, "body splash," and other scented products to give themselves an odor that others will presumably find pleasant. Although women used to be the target market for scented bathing and after-bath products, more and more men now use them also. Perfumed soaps, scented aftershave lotions, and colognes intended for men (to give a "manly smell" that "women find attractive" or even "irresistible," as the commercials say) are widely available. The ideal person does not use too much of a scented product, however. *Too much* means that the scent is discernible more than three or four feet away from the person's body.

Many Americans regard the sight of hair under a woman's arms or on her legs as masculine, unattractive, or unhygienic; most American women shave their legs and under their arms. A small number of women choose not to shave at all.

Many American women also wear some makeup on their faces. Too much makeup is considered to make a woman look "cheap"—that is, more or less the way a prostitute is presumed to look. What is "too much" makeup, however, varies from time to time and place to place. It is often said that women in northern states wear less makeup than women in the South. Women from other countries wanting guidance on how much makeup is considered appropriate for them can observe American women whose age and social status resemble their own.

According to the general American conception, clothing, like bodies, should not emit unpleasant aromas. Americans generally believe that clothing that has taken on the smell of the wearer's perspiration should be washed before it is worn again. For many, this means washing their clothes after each wearing, particularly during warm summer months. International visitors will find a wide variety of laundry products that promise to keep their clothes smelling "fresh and clean."

VARIATIONS

Some Americans do not follow the hygiene practices described above. Some women, for example, do not use makeup or perfume. Makeup and perfume are not required for social acceptability, as long as the person is clean and free of body odor.

Another variation is people who do not use deodorants or other products intended to make them "smell good." And some people fail to keep themselves clean. There are various explanations for such behavior, including poverty, a wish to show independence or to protest against standard practices, and a conviction that natural smells are better than artificial ones.

International visitors should keep in mind that the basic guidelines given at the beginning of this chapter are those followed by what Americans call "polite company"—that is, middle-class, "average" people. Those who fail to keep themselves clean are regarded as inconsiderate, rebellious, disgusting, or worse. Foreign visitors who want to stand in good stead with mainstream Americans will want to adopt the prevailing personal hygiene practices, even though doing so is not always easy or even acceptable in their own country.

OTHER ISSUES CONCERNING HYGIENE

Americans who encounter a foreigner they think "smells bad" can be heard to ask, "Why doesn't he take a shower more often?" or "Why doesn't she use some deodorant?" or "Why doesn't he use mouthwash? He smells like a garlic factory!" Similar questions, though they are virtually never addressed directly to the offending person, are "Why does she wear so much makeup?" or "Why doesn't she shave under her arms? That hair is so ugly!"

Many international visitors find the hygiene-related notions and practices of Americans unnatural. They may consider it unmanly for men to mask their natural odors and unfeminine for women not to use a considerable amount of makeup.

Even those with a sophisticated understanding of cultural differences are unlikely to realize that other people's hygiene habits are as deeply ingrained as their own. They may not recognize that issues of identity and integrity can result when a person feels pressured to change hygiene habits. For many people visiting the United States from other countries, it is not easy to say, "Well, the Americans think I should take a shower every morning, shave under my arms, use deodorant, and launder my clothes more often. So I'll do all that, just to make them happy."

Interestingly, Americans themselves "smell bad," according to the Japanese stereotype of them. They say Americans smell of milk. People from India often complain of a meat odor emanating from Americans. What smells "good" and what smells "bad" turn out to be matters of personal and cultural experience. Ideas and practices related to personal hygiene are complex and perplexing and can produce significant disharmony in intercultural relationships.

SUGGESTIONS FOR INTERNATIONAL VISITORS

Take note of the aromas of individuals and compare them with those you would expect to find in your own country.

In a shop, particularly a bath and body shop, look at the array of personal care products and compare them with those that you would find at home.

Pay attention to advertisements for personal care products, and think about the assumptions that underlie them and the messages they use to persuade potential buyers.

Ask Americans you meet how they decide what personal care products to use.

Particularly if your stay in the United States will be long and you expect to be interacting with many Americans, ask yourself what changes in your hygiene practices you might be willing to make in order to "fit in."

CHAPTER 17

Getting Things Done
in Organizations

"Will you tell him?" my secretary asked me many, many times. Usually the issue was with a male Middle Eastern or Nigerian student. She had told the student that he could not get some document he wanted or that he was not eligible for some benefit he was seeking; he wouldn't accept her answer and became "pushy." "I think he needs to hear it from a man," the secretary said.

I would talk briefly with the student and explain that the secretary's answer was correct. The student cordially accepted the answer and departed. Meanwhile, my secretary was annoyed and insulted. That student wouldn't be likely to get her cheerful assistance in the future, even if he was asking for something she could readily supply.

One of the misconceptions that many international visitors bring to the United States is that women cannot hold responsible positions in businesses and organizations. Such visitors have been trained to believe that women are inferior or subordinate or that they cannot properly be in positions of authority. In American organizations, though, many women do hold responsible positions. Many foreign student advisers and university professors, for example, are women, as are an increasing number of managers and executives in corporations and governmental agencies.

Like many intercultural interactions, these situations of male clients insisting on talking with male officials are subject to more than one interpretation. Perhaps the clients want to talk to someone with more authority than the secretary, no matter the gender of either person.

Perhaps, but during the periods when I had a male secretary, incidents such as these occurred far less frequently.

International visitors handicap themselves if they make invalid assumptions about U.S. American organizations. We just discussed the invalid assumption that women cannot have authority in important matters. This chapter addresses four other common misconceptions, then discusses some characteristics that distinguish U.S. American organizations from those in many other places. This chapter ends with some guidelines for international visitors who must deal with organizations in the United States.

MISCONCEPTIONS

"I have to see the boss." Many visitors come to the United States from countries where the only people in organizations who are considered capable of meeting a request, making a decision, or carrying out a procedure are the supervisors, the bosses, the "higher-ups." When such visitors get to the United States, they may resort to a wide array of tactics to bypass the receptionist, the secretary, and other subordinate staff members in order to see the "boss," the one person they believe will be able to help them. Sometimes it's true that only the boss can help, but far more often a subordinate employee can do so. The most common results of bypassing subordinates to reach the boss are delays and irritation on the part of all the Americans involved, including the boss. As will be discussed shortly, American organizations are normally based on the idea that people at all levels are intelligent and can—in fact should—make decisions appropriate to their position.

"If I refuse to take no for an answer, I will eventually get my way." In cultures where negotiation is widely used in dealings with organizations or where organizational employees have wide latitude in making decisions, persis-

tence might well be rewarded with an affirmative answer. In the United States, though, employees are typically bound by written rules limiting their discretion. Faced with a person who refuses to take no for an answer, they must still persist in saying no. Meanwhile they become increasingly annoyed and decreasingly likely to give any form of assistance.

"Most organization employees are incompetent." In many countries people get jobs in organizations on the basis of personal or political relationships, and people believe that the employees' main interest is in drawing their periodic pay rather than in working. Of course, there are examples in the United States of people getting jobs for reasons other than their interest in the work and their ability to perform their duties, and of course there are people who do not work hard. But the general belief among Americans is that people who work in organizations are capable of carrying out their assigned responsibilities and feel at least some obligation to do so.

"Paperwork doesn't matter; all I have to do is know somebody." In many countries impersonal procedures in organizations do not work or work only very slowly. It is not enough to fill out an application form, for example. One must take the completed form personally to the boss or to some person with whom one has a connection and see to it that the application gets processed. Such countries can be said to have a "personal" orientation to an organization's workings. The underlying assumption is that issues should be resolved by understanding and acting on the particular circumstances of the people involved. Fairness is ensured by treating people differently, depending on the circumstances.

By contrast, what prevails in the United States can be called the "procedural" approach. The assumption is that issues should be resolved by adhering as much as possible to standard rules and procedures, so no one is discriminated against. Fairness is ensured by treating people similarly. The rule of law, discussed in chapter 5, prevails. Acting in someone's favor on the basis of a personal relationship, often termed *favoritism*, is considered bad practice and can even be punishable by law or by the employer.

A graduate student from Brazil said that before he came to the United States he supposed it would be impossible for him to get financial aid from any American university because he did not know anyone at any of them. He came to the country without financial aid, and later he filled out a scholarship application and submitted it to the appropriate university office, following the instructions printed on the form. Even though he did not know anyone who worked in the financial aid office and even though he had not talked to anyone other than the secretary to whom he submitted the application form, he was awarded a scholarship.

"I didn't believe that could happen," the student said. "A friend in Brazil wrote to me a couple of months ago and asked if I could help him get some financial aid. I told him just to fill out the form and send it in. Things work that way here. I know he won't believe it. He'll think I have to help him, but in fact there's nothing I can do."

CHARACTERISTICS OF U.S. ORGANIZATIONS

Many of the points discussed next have already been mentioned, so this section will be brief.

Competence is the key to being hired by most U.S. organizations. Applicants must have completed certain educational or training programs; often they have taken some sort of examination to demonstrate that they are prepared to do the work involved. For example, attorneys must pass a state licensing examination (the "bar exam") in order to practice law. Licensing examinations or other types of certification are also required for many other occupations, including doctors, dentists, electricians, plumbers, contractors, law-enforcement officers, certified public accountants, physical therapists, and public-school teachers. In large organizations, clerks, secretaries, and office assistants often have to pass some kind of screening to obtain their jobs.

Efficiency is a primary concern of most organizations. Some are more efficient than others, but most strive to carry out their work as quickly as possible while maintaining certain standards of quality. Organizations typically develop "performance management" or scorecard systems in order to ensure that everyone is working efficiently and effectively.

International visitors are often struck by the relative efficiency of U.S. organizations. "You can get things done so easily here," they say, observing how one telephone conversation is able to accomplish what might require two personal visits and three supporting documents at home.

One manifestation of the drive for efficiency is Americans' increasing reliance on recorded responses to telephone calls for everything from airline arrival and departure schedules to banking information to billing inquiries. The recorded telephone responses may be efficient from the viewpoint of the organizations that use them, but from the customer's standpoint they may entail frustration and long waits for "the next available associate." Many Americans dislike having their calls answered by recordings ("Press '1' for this, press '2' for that," etc.), and foreign visitors with limited English proficiency can find these recorded responses even more troublesome.

So it is not surprising that many people turn to the Internet to do their business with large organizations.

On the other hand, organizations in all sectors reduced their work-forces, or "downsized," in the 1990s and even more so during the recession of the late 2000s. In at least some cases, organizations left themselves with too few employees to get the organization's work done efficiently. Employees in these organizations are often tired and anxious from having to do more than one person's work.

SUGGESTIONS FOR DEALING WITH U.S. ORGANIZATIONS

These guidelines follow from what appeared earlier in this chapter about American organizations and from what has been said in this book about Americans and their values of individualism, equality, and respect for the rule of law.

1. Be courteous to all employees, both male and female, even if they hold what you might think are low-level positions.
2. Explain your request or question to the person who answers the telephone or greets you at the office. Let that person decide what procedure you must follow or what other person you need to see. Being gracious may earn you better service.

3. If there is some procedure you must follow, ask about it so that you understand it clearly and completely. Find out what papers are involved, where the papers must be taken or sent, what steps are involved in the procedure, and how long the procedure normally requires.

4. Make a note of the date and the names and telephone numbers of the people you deal with in case some delay or complication arises and you need to make further contact.

5. If the procedure takes more time than you have been told it would (or if you learn that a deadline has passed and you have not received an expected notification, or you learn that a case similar to yours has already been processed), it is appropriate to follow up to see if there is some problem. In following up, take these steps:

- Plan your telephone call or your presentation carefully, so you can explain your situation concisely and make clear what you want.

- Begin with the lowest-level person who is in a position to know about the procedure.

- In a pleasant, conversational manner, explain who you are, what you have done, and why you are inquiring about the status of your case.

- Seek some statement about the projected completion date for your case.

- Again, note the date and the names and telephone numbers of anyone you talk to.

- Avoid showing anger or impatience. Anger might induce quicker action on your case, but it might also provoke resentment, defensiveness, and further delays. It could reduce your chance of getting a positive reaction in future dealings with the organization.

- Call on a higher-level person (the manager or supervisor) or an influential outsider only as a last resort, if you are convinced that the normal procedure is not working.

- If the procedure works out in a way that is against your interests, ask what appeal procedure is open to you. If there is a way to have your case reconsidered, you will normally be told about it.

- Keep in mind that in the United States people use e-mail, the telephone, and the mail for many more things than they might elsewhere. Inquiries and procedures that an international visitor might think require a personal visit may be taken care of with those alternative methods. It is quite acceptable to e-mail or telephone an organization, state what you want, and ask for instructions about the most efficient way to proceed. Remember that Americans do not generally believe that they need a personal relationship with another person in order to have successful business dealings with him or her.

CHAPTER 18

Behavior in Public Places

When they are out in public—on sidewalks or in stores, restaurants, or an audience—international visitors are constantly reminded that they are indeed foreigners. This is not just because the people around them differ in color, stature, dress, and language but also because the other people behave in unfamiliar ways. People's behavior in public places, like their behavior anywhere else, is subject to cultural influence. The American belief in equality and individuality is reflected in the informal rules Americans follow in public places. Aspects of their communicative style are also evident when they are out in public.

RULES FOR BEHAVIOR IN PUBLIC PLACES

Keep to the right. When they are walking on sidewalks, in hallways, or on stairways—wherever groups of people are going in two opposite directions—Americans stay on the right side. This enables them to pass each other without physical contact and to progress as quickly as possible.

Line up, and wait your turn. When a group of Americans want attention or service from someone, they line up (or "queue," as some people say). In the bank, at the theater box office, or at the university registrar's counter, the latest person to arrive is expected to step to the end of the line and patiently (patiently unless it becomes clear that the service the people are waiting for is slower than it ought to be) wait his or her turn. This behavior reflects their notion that all people are equal, in the sense that no one has the privilege of going directly to the front of a line. It also reflects their aversion to touching, which is much less likely to happen in a line than in a jostling crowd. Furthermore, it satisfies Americans' need for order and rules.

People who do not go to the end of the line to wait their turn but instead go to the head of the line and try to push their way in front of others will usually evoke a hostile reaction.

First come, first served. Related to the "line-up" rule is the first-come, first-served rule. The general notion is that the person who arrives first gets attention first. Alternative notions, such as giving priority to the elderly, the wealthy, or males, do not normally occur to equality-minded Americans. They will, however, give priority to people with an obvious physical disability—people in wheelchairs, for example, or on crutches.

If several customers are standing near a counter awaiting service, the employee might ask, "Who's next?" or say, ungrammatically, "I can help who's next." A truthful response is expected: if you aren't next, don't say you are.

Don't block the traffic. Generally, Americans give priority to people who are moving rather than to those who are stationary. A person in a moving crowd (on a sidewalk or a moving walkway at airports, for example) who wishes to stop or to go more slowly than others is expected to move to the side or otherwise get out of the path of those who are continuing to move. It is considered inconsiderate to obstruct other people's progress.

Don't block the view. It is also deemed inconsiderate to obstruct another person's view when that person is trying to watch a public event, such as a parade, an athletic contest, or a theater performance. People toward the front of an audience or crowd are expected to remain seated so that people behind them can see. This rule can be interpreted as yet another manifestation of Americans' assumptions about equality and individualism.

Be cautious about where you smoke. "I never thought much about when and where I smoked when I was at home," a German said. "But here I notice that people sometimes look at me unpleasantly if I light a cigarette. Several people have even asked me to put my cigarette out!"

In recent years an antismoking movement has gained strength in the United States, and a declining number of Americans smoke. Many states and localities have outlawed smoking in public accommodations, including restaurants, bars, theaters, and shopping malls. College and university buildings are generally smoke-free, and indeed some entire campuses bar smoking. Many organizations have formulated rules about smoking, usually rules that specify where people can and cannot smoke. Even at social gatherings in their homes, American hosts who are nonsmokers generally ask people to step outdoors to smoke. It is polite for visitors who want to smoke to ask their host whether or not they may smoke indoors. Such visitors should not be surprised if they are asked to go outside to smoke, even if a snowstorm is in progress.

Nonsmokers who are bothered by cigarette smoke often ask (or tell) smokers to extinguish their cigarettes. People who do smoke are likely to postpone having a cigarette until they are in a situation where they can smoke without "polluting" the air around nonsmokers.

Many international visitors, like the German mentioned here, come to the United States from countries where a higher portion of the people smoke, and where the "right of nonsmokers to a smoke-free environment," as the Americans say, gets little or no attention. Such visitors, if they smoke without regard to local laws or the sensitivities of nonsmokers, are likely to give offense and be regarded as inconsiderate or worse.

Foreign visitors who smoke and who wish to avoid offending Americans will want to notice whether others in the group are smoking and, if they are, whether they are confining themselves to a particular part of the room or building. Asking those around them, "Do you mind if I smoke?" is a good idea, and so is acceding to the wishes of those who say they do mind.

COMMUNICATION BEHAVIORS

Voice volume. Words on a page cannot describe how loud sounds are. Suffice it to say that when they are in public places, Americans are generally louder than Germans or Malays but not as loud as Nigerians or Brazilians. Of course, the volume at which people speak when they are in public varies from one sort of situation to another. A crowd at a baseball game will make more noise than a theater audience. Patrons in a fast-food restaurant are likely to be noisier than those in a fashionable restaurant, although restaurants in general seem to be getting noisier.

International visitors who do not want to draw attention to themselves will want to note how loudly others around them are talking and adjust accordingly. Talking more softly than the people nearby will cause no problems, but making more noise than they do will draw attention and, perhaps, adverse comment.

Touching. Americans' general aversion to touching others and to being touched (discussed in chapter 2) is clearly evident in public places. The "keep to the right" rule discussed earlier is one means of reducing the likelihood that strangers will have physical contact with each other.

Americans will rarely crowd onto a bus, train, or other public conveyance the way Japanese and Mexicans are famous for doing. They will simply avoid situations where extensive and prolonged physical contact with strangers is inevitable. Pushing one's way through a crowd is considered quite rude.

When in a situation where physical contact is unavoidable, Americans will typically try to draw in their shoulders and arms so as to minimize the amount of space they occupy. They will tolerate contact on the outsides of their arms when their arms are hanging straight down from their shoulders, but contact with other parts of the body makes them extremely anxious. When they are in a crowded situation, such as a full elevator ("lift") or bus, they will generally stop talking or will talk only in very low voices. Their discomfort is easy to see.

In cases where they bump into another person or otherwise touch the other person inadvertently, Americans will quickly draw away and usually apologize, making clear that the touch was accidental. "Excuse me," they will say, or, "Sorry."

Foreign visitors who violate Americans' notions concerning touching, in public places and elsewhere, are likely to be regarded as "pushy" or "aggressive." Uninvited touching of members of the opposite sex can bring legal charges of harassment and even assault. Visitors from abroad, particularly male visitors, need to keep in mind that most American women will not welcome any sort of sexual comment, let alone touching, from a stranger.

SUGGESTIONS FOR INTERNATIONAL VISITORS

Aside from noting the points mentioned in this chapter about typical American behavior in public places, international visitors should spend some time observing Americans going about their daily routines. Try some of the activities mentioned in chapter 22 under the heading "Take Field Trips."

CHAPTER 19

Studying

Many foreign students in the United States have trouble under-standing and adapting to the behaviors Americans expect from college or university students. "I am sorry I came here," a recently arrived Korean student said. "Many times I think about just quitting and going back home. It's not what I expected. At home I was a good student. Here I don't know how to be a good student, and I can't make any friends."

International students often feel frustrated and confused, lonely, iso-lated, misunderstood, and even abused because they do not understand how American students act in relationships with each other and with their teach-ers. This chapter discusses some assumptions that underlie the American system of higher education, student-student and student-teacher relation-ships, roommate relationships, and the important topic of plagiarism.

ASSUMPTIONS UNDERLYING THE HIGHER EDUCATION SYSTEM

An educational system is both a manifestation and a carrier of a culture. People in a particular educational system, like people in a particular culture, may be unaware of the fundamental assumptions they are making and thus may be unable to articulate them to people from other systems. This leaves international students (in any country) on their own to figure out how the system works and what is expected of them.

For students in the United States from other countries, the challenges may not be in the intellectual realm. "To be honest," an East Asian student told researcher Alisa Eland (2001), "I think that if you want to survive [as a student] in [my country], you have to have more intellectual skills than here [in the United States] . . . . It is kind of easy after I came here . . . . It is tougher to be a student in [my country]." If it is not the intellectual aspects of higher education in the United States that can cause problems for foreign students, it is the mechanical aspects, and the cultural assumption that underlie them. For example, a Western European student told Eland, "My papers here have been more superficial due to time limitations" (83).

Using interviews with graduate students from other countries, Eland identified several aspects of the educational system where fundamental assumptions differed along cultural lines. One difference had to do with "content breadth and depth." In the minds of the two students just quoted, the American system's emphasis on breadth of learning made classes less intellectually demanding than their own systems, where a high value was placed on depth of learning—that is, studying fewer subjects in greater detail and at greater length.

Eland also identified differences in what she called "valued knowledge." Some foreign students, she wrote, "found that, in the United States, in contrast to their countries, only information that is rational, logical, objective, and verifiable is valued" (83–84). One student explained, "You have to provide reasons [for what you say or write]. Almost everything you say in your paper has to be backed up" (84).

By contrast, some students said that at home they could express their own feelings and opinions or quote respected elders or other authority figures. Such sources of knowledge were considered valid, and they did not always have to find support in academic publications for what they wrote in their papers, as they did in the United States.

The American demand for "facts and figures" or "hard data" is reflected in the corporate world, where decisions are so often made, or at least claimed to be made, on the basis of "the bottom line." "You can't argue with the facts," Americans will say.

The students Eland interviewed also commented on differences in what she called "ownership of knowledge." She wrote, "A West African student found that once knowledge is on paper [in the United States] it belongs to the author." The student remarked that "[for] everything you say, you have to put someone's name and the date and the page, to look scholarly" (85).

Eland also mentions a difference in "theory and practice balance." She quotes one student: "The [Francophone educational] system is much more intellectual, much more academic. Here, it is much more practical" (86).

The American preference for the practical over the theoretical (discussed in chapter 3) will, of course, be evident in the educational system.

Not only are students surprised by American classroom practices, but at a deeper level by powerful differences in thinking styles—that is, the way people process information. Richard Nisbett's stimulating book *The Geography of Thought* (also referred to in chapter 3) provides an intriguing glimpse into how differently people perceive and construct reality. He and other researchers describe Western thinking styles as more abstract, digital, objective, analytical, rational, detached, and concerned with validity. Meanwhile, Eastern styles are described as more concrete, analogic, subjective, holistic, global, metaphorical, empathic, and concerned with relationships.

As people from other cultures enter the classroom (and the workplace), they come to recognize that certain thinking patterns are assumed, and that they may not share those patterns. To succeed, they need to adapt to the local style. This adaptation requires a substantial shift, adding to the fatigue that occurs for those studying (or working) outside their own cultures.

STUDENT-STUDENT RELATIONSHIPS

The American values of independence and self-reliance are reflected in the way that American students interact with each other at school. American students, especially at a university, generally do not go out of their way to have conversations with classmates or to begin friendships with students outside of class. Some American students go to college classes and never speak to the person sitting next to them. In other cases, students may exchange e-mail addresses or phone numbers to form study groups or to discuss school-related matters, but such contact often takes place just before an assignment is due or the night before an exam. American students usually prefer to keep their schoolwork separate from their personal lives.

Many international students are dismayed to find that American students do not help each other with their studies in the way students in their own countries do. Indeed, American students often seem to be competing rather than cooperating with each other. International students who understand the degree to which Americans have been taught to idealize self-reliance will understand much of the reason for this competition. Another part of the explanation is that many instructors in American schools assign final class grades "on the curve," meaning that they award only a small—sometimes predetermined—number of high grades to the students who perform best in the class. When the instructor grades on the curve, the students in the class are in fact competing against each other to get one of the limited number of high grades.

Eland quoted an Asian student:

> [In the U.S.] all the students [are graded] on a curve. I came from where you always share your notes and common papers. . . . What I study for and what the other person is studying for is not going to be on a curve. . . . We would kind of divide the work up and if I wrote an answer I'll give it to my friend. . . . It was very community-based. . . . [In the U.S.] they prefer learning and studying alone. (104)

An alternative to grading on a curve is grading with an absolute scale, in which case every student in a class could possibly get a high grade. Some teachers in the United States do use that method.

Some American students may also be reluctant to help others study because they fear being accused of cheating. See the remarks about plagiarism, which follow.

The degree to which American students pay attention to foreign students, and the forms that attention takes, will vary according to many factors. A primary factor is the amount of experience the U.S. Americans have had interacting with foreign students or with other people who are different from themselves. For instance, American students who have studied or traveled abroad will often seek out international students in their classes.

STUDENT-PROFESSOR RELATIONSHIPS

"My adviser wants me to call him by his first name," many international graduate students in the United States have said. "I just can't do it! It doesn't seem right. I have to show my respect."

On the other hand, professors have said of international students, "They keep bowing and saying 'yes, sir, yes, sir.' I can hardly stand it! I wish they'd stop being so polite and just say what they have on their minds."

Differing ideas about formality and respect frequently complicate relationships between American professors and students from abroad, especially Asian students (and most especially female Asian students). The professors generally prefer informal relationships (sometimes, but not always, including the use of first names rather than titles and family names) and minimal acknowledgment of status differences. Many foreign students are accustomed to more formal relationships and sometimes have difficulty bringing themselves to speak to their professors at all, let alone address them by their given names.

The characteristics of student-professor relationships on American campuses vary, depending on whether the students involved are undergraduate or graduate students, on their age (younger Asian students may be more comfortable with informality), and on the size and nature of the school. Graduate students typically have more intense relationships with their professors than undergraduates do; at smaller schools, student-professor relationships are typically even less formal than at larger ones.

To say that student-professor relationships are informal is not to suggest that there are no recognized status differences between the two groups. There are. But students are expected to show their deference only in subtle ways, mainly in the vocabulary and tone of voice they use when speaking to professors. Much of their behavior around professors may seem disrespectful to foreign students. American students will eat in class, use their cell phones, surf the Internet on the laptops they bring to class allegedly to take notes, read newspapers, and often assume quite informal postures.

They may arrive at class late or leave early. Professors might dislike such behavior, but they usually tolerate it. Students, after all, are individuals who are entitled to decide for themselves how they are going to act.

American professors generally expect students to ask them questions or even challenge what they say. Professors do not generally assume they know all there is to know about a subject nor do they assume that they always explain things clearly. Students who want clarification or additional information are expected to ask for it during the class, just after class ends, or in the professor's office at the times she or he has announced as "office hours." Students who do not ask questions may be considered uninterested or uncommitted.

While some professors, particularly at smaller institutions, will take the initiative to contact students who appear to be having trouble in their classes, the normal expectation is that the student will take the initiative.

While most professors welcome students' questions and comments about the course, they do not welcome student efforts to negotiate for higher grades. Professors normally believe they have an acceptable system for determining grades, and unless it seems possible that a mistake has been made, professors respond negatively to students who try to talk them into raising a grade. Some foreign students, particularly ones from countries where negotiating is a common practice, severely damage their reputations in professors' eyes by trying to bargain for better grades.

ROOMMATE RELATIONSHIPS

International students may find themselves sharing quarters with American students, whether they deliberately sought out such an arrangement or the college housing office set it up for them. These arrangements can be enjoyable and educational or stressful and difficult, depending on a number of factors. One factor is the international student's knowledge of American culture. Another is of course the American student's knowledge of the international student's culture, but American students do not generally enter into roommate relationships with the idea that they will have to accommodate an international student's way of seeing and thinking about things.

Once again, what has already been said about Americans' values, thought patterns, and communicative style is consistent with what is said here about Americans and their relationships with roommates. It is important to remember that the ideas offered here are generalizations. Individual roommates will have their own personalities, and foreign students need to keep that fact in mind.

General Comments

It is not possible to generalize about the assumptions American students make about the kinds of relationships they will have with their roommates. While some—more often females than males—may be looking for close friendship, others may simply want another person to share housing costs and may not want any more involvement with the roommate than a periodic reckoning of accounts. The remainder of this section discusses the minimal expectations that Americans are likely to have about desired roommate behavior.

Respect for privacy. Americans are likely to respond quite negatively if their roommates open or otherwise read their electronic or other mail, listen in on their telephone or private conversations, enter their bedrooms uninvited (if they have separate bedrooms), or ask questions they consider "personal." The Americans' notion of privacy generally means that their personal thoughts, their belongings (see the next paragraph), their relationships, and their living quarters are to be shared with others only if they themselves wish them to be shared.

Respect for private property. Americans generally see their material possessions as, in a sense, extensions of themselves. Just as they do not readily share their innermost thoughts or feelings with others, they generally do not share their possessions with others until they have agreed about the terms of the sharing. Roommates, whether from the U.S. or abroad, do not share their clothing, toiletries, appliances, books, and other possessions without prior agreement. You should therefore not borrow, use, or even touch a roommate's possessions without permission.

Consideration. Americans will generally expect an even sharing of duties such as picking up your things and cleaning. If there are two roommates, then the sharing is expected to be, as the Americans often say, "fifty-fifty."

Doing your part is being considerate. Most Americans will extend consideration to and expect consideration from their roommates concerning noise levels, smoking habits, and schedules for using joint facilities. If one roommate wants to use the shared quarters for a party on Friday night, for example, that roommate is expected to confer with the other to make sure that some conflicting event or activity is not planned. Roommates are expected to take telephone messages for each other and to let one another know if a visitor has dropped by in the other's absence.

A particularly touchy issue has arisen more and more frequently in recent years—the issue of hosting overnight guests, particularly guests of the opposite sex, in shared quarters. Countless foreign students have talked about the great embarrassment they felt when their roommate was having sex with someone while they were, unwillingly, present. Considerate roommates avoid imposing such situations on each other.

Directness. Americans typically expect their roommates to be direct and assertive in expressing their preferences and in making it known when they are inconvenienced or otherwise negatively affected by something the American is doing. "How would I know he didn't like the music playing loud?" an American might ask. "He never said anything to me about it."

This orientation on the part of the Americans contrasts with the orientation some people bring from other cultures, where the burden is on the aggressor (in this example, the person playing the music) to make sure no one is bothered by the behavior in question.

PLAGIARISM

To plagiarize is to represent someone else's academic work—in the form of writing or ideas—as one's own. The American belief in the value of the individual and the sanctity of the individual's property extends to ideas. Ideas belong to people; they are a form of property. Scholars' writings and ideas are considered their intellectual property, as was mentioned earlier. Students and other scholars are not supposed to use those ideas in their own writing without acknowledging where they came from. To leave out the acknowledgment and thereby convey the impression that another's words are one's own is considered plagiarism.

International students are sometimes accused of plagiarizing the works of other people, as are younger American students who often seem to regard anything they find on the Internet as freely available for anyone's use. Much of the plagiarism international students commit (usually by copying the words of another writer into a paper they themselves are writing and failing to include a footnote or citation giving credit to the original author) is the result of habit and misunderstanding rather than dishonesty. To American scholars the notion of "intellectual property" is generally clear and sensible. It is obvious to them when an idea has been "stolen." And stealing ideas is a cardinal sin in the American academic world.

Many foreign students do not share the Americans' conceptions about private property and the ownership of ideas, however, and see nothing wrong in copying relevant, well-expressed ideas into a paper they are writing. But the faculty will see it as wrong, and international students need to know that and behave accordingly. Many colleges and universities have explicit regulations with respect to plagiarism and other forms of academic dishonesty. All students are expected to understand and comply with these regulations, and the penalty for noncompliance can be severe, ranging from a failing grade on a paper or an assignment to a failing course grade. In extreme cases, a student may be expelled from the college or university.

The rules for acknowledging sources of ideas other than one's own differ somewhat from field to field. Before students turn in any written paper, they should be sure they know and have used the rules for attribution that are customary in their field of study. It is part of the professor's job to guide students in this matter. When in doubt, students should acknowledge their sources.

This does not mean that American students (and, indeed, sometimes their professors and even their institutions' presidents) never engage in plagiarism or any other form of academic dishonesty. They do, and reportedly with increasing frequency. Still, plagiarizing entails risks that are probably not worth taking.

SUGGESTIONS FOR
INTERNATIONAL STUDENTS

In most cases you will find that you must exercise some initiative if you want to have conversations or relationships with American students. The latter will not generally approach international students with unsolicited offers of companionship or friendship.

Although American teachers often respond negatively to students' requests to bargain for higher grades, it is acceptable for students to speak with their teachers about concerns they have regarding their grades. For example, students may arrange to meet with a teacher to talk about their progress in class. Students may inquire about the criteria for a specific grade. Students may also ask questions that help them clarify their teacher's expectations about an assignment or the material that will be covered on an exam. Generally, teachers are willing to discuss how students can improve their performance. You can ask the professor, "How can I do better in your class?"

Asking to be included in a study group, if there is one, can require considerable courage on the part of a foreign student, particularly one still working to improve his or her English proficiency. But asking is probably worth the risk.

A noticeable number of classes, particularly in business schools, entail assignments to *teams* of students. Both international and domestic students often find these team experiences unpleasant, in part because not all students actively participate. Students from abroad will want to do their best to overcome shyness or other reservations about participating fully in their teams.

CHAPTER 20

Business

"The business of America," said former U.S. president Calvin Coolidge, "is business."

In some nations a society's religious sector plays a predominant role in politics or governmental affairs. In the United States the business sector plays that role. The business world rewards the values and virtues Americans admire: hard work, achievement, competitiveness, materialism, rationality, perseverance, and building toward the future. Successful businesspeople are well-known in their communities, usually more so than clerical, literary, or academic people. The very successful, such as Bill Gates (Microsoft), Steve Jobs (Apple), Jeff Bezos (Amazon), Warren Buffett (investor), Sergey Brin (Google), Oprah Winfrey (television talk show, magazine, production company), and Sam Walton (Walmart), become cultural heroes whose thoughts and lives are deemed worthy of study and emulation. This remains true despite the major corporate scandals (Enron, WorldCom, and others) of the early 2000s and the banking and investment busts (Bank of America, Bear Stearns, and others) of the late 2000s.

American values are reflected not just in the general status of business within the society but also in the operations of each business organization.

A female colleague who formerly worked for an oil company in the Southwest told this story:

> One summer the president of my company had a party at his house. The president is tall and is sometimes compared to a polar bear.
>
> At the party, the executive vice presidents bet me that I couldn't throw the president into the swimming pool. I am quite short and slight. I accepted the bet.
>
> I took a drink to the president and lured him to the edge of the pool. I explained the bet to him. He was most sympathetic to my situation. To have refused the bet would have shown either timidity (a horrible affliction in a high-risk business) or that I couldn't "play" with the "boys"—a rejection of their offer of equality. The president told me to put my hand on his back, count to three, and push, saying he would jump in. I did. As I pushed, he turned to me, smiled, picked me up and tossed me into the center of the pool. When I surfaced, I saw the vice presidents throwing the president in (it took three of them). By the end of the afternoon, everyone, including the hostess, had been thrown into the pool.

This story illustrates at least three aspects of American business life that people from abroad notice very quickly. The first may not seem to be a matter of culture, but it probably is. American executives (if they are male) are likely to be tall. Numerous studies have shown a correlation between a male executive's height and his status in an organization. Taller men are more likely to be selected for higher positions in their organizations and to be paid higher salaries. International visitors who meet high-level American executives are likely to be dealing with tall males. In many people's minds height is associated with the strength, power, and competitiveness that are idealized in American business.

Another characteristic of business life in the United States that international visitors notice is its informality. You may not see a president being tossed into a swimming pool by the vice presidents, but you are likely to witness much more informal behavior than you would among colleagues at home. U.S. American businesspeople, at least as much as so-called average Americans and probably more so, address others by their first names, make jokes, and use a vocabulary and tone of voice suitable for informal relationships. Because they are likely to equate formality with discomfort,

Americans want to encourage others to relax during their business dealings. They may dress relatively casually, and men may remove their coats
and loosen their neckties if they are in a long meeting. Some companies
encourage their employees to abandon coats and ties in favor of "business
casual" dress on Fridays. High-tech companies such as Google, Apple, and
Microsoft are famous for the informality of their workplaces, where people
dress casually, play games with others at the office, and even get massages
at their desks. Bill Gates and Steve Jobs are rarely seen in neckties; in his
public appearances, Jobs is usually wearing blue jeans.

Of course, such informality is not always the rule. Investment bankers
are rarely photographed in anything but suits and neckties.

Americans' notions about equality also strongly influence what happens throughout business organizations. Although people at various levels
are quite aware of the status differences among them, they are unlikely to
overtly display superiority or inferiority, as the poolside behavior recounted
here makes clear. Rank-conscious foreign visitors often feel uneasy around
the relatively relaxed and informal interactions they will see between lower-
and higher-status employees.

Another manifestation of the equality assumption is the prevalence
of written rules and procedures in the workplace. If people are considered
equal, then they must be treated fairly or impartially—that is, without
reference to their own particular personalities. Fairness is best assured,
as we have seen, if there are written rules and procedures that apply to
everyone equally. So there are written procedures for hiring, training,
evaluating, rewarding, disciplining, and terminating employees. There are
written procedures for handling employee complaints as well as written
job descriptions, safety rules, policies on sexual harassment, and rules for
taking "breaks" (rest periods) from work.

Foreign visitors are likely to think that the constraints Americans
impose on themselves by means of their rules are excessive, especially if
labor-union rules are added to those of a company.

Finally, the swimming-pool story illustrates the presence of women
in American executive circles. Women are still in the minority, and they
encounter many obstacles in their efforts to advance (sometimes referred
to as the "glass ceiling"), but they do hold powerful positions in a growing

number of organizations. According to statistics compiled by About.com, between 1997 and 2006 businesses owned or controlled by women had a growth rate nearly double that of American firms overall: 42.3 percent versus 23.3 percent.

DOING BUSINESS IN THE UNITED STATES

Some international businesspeople stay for extended periods in the States and have opportunities to observe American business operations in detail. While it is impossible to list all of the characteristics of U.S. American companies here, it is safe to say that the more a foreigner understands about how an organization is set up and how it operates, the more effectively he or she can work within that organization. The comments that follow represent a few aspects of American business operations that stand out in the minds of many international visitors.

Hard Work

While they may appear to be informal and relaxed, Americans generally work hard. They may devote long hours—as many as 16 or 18 per day—to their jobs. They may consider their work more important than family responsibilities and social relationships. Americans use the term *workaholic* to describe a person who seems addicted to work—one who spends as much time as possible on the job and seems to think of little else. Workaholics are by no means rare in the American business world.

Some observers see a change in this "work ethic" as more young people make their way into organizations. More so than their elders, members of the upcoming generation may resist putting long hours into their jobs, preferring to spend time with their families or pursuing their private interests.

American executives and managers often embarrass their foreign counterparts by performing manual work or other tasks that elsewhere would be done only by lower-status people—tasks such as serving coffee, rearranging the furniture in a meeting room, or taking out a calculator to solve a problem during a meeting.

Punctuality

Promptness and schedules are important. Meetings and appointments ideally begin and end on schedule. The topic that is supposed to be addressed during the meeting or appointment is generally expected to be covered by the scheduled ending time. Delays cause frustration. Getting behind schedule is likely to be considered an example of bad management. In keeping with their notions about the importance of using time wisely and getting the job done, American businesspeople generally want to "get right down to business." They do not want to "waste time" with "formalities" or with long, preliminary discussions. In fact, they are usually uncomfortable with purely social interactions while they are working.

Impersonal Dealings

Americans generally have no particular interest in getting personally acquainted with the people with whom they work. As long as they believe the other party is trustworthy in business dealings and has the ability to deliver whatever product or service is being discussed, they will proceed in a relatively impersonal manner. They value decisiveness and efficiency. For many Americans, the saying "time is money" reflects their belief that what is important is getting things accomplished as quickly as possible. Some European people behave similarly, but people from many other parts of the world may find the typical American approach cold or otherwise uncomfortable.

Even when they seem to be socializing, as at a dinner or reception with business colleagues, Americans' main purpose is more likely to be discussing business or networking than becoming personally connected to other people. "Shop talk" will dominate the conversation.

Quantitative Reasoning

American businesspeople, probably even more noticeably than Americans in general, prefer to think and analyze in quantitative terms. They want "hard data" when they are analyzing a business situation and trying to make a decision. The assumption is that wise decisions are made on the basis of "objective" information uncontaminated by considerations of personal feelings, social relations, or political advantage.

American executives frequently use the term *bottom line*, which refers to the final entry in an accounting statement. They want that statement to show a profit. Nothing else is as important as "return on investment." The purpose of a business is to make a profit and to do so in the short run. Executives are often evaluated on the basis of their contribution to the company's bottom line.

Writing It Down

The written word is supremely important to American businesspeople. They make notes and send "memos of understanding" about conversations, keep files on their various projects, and record the minutes of meetings, whether on paper or using the company's "intranet," an internal Internet where company documents are stored so as to be readily available to employees. A contract or agreement must be written down in order to be taken seriously, and every written word in it is important. It must be the correct word, the one that most clearly states each party's rights and obligations.

To Americans in business, then, it seems perfectly natural to consult lawyers about contracts and agreements. Lawyers are trained to select the proper words for important documents and to correctly interpret them. Americans have difficulty understanding that people from other parts of the world might consider oral agreements adequate. Businesspeople from abroad might feel insulted by the Americans' insistence on having written agreements, viewing the Americans as distrustful.

Self-Improvement

The American belief in self-improvement, mentioned elsewhere, is quite evident in the business world. Managers might attend seminars on public speaking, conflict resolution, delegating work, or time management. Clerical staff might attend training on telephone manners or spelling and grammar. Employees at any level may study videotapes about stress management or new computer software. Whole organizations might adopt some new approach to management, such as appreciative inquiry, balanced scorecards, talent management, or benchmarking.

Behavior in Meetings

Meetings are of course common in the business world, but what actually happens in meetings varies greatly, not just from country to country but from organization to organization. Meetings can have a variety of purposes—sharing information, giving instructions, heightening employee enthusiasm and dedication, discussing issues and problems, suggesting solutions, making decisions, and no doubt others. Americans like to know explicitly what a meeting's purpose is. "What's the agenda?" they may ask. "Why are we here?"

The leader's role in meetings also varies. The leader might be the one who opens the meeting, does all the talking, and then dismisses everyone. Or the leader may play the role of a moderator, opening the meeting and then allowing others to discuss matters and make decisions. The role of those attending the meeting differs too. They may sit quietly and listen, or offer suggestions or comments, or even to challenge ideas others put forth.

In the ideal American meeting, the leader encourages participation from all those who might have ideas to contribute. Attendees offer ideas and information intended to help illuminate the subject under discussion. They may openly and bluntly disagree with each other. Witnessing such meetings can shock foreigners who are accustomed to more formal, hierarchical arrangements, where the leader firmly controls what takes place and participants either remain silent or mask any disagreement with what others say.

In American meetings, issues are often resolved by means of a vote. "The majority rules," Americans often say—not just in this context but in others too. The practice of voting in meetings might disconcert international visitors who are accustomed to a system in which decisions must be unanimous or one in which the person in authority makes the decisions.

Turnover

International visitors may see more employees joining and leaving the organization than they are accustomed to. America is still a more mobile society than most, so people change jobs relatively readily. Studies suggest that the average thirty-eight-year-old will have had 13 or 14 different jobs. A neighbor of mine, still under thirty, is now in her sixth job since moving into her house about three years ago. The strong sense of company loyalty, still prevalent in some countries, is harder and harder to find in the United States, particularly among young people. Even many senior executives are ready to change employers when a promising opportunity arises. Many people view their jobs as a means to earn a living, and in most cases it does not matter to them where that living comes from. They do what they are supposed to do (according to a written job description, usually), collect their pay, and go home. Supervisors are often seeking ways to enhance employee allegiance to the company, believing that employees who are more loyal will also be more productive.

On the other hand, a manager is considered to be doing a good job if she mentors her employees to prepare them for a higher-level position, even if that position is with a different organization.

It is not just employees who are mobile but companies as well. Giant corporations may shift their headquarters from one city to another. For example, in 2001 the aircraft manufacturer Boeing moved its headquarters from Seattle, Washington to Chicago, Illinois. Company executives believed that the new, centrally located offices would allow Boeing to better serve their customers and expand their business potential. And besides, Boeing's new president liked Chicago better than he did Seattle! Meanwhile, thousands of workers were forced to relocate or be left unemployed.

In an age of mergers and acquisitions, businesses are continuously being bought and sold. Any business might be taken over by another at any time, a process most Americans seem to view as a normal development in a capitalist system. Since the capitalist system (or "the marketplace," as it is often called) is seen as rewarding virtues Americans generally value—hard work, decisiveness, rationality, and so on—these shifts in ownership and location are generally accepted as "necessary evils," actions that many people may not like but are required to accept in the name of progress. When reciting their history with a company, many employees can cite five or six mergers or acquisitions that have taken place since they started with the firm.

By the time the late-2000s depression slowed the rate of mergers and acquisitions, major industries such as entertainment, finance, media, petroleum, pharmaceuticals, and automobile manufacturing had come under the control of fewer and fewer organizations that had grown larger and larger.

Companies may change their names as they grow, often inventing a word for the new name. Take, for example, the case of a company called Phillip Morris. For decades Phillip Morris made cigarettes, including the well-known Marlboro brand. Along the way Phillip Morris bought Kraft Foods, maker of many common grocery items. It also acquired Miller Brewing, a beer maker of long standing. In 2001 Phillip Morris changed its name to the Altria Group, Inc. Though *Altria* is not a real word in the English language, to the ear of a native speaker of American English, it has a modern, progressive sound.

Companies may change their names for other reasons as well. In 2009, the company formerly known as Blackwater adopted the meaningless name of Xe Services. Blackwater provided "private security services" to, among others, American agencies operating in Iraq and Afghanistan. Blackwater's name became affiliated with an array of questionable activities, and the company then adopted a new name.

Diversity

In the last three decades, America's population has changed rapidly in at least two important ways, as has been mentioned in other chapters. First, the proportion of European Americans is diminishing, so their traditional dominant role in the society—holding positions of power and influence, defining the terms of public issues, being the arbiters of values and tastes— is arguably coming to a close. The declining birthrate among European Americans, immigration from other parts of the world, and the higher birthrates among many nonwhite immigrant groups together are making nonwhites ever more salient in defining the nature of American society.

Another way in which the population is changing is with regard to public attitudes. Some examples:

- Increasing acceptance of females in fields of endeavor and at organizational levels formerly dominated by males
- Increasing acceptance of nonwhites in fields and at levels formerly restricted to European American people

- Realization that people with physical and mental disabilities can in many cases be contributing members of society
- Increasing acceptance of lesbian, gay, bisexual, and transgendered people
- Legitimation of the idea that people ought to be open and accepting toward other people who are different from them in whatever respect—race, gender, religion, nationality, physique, sexual preference, and so on

This is not to say that all Americans are accepting of these human differences. Many are not; in fact many are deeply disturbed by the changes they see going on around them.

But these changes are under way, giving rise in nearly all organizations to a commitment to understanding cultural differences and working effectively with others who have a different worldview. In keeping with the general American belief that people can change through conscious effort, countless organizations now have some official component—a staff member, or maybe even an office—whose job it is to try to ensure that no one (employee, prospective employee, customer, supplier) is harassed or treated unfairly on account of race, gender, religion, age, nationality, physical limitation, or sexual orientation. These diversity offices operate within the framework of written rules and procedures intended to ensure fair treatment of all.

Governments at all levels have "anti-discrimination" laws and ordinances intended, again, to ensure that everyone is treated fairly. People who believe they have been mistreated as a result of being a member of some protected category can file complaints with anti-discrimination agencies and can sue alleged offenders in court. Some well-known businesses, including Walmart and Denny's, have been required to pay heavy fines for discriminatory conduct. In Walmart's case the mistreated group was female employees; in the case of Denny's, it was black employees and customers.

The concern with diversity has given rise to a field of endeavor called "diversity training," a term that encompasses a range of educational and training programs originally intended to help people learn how demographic trends were transforming the workplace. More recently, this training has addressed the matter of intercultural competence, trying to help organizational members at all levels work, teach, and manage in intercultural settings.

THE GLOBAL ECONOMY

No chapter about business would be complete without mentioning globalization's effects on business life in the United States. From a cultural perspective, globalization has increased and intensified interactions between Americans and people with other cultural backgrounds. It is not just business executives who are posted abroad but technicians, various specialists, and their family members as well. Books, videos, and training programs on doing business internationally are far more common than they were before "globalization" became an everyday term.

Many more Americans are gaining experience abroad, then, while many foreigners are seeing American life from the inside. Presumably, this exchange will produce more understanding of (if not appreciation for) various culturally based assumptions, values, and customs.

From a practical perspective, globalization has accentuated the uncertainty surrounding the future of many American businesses. Relocations, buyouts, takeovers, downsizings, bankruptcies, outsourcing, and closures attributed to competition in the global marketplace are frequently in the news. Executives and workers in many industries are often doing the work of two or three people and even then cannot be certain whether they will have a job the following week.

SUGGESTIONS FOR INTERNATIONAL BUSINESSPEOPLE

Businesspeople from abroad can use this chapter as a framework for what they observe in the business organizations with which they interact.

If you work with American companies, take every opportunity to meet and socialize with your American coworkers. You can discuss the ideas in this chapter with coworkers and find out how the ideas fit with their experience.

Business-oriented newspapers such as *The Wall Street Journal*, *Barron's*, and *Investor's Business Daily* are widely read by American businesspeople and will offer insight into American business issues and practices.

Television programs such as *Nightly Business Report* and *Wall Street Week in Review* (both aired on many public television stations) offer useful information and insights. So do cable news stations such as MSNBC and CNN, which frequently highlight business-related stories.

Foreign students who want to work in the United States can find workshops or one-on-one assistance in writing resumes and preparing for job interviews (which are ever more frequently carried out by telephone). The entire job-search system is, of course, culturally based and requires applicants to "sell themselves" in ways that people from less individualistic and assertive societies can find uncomfortable.

If you are an international student, you may also want to participate in student organizations that promote networking and skill building in specialized business fields. Whether you are a student or are in the United States for business, you can learn more about business practices by enrolling in business courses at a college or university.

CHAPTER 21

Healthcare

People travel to the United States from all over the world to obtain high-quality medical care. Well-to-do people, that is. While the United States offers what many regard as the most advanced medical care in the world, the fact is that many Americans cannot afford the care they need.

Doctors in America (one cannot safely say "American doctors," because many doctors practicing in America are from other countries) have access to the most sophisticated training, diagnostic equipment, treatment techniques, and pharmaceuticals. They can identify and treat rare diseases, repair the gravest of injuries, and prolong the lives of the most critically ill. But providing these services is expensive, so much so that some Americans delay or forego treatment for their maladies, or are forced to choose between paying for their medical care and paying for daily necessities.

How can it be, many visitors from abroad wonder, that a country as wealthy as the United States can have a healthcare system that many of its own citizens are unable to use?

The answer, as usual, lies in the system's cultural underpinnings.

CULTURAL UNDERPINNINGS

Very generally speaking, the American healthcare system brings together the practice of what is known as "Western medicine" with political and economic arrangements compatible with the notions of individual independence, freedom, and free enterprise.

Western medicine is presumably based on science, the systematic study of natural structures and phenomena. The disciplines underlying Western medicine are anatomy and physiology—the study of the body's structure and systems.

Western medicine is based on assumptions that are incompatible with the assumptions that underlie medical traditions found in other parts of the world. It generally assumes that illness has specific physical (if sometimes undetectable) causes, and it uses specific, physical means of treatment. These means are mainly pharmaceuticals and surgery.

The fundamental concepts of Western medicine do not address animistic or spiritual forces, the concepts of balance and energy flow (*qi*) that underlie traditional Chinese medicine, or concepts related to energy centers such as *chakras*, found in traditional Indian medicine.

In its search for the causes of illness, its diagnosis of injury, and its treatment of illness and injury, Western medicine relies on doctors who have undergone lengthy training in high-priced facilities. These doctors and their associated specialists use costly equipment such as x-ray machines, CAT scanners, magnetic resonance imaging (MRI), laboratory testing, microsurgical equipment, man-made replacements for various body parts, and a vast array of pharmaceuticals.

All these components of Western medical practice make it very expensive. Medical care in America is made all the more expensive by the emphasis its practitioners place on prolonging life and on treating the most seriously ill or injured. American culture supports the notion that humankind can achieve mastery over nature, or at least many aspects of it. In the context of medical care, this includes, among other things, forestalling the natural forces of aging and death. Whether through organ transplants, replacement of body parts, plastic surgery, liposuction, Botox injections, pharmaceuticals, or other interventions, Americans in general believe their technological inventiveness will enable them to improve and lengthen their lives.

Who pays the cost of this expensive system? In most industrialized countries, and indeed in a number of countries that are not so industrialized, the government pays for most if not all of its citizens' medical expenses. Healthcare is viewed as a right that all citizens deserve, rather than as a product available, like other products, on the open market. In these systems, peoples' access to healthcare is not determined by their level of wealth.

POLITICAL RAMIFICATIONS

But many Americans, as we have seen, traditionally distrust government. They value individual choice and freedom from external direction or restraint. Their political system is based on a constitution that intends to limit the government's size and scope. Their constitution does not explicitly give the government responsibility for healthcare. As matters have evolved, the government, through the people's representatives in the Congress, has assumed responsibility for paying at least a share of the health costs of Americans aged 65 and over. This is done under a program called Medicare. For those under 65, free enterprise prevails. This means that people must pay for their own healthcare. They use various means to do this, including the following:

- They pay "out of pocket," using their own money.
- They buy health insurance, which spreads the cost of healthcare among a group of people. In some cases their employers pay a portion of their health insurance premiums; otherwise, they buy insurance themselves. In either case, the cost of health insurance, reflecting the cost of healthcare itself, is high and growing higher.
- If their income falls below certain thresholds, they apply for aid from programs that state and local governments have established to help impoverished people pay for medical treatment. Most of these programs have not been able to meet the demands placed upon them.
- They turn to "alternative medicine," the label generally given an array of healthcare and health-maintenance approaches not usually considered part of Western medicine. Alternative medicine includes such approaches as acupuncture, chiropractic, homeopathy, massage, natur-

opathy, and Chinese medicine, which generally entails acupuncture and herbal preparations. It should be noted that some of these approaches, particularly chiropractic and acupuncture, have slowly been gaining acceptance among Western medical practitioners.

- They travel to other countries, such as Mexico, Costa Rica, Thailand, and India, to obtain medical and dental care.
- They forego medical care, either because they cannot afford it, are physically unable to transport themselves to a healthcare facility, have a strong fear or dislike of doctors, or do not believe in the effectiveness of Western medicine.
- In extreme circumstances, they go to a hospital emergency room, from which, by law, they cannot normally be turned away despite an inability to pay for care.*

By the late 2000s, America's healthcare system was widely considered to be "in crisis." Even before the economic downturn of that period, healthcare costs were rising faster than most other components of family budgets, and the cost of health insurance was rising. A growing portion of the population was reaching age sixty-five, when it became eligible for Medicare, putting increasing demands on that government program.

With the economic downturn, tens of thousands of people lost their jobs and thus, in many cases, their employer-supported health insurance. Millions saw their incomes decline, reducing their ability to pay for health-care and health insurance.

This crisis produced yet another federal-government effort (there had been several such efforts in previous decades) to "reform" the healthcare system. The contentious debate about that reform once again highlighted the cultural themes that underlie the way Americans think about healthcare.

Those supporting healthcare reform generally argued that it was unfair, or even immoral, to maintain a system in which some people could not get necessary medical care because, for whatever reason, they did not have money to pay for it. Everyone should be entitled to medical care, their argument proposed. They went on to suggest various ways in which the system

---

* A fuller description of the components and workings of the U.S. health-care system can be found in chapter 21 of Diane Asitimbay's *What's Up, America?*

could be changed in order to provide all Americans, or nearly all of them, with access to basic medical services.

On the other side were those who, while perhaps agreeing that wider access to medical care would be good, rejected the notion of a governmental program that might limit individual citizens' choices or restrict the operations of businesses such as health-insurance companies or pharmaceutical firms. Citizens should be able to choose their own doctors, the argument went, rather than being required to see particular doctors available through some government-managed program. The free market, rather than the government, should determine healthcare prices.

Clearly this is a political issue, determining the government's role in a major component of a country's economy. The future of the 2010 "healthcare reform" legislation remains uncertain. The measure faces court challenges, and its implementation is scheduled to take place over several years.

SUGGESTIONS FOR
INTERNATIONAL VISITORS

It is vital for international visitors to the United States to have health insurance that covers them during their time in the States. Of course no one plans on having an accident or falling ill, but those things do happen, and the resulting medical bills can be crippling. Insurance will help pay those bills. Wise travelers get insurance before leaving home, so they are covered from the beginning of their stays.

Visitors interested in a more complete understanding of the healthcare system can talk with Americans they meet about their own experiences with doctors, hospitals, pharmacies, alternative medicines, and insurance companies. Such a talk can begin with questions such as, "Have you been sick or hurt and needed medical care? If you have, what was your experience with the system?" Or, "I understand that healthcare is a hot topic in this country. What's your opinion about that?"

Many Americans are pleased by an opportunity to tell their healthcare stories. Some will do so with considerable emotion. Be prepared for that!

Coping with Cultural Differences

S ome people find cultural differences interesting and exciting. They feel challenged and stimulated by encounters with people from other cultures, and they want more. Other people have a different reaction. In the presence of people from different cultures, they feel uncomfortable, anxious, and confused. They have a strong tendency to judge or evaluate other people and to reach negative conclusions about them.

People of the first type are of course more likely to have constructive experiences with people from other cultures than are those of the second type. Can anything be done to help people react more constructively than they might otherwise? Part III is based on the assumption(perhaps typically American!) that some things can be done.

Chapter 22 offers ideas about intercultural relationships and adjusting to new cultures. Chapter 23 suggests some activities that can help you understand your own ideas about intercultural encounters and also understand Americans better. These suggestions supplement those given at the close of earlier chapters.

CHAPTER 22

Some Helpful Ideas

Two Japanese businessmen are assigned to work in the United States. They are just a year apart in age. Both work for the same large automobile corporation, both are trained as mechanical engineers, and both are sent to the same American city to help test their company's cars under mountain and winter driving conditions.

One is miserable in the States. He cannot wait to get back home. The other has an interesting and enjoyable time and would like to stay longer. What accounts for the difference? It is not possible to say for certain, but it is clear that the ideas and attitudes people bring to the States from other countries, as well as their knowledge of U.S. American society and culture, strongly influence what kind of experience they have. Each of the Japanese engineers, it is safe to say, had some ideas that the other did not have. This chapter presents an assortment of ideas that can help you, as a visitor to the United States, to respond constructively to your experience.

INTERCULTURAL COMPETENCE

Thinking about the concept of "intercultural competence" is a way to start. In material she uses in her intercultural-training sessions, my colleague

Janet Bennett defines intercultural competence as "a set of cognitive, affective and behavioral skills that support effective and appropriate interaction in a variety of cultural contexts."

To make this definition more practical and memorable, Bennett uses the term "mindset" to refer to *knowledge*, "skillset" to refer to *skills*, and "heartset" to refer to *attitudes*. People who are (or are going to be) foreigners in the United States or anywhere else can assess their cultural competence by asking themselves some question about their mindset, skillset, and heartset.

With respect to your *mindset*, ask yourself:

- *Cultural self-awareness:* What are some of your most important culturally-based values and assumptions?
- *Culture-general knowledge:* What are some of the ways in which cultures (in this case, national cultures) vary?
- *Culture-specific knowledge:* How much do you know about the culture of the place you plan to visit or are now visiting (in this case, the United States)?
- *Interaction analysis:* Can you accurately assess what is happening in interpersonal interactions?

Ask yourself these questions about your *skillset*:

- *Relationship-building skills:* Can you attract people's attention, begin and sustain an interaction with them, and develop bonds with them?
- *Behavioral skills (listening, problem solving):* When other people have spoken with you, do they go away with the feeling that you heard what they had in mind? When faced with a problem, can you readily find ways to address it?
- *Empathy:* How readily can you understand and share someone else's perspectives? Do you feel understood?
- *Information-gathering skills:* Are you resourceful at finding out things you want or need to know?

Finally, about your *heartset*:

- *Curiosity:* Do you want to learn and understand more and to have new experiences? When you experience an interaction you don't understand, do you seek further information?

- *Cognitive flexibility:* Can you readily reframe situations—that is, see them from different points of view?
- *Motivation:* Do you *want* to succeed in your intercultural situation?
- *Open-mindedness:* Can you avoid judging others, and simply try to understand what is behind their behavior?

EXPECTATIONS

Be aware that your reactions to your experience in another country have as much to do with your *expectations* as with *what actually happens* to you. When you find yourself disturbed or upset about your interactions with Americans, ask yourself, "What did I expect? Why did I expect it? Had I known more, would I have expected what I actually experienced?" Unrealistic expectations create much unhappiness for international visitors anywhere. That graduate student in Pittsburgh who could not find an apartment building that housed attractive female tenants had some unrealistic expectations, as he came to realize after he talked with other people who had spent more time in the United States.

PERSONALITY CHARACTERISTICS

Scholars and researchers have attempted to determine what personality characteristics are associated with successful intercultural experiences. Although their findings have often been unclear or inconclusive, four characteristics recur in their reports: patience, curiosity, a sense of humor, and tolerance for ambiguity.

Patience, of course, is the ability to remain calm even when things do not go as you want them to, or hope they will, or have even been assured they will. Impatience is usually counterproductive.

Some people seem naturally more *curious* than others. They notice what goes on around them. They wonder what factors can explain what they are experiencing. They want to know more. Curious people are more likely to be stimulated by an intercultural experience, and less likely to feel frustrated or overwhelmed by it.

If you have a *sense of humor*, you will be less likely to take things too seriously and will be more ready to see the humor in your own reactions. The value of a sense of humor in intercultural relations is difficult to overestimate.

Tolerance for ambiguity is a more difficult concept to define than patience, curiosity, or sense of humor. International visitors often find themselves in situations that are ambiguous to them—that is, they do not know what is happening around them. Perhaps they do not understand the local language well enough; they do not know how some system or organization works; they cannot determine different people's roles in what is going on; they do not know what assumptions the people around them are making; or they do not know what is expected of them. "It's like I just got here from the moon," a Chinese graduate student newly arrived in the United States said. "Things are just so different here." The student did not know what to expect of university teachers or administrators, clerks in stores, the bank teller, or the government agents he supposed were everywhere. He did not know how he was expected to behave.

Some people have little tolerance for ambiguity. They want to know what is happening at all times; indeed, they may even want to be in control of what is happening. Such people are usually unhappy when they leave their own countries (if not their own hometowns) because as foreigners they inevitably encounter situations that, to them, are ambiguous.

Tolerance for ambiguity is the ability to say to yourself, calmly, "Well, I don't know what's going on here. I'll just have to wait and see, or try to find out." People with a high tolerance for ambiguity have a much easier time in intercultural encounters than do those who feel a constant need to understand what is happening in their surroundings.

TRAITS AND SITUATIONS

A server comes to your restaurant table, looks at you coldly, and says, "What do you want?!" You are startled by her unpleasant behavior. If you are like most people, you search your mind for an explanation for her conduct. One sort of explanation you might settle on has to do with the woman's *personality traits.* "What an unfriendly person!" you might say to yourself. Or, "She obviously doesn't like foreigners. She must be narrow-minded and prejudiced."

Another sort of explanation has to do with the woman's *situation*. Perhaps the other two servers who were supposed to be on duty failed to appear for work, and your server is trying to do three people's jobs. Perhaps her two teenage children had a loud argument about using the bathroom early that morning, and the woman was awakened from a deep sleep by the sound of their yelling. Perhaps her husband is in the hospital. Perhaps another customer just shouted at her because the chef (not the server) had overcooked his meat. Any of these possible circumstances (and any of dozens of others) might account for the server's unfriendly manner.

People's behavior stems from some combination of their personality *traits* and the *situations* in which they find themselves. When we are familiar with other people, we know what their situations are—how their health is, what pressures they are under, what role they are currently in—and we are more likely to tolerate what might otherwise be unacceptable behavior from them. When we are unfamiliar with other people's situations, however, we tend to attribute their behavior solely to their personality traits. Often their traits explain far less about their behavior than their situations do.

In intercultural encounters, psychologist Richard Brislin (1981) points out, we typically know little if anything about other people's situations. We do not know them as individuals when we are new in their country. We do not know what their personal or work lives are like, and we do not know how they perceive what is going on around them. Since we are unfamiliar with their situations, we tend to attribute their behavior to personality traits—this person is unfriendly, that one is prejudiced, the one over there seems nice, and so forth. By overlooking the influence of other people's situations on their behavior, we misunderstand and misinterpret much of what they do.

Keeping in mind the distinction between traits and situations helps you remain aware that the reasons for other people's actions are complex and often unknowable. That awareness makes it easier to avoid misunderstandings and misinterpretations of what individual Americans do.

CULTURE SHOCK AND STAGES
OF ADJUSTMENT

The process of adjusting to a new culture begins when you decide to go abroad. From that point on, you start paying more attention to news and information about the destination country. You seek out people who have been to that country, ask questions, and pay attention to the answers.

Most people who come to the United States from elsewhere have been hearing about American life for most of their own lives. They have seen movies and television programs from the States. Perhaps they have known some Americans. Now, at last, they are in the country to experience it for themselves. They assume they will experience some "culture shock," the term commonly used to refer to people's initial reactions to a new country.

Some social scientists suggest that "culture shock" covers an array of reactions and needs to be thought about more carefully. In her intercultural training materials, Janet Bennett distinguishes *culture surprise, culture stress*, and *culture shock*.

Culture surprise relates to unexpected or unfamiliar things one encounters in a new country—the way people dress, the smells pervading the streets, or the sound of birds singing.

Culture stress relates to the feeling of being overwhelmed by trying to accomplish routine things but not knowing how to get them done, like sending a package abroad, getting a necessary legal document, opening a bank account, or buying a car.

Culture shock is the sense of disorientation or loss that comes with encountering fundamental differences in values and way of life.

Most people who go to another country respond initially with excitement, curiosity, and stimulation. They enjoy the cultural surprises, and they work through the stresses. Then comes the culture shock, as the nature and number of unfamiliar things grows, along with a longing for the familiar people and way of life they have left behind.

The notion of culture shock calls to mind two useful points. First, most people experience some degree of culture shock when they visit a new country, whether they admit it to themselves and others or not. Culture shock is more a product of the situation of being in a new culture than of the traveler's personal traits. However, your traits—including patience, curiosity, sense of humor, and tolerance for ambiguity—can influence how deep or long-lasting the culture shock will be.

For a few people, the shock is too much to bear. Journalist Alexei Barrionuevo reported on an attractive, 16-year-old Brazilian girl who lived in a remote area of her country. A "model scout" looking for people who might follow in the footsteps of other attractive Brazilian women who became internationally famous as fashion models, "discovered" the girl as she was "riding her bicycle to school." She was a shy girl, the report explained. She cried the first time she went to São Paulo. The second time, she stayed six days before the model scout sent her home.

Until the girl's mother went on the São Paulo trip, she had never been out of her town. The girl and her parents shared a four-room house with their chickens and dogs. For lack of space elsewhere, their freezer was in the girl's room.

The girl said she wanted to give her parents a better life.

"Recently," Barrionuevo reported,

> she went to São Paulo again, where the scout put her in a three-bedroom apartment with 11 other girls. Two weeks before São Paulo Fashion Week, [she] packed up and left. (2010)

In thirty years of working with foreign students and scholars, though, I was aware of only one case—a visiting scholar from an Asian country—who after less than a week in the States packed up and left. For most people, culture shock passes with time.

Academic analysts point out that the experience of culture shock need not be negative. While there may be some unhappiness and unpleasantness along with confusion and disorientation, the discomfort is a necessary step in learning about the new culture. If everything in the new place were just like home, no learning would come from being there.

Culture shock is usually followed by the next stage of adjustment when more negative feelings—disappointment, frustration, depression, anger, and hostility—surface.

When I was serving as an adviser in an international student office, I told new students, who were usually in the initial excitement period when I first met them, that the time would come when they would find themselves in the company of other foreigners who would be sharing stories about how "stupid" the Americans are. I told them they would try to outdo each other with examples of Americans' ignorance, selfishness, insensitivity, or other negative qualities. The new students smiled and said they didn't believe they would do such a thing. After a few months, though, they often admitted that they had had such conversations, sometimes many of them. This period of hostility toward the local people, born of frustration and confusion, is a common stage in adjusting to a new culture.

The next stage comes when you begin to learn and understand more about the host society and perhaps become better acquainted with some local people. In this stage the negative feelings decline, and you begin to feel more competent and comfortable.

The final stage of adjustment entails general feelings of accomplishment and acceptance of your place in the new situation, whatever that place may be.

If you are aware of these stages of adjustment, you will have a useful perspective on your own reactions. You will realize that your periods of intense happiness and excitement as well as periods of animosity and depression are probably going to pass as you find your way to some reasonably stable accommodation to your new setting. You will realize, too, that getting adjusted requires some time.

D-I-E

For many people the single most helpful idea on how to cope with a new culture comes under the easy-to-remember acronym *D-I-E*, which stands for *Describe-Interpret-Evaluate*.

"These Americans are crazy!" a visiting Brazilian engineer said. "They have no sense of humanity, of aliveness! They follow their rules like a bunch of robots. I've seen them out driving late at night when there are almost no other cars around. They come to a red light and they stop, even when there are no other cars within miles. They stop and they wait until the light turns green! They just aren't human!"

What has the Brazilian engineer told us about Americans? Almost nothing. Only that he saw at least one American stopping for a traffic signal when it was late at night and no traffic was in view. The rest of what the engineer said was his interpretation and evaluation of what he saw.

When talking about their experiences with others, people quite often blend description, interpretation, and evaluation together, as the Brazilian engineer did. For those in intercultural situations, learning to distinguish among these three reactions is most helpful.

Description refers to what one actually sees: the "objective facts," or the events various observers would agree took place. The engineer saw a person who might have been an American stop at a traffic light under certain conditions. Anyone who was with him at the time, asked to describe the situation without any interpretation or evaluation, would portray the same general scene.*

Interpretation has to do with what one *thinks* about what one sees. The engineer thinks the car's driver, presumably an American, is very concerned with rules. He also thinks it is not necessary to follow rules when no one is around and no one will be harmed by the rule-breaking. Americans are *too* concerned about rules, in his view. They are afraid to live spontaneously. That is his interpretation of what he saw, though not what he actually saw. His interpretation is, of course, based on his own perceptions, assumptions, and values, which are in turn based in part on his own cultural background. Perhaps most Brazilians would consider a person too rule-obsessed if he stopped at that traffic signal, but most Americans would not.

Evaluation has to do with what one *feels* about what one sees. The engineer feels that Americans are "crazy," not really human, not really alive. He feels uncomfortable around them, confined, unable to exhibit his personality. Once again, though, it is the engineer's values that are at issue, not Americans' actual behavior. What the Americans would regard

---

* This does not mean that eyewitnesses always agree. They do not. Different people notice different things. For example, a passenger with the Brazilian might have noticed what time it was when the car stopped, while the engineer himself was not aware of the hour.

as good, law-abiding behavior, the Brazilian feels is crazy or at least inhuman. Which evaluation is correct? Neither, of course. It is strictly a matter of point of view.

Books about intercultural relations usually urge international visitors not to be judgmental. This is another way of stating what we are saying here about evaluation. Starting with judgments about other people's behavior is not usually constructive. Statements that contain the words *right, wrong, should, ought, better, abnormal, weird,* and *crazy* are usually evaluative or judgmental.

There are two ways you can use the D-I-E idea. First, you can learn to distinguish, in your own reactions to other people, among description, interpretation, and evaluation.

Second, you can learn to stop, or at least delay, evaluating. We have seen that evaluations and interpretations are inevitably based on your own standards, standards that are based in part on your culture and may be inappropriate in another. Quick, judgmental reactions can lead to misunderstandings, misjudgments, and negative opinions. The Brazilian engineer conflated his descriptions, interpretations, and evaluations. The result was misunderstanding and unwarranted negativism. Had he been aware of the D-I-E idea, he might have realized how he was misleading himself and reducing the likelihood that he would have an accurate understanding of or constructive interactions with Americans.

CHAPTER 23

Activities for Learning
About American Culture

This chapter suggests activities intended to help foreign visitors learn more about American culture. These activities supplement those suggested at the close of earlier chapters. Although a few are appropriate for short-term visitors, most are intended for people who will be staying in the United States for a longer time.

You are encouraged to do as many of these activities as you can—even ones that seem inconvenient or uncomfortable—because the potential benefits are great. Doing them can increase your understanding of Americans (and of yourself and people from other cultures as well), which will help you get maximum benefit from your time in the United States.

The first two items are rather general and are extremely important. You should keep them in mind at all times. The subsequent items are more specific. They are not in any particular order of priority.

ASK QUESTIONS

Many international visitors are reluctant to ask questions of the local people. They feel embarrassed by their ignorance of simple things or by their limited

English proficiency. It is important for you, as a foreigner, to remember that you are the one unfamiliar with the local culture, society, and ways of doing things. Your limited knowledge can make even simple tasks like going to the bank more difficult than necessary. Remember, the more you know, the better off you will be, and the best way to learn more is to ask questions.

Whenever I talked with newly arrived international students about asking questions, I advised them how to do so without embarrassing themselves. I suggested that they begin their questions by saying, "Excuse me. I'm new here, and I have a question." If you introduce your question that way, I told them, people will understand that you have a valid reason for asking your question and they will not consider you ignorant or childlike.

Once I was talking to a student who had come to my university five years previously. "I still remember your advice about how to ask questions," he said, "by explaining that I'm new here." He smiled and said, "I still use that."

When you have questions, ask them. If the first person you ask is not helpful (or patient), ask someone else. But do ask. If you were in your home country, you would probably offer the same advice to travelers there.

Some of your questions will be requests for practical information. "How does this copy machine work?" for example, or "Where can I get my hair cut?" But you can also ask more general questions. Ask people for their opinions about things (particularly things that are harder to find out about online) and about their experiences. Ask for their reactions to some of the generalizations about Americans that appear in this book. You will find that people have differing views about them, and you will begin to see that this book's generalizations are indeed merely generalizations and are therefore subject to exception and qualification.

LEARN AND PRACTICE
LOCAL ENGLISH

Most Americans cannot use any language other than English. While they may admire a person who speaks more than one language, most of them do not place a high value on learning another language themselves. They expect other people to learn or to already know English. International visitors who can speak and understand English will have a far better opportunity than non-English speakers to learn about the American people.

"Local English" is the version of English spoken in the locality where you are staying. Although American linguists have a concept of "Standard American English," regional and local variations strongly influence idiomatic usage, colloquialisms, pronunciation (accent), rate of speech, and even aspects of communicative style (see chapter 2). You will want to learn the version of English that prevails in the part of the United States where you find yourself.

There are many ways you can improve your English while you are living in the United States:

- Watch television (for Standard American English), including programs for children.
- Listen to the radio, especially to local news programs.
- Read a local newspaper regularly.
- Read children's books. They offer a good way for beginners to practice their English reading skills, and they provide interesting insights into American culture.
- Read short books for adult learners of English.
- Enroll in an English class, which can be very helpful for beginners and intermediate-level users of English. More advanced learners may want to hire a tutor. Whatever your English-language ability, it is important for you to talk with as many people as possible: neighbors, bus drivers, fellow bus passengers, people on the streets, colleagues, and so on. Look for people who are not obviously busy. Not all people will respond positively to your initiatives. Keep trying until you find people who do.
- Search the Internet for "practice English," and carry out some of the many activities you find there.
- Record some of your own conversations. Listen to them, and seek ways to improve the defects you hear.
- Record things other people say in English (with their permission, of course), so you can review them.
- Make a note of any unfamiliar vocabulary and idioms you hear, and ask an American what they mean. (Before you use them yourself, however, make sure that they are appropriate for "polite company.")

TAKE FIELD TRIPS

A field trip is a visit to a "real" place where you can observe what happens. Some of the field trips suggested here are for international visitors with particular interests (for example, businesspeople) or for those who are staying for a relatively long time. Others are suitable for anyone.

Stand at a busy intersection. Watch the people and the traffic. Listen. Here are but a few of the many questions you can ask yourself as you watch: How do drivers respond to traffic signals? How fast do drivers go? How do drivers proceed with left turns in front of oncoming traffic? How frequently do drivers honk their horns? If traffic becomes obstructed, what do drivers do? Where do pedestrians walk? How fast do they walk? Do they touch each other? Where do they direct their eyes? How loudly do they talk? What do they do when they want to cross the street? How many drivers and pedestrians are using some electronic communications device?

Observe parent-child interactions. At many of the field-trip sites suggested here you will see children with their parents. Watch their interactions, and try to hear what they say. By what name do children address their parents? What volume and tone of voice does each use? How do the parents convey their wishes or opinions to the children and vice versa? What do the parents do if the children misbehave? How would all this compare with what you would see in a similar setting at home?

Observe male-female interactions. You can watch male-female interactions during many of these field trips. How old do the male-female pairs you see appear to be? Do older pairs behave differently from younger ones? How close do they get to each other? Do they touch? If so, how? Try to hear them talking, so you can hear what they are talking about and how they use their voices.

Enter a public or commercial building. Choose a bank, department store, post office, or some other public building. How quickly do people walk around? What do they do when more than one person wants attention or service from an employee? How close do they get to each other? How loudly do they talk? In what tones do employees and members of the public speak to each other? Where do they direct their eyes?

Walk inside a restaurant. Take a seat and order a meal, snack, or beverage. Then watch and listen. How do the servers and the customers talk to each other? What questions do the servers ask their customers? At what volume? How loudly do diners converse? What subjects do they talk about? How do patrons get a server's attention if they want additional service? What do patrons do to get their checks when they are ready to pay for their meals?

Sit in the reception area of a business or an office. Observe and listen. How is the furniture arranged? What decorations are hung on the walls or placed elsewhere? What magazines, newspapers, or books are available? Are there provisions for children who might be waiting? How does the setting compare with the same type of setting at home? How do the employees interact with each other? Does their behavior change in the presence of customers? In the presence of higher-ranking people in the office? When an employee answers the telephone, try to hear what is said and how it is said. Do you notice any change in vocal volume or tone?

Attend an American business meeting. How is the furniture arranged? Where do people sit, and what can you tell from the seating pattern about participants' status in relation to each other? Who participates (speaks) in the meeting and in what way? How long do people speak? Where do they look when they are talking and when they are not? Do they interrupt each other? If so, do some interrupt more frequently than others? How many charts or PowerPoint slides are used? Pictures? Statistics? How does all this compare with what you would see in a similar type of setting at home?

Board a public bus, train, or streetcar. Take a map, if one is available, and follow the bus route on it. But watch the passengers too. Notice where they sit, where they look, and how they talk (if they do). Do some people give up their seats so others may sit? If so, what pattern do you see? How are the stops arranged and decorated?

Walk around a neighborhood. If possible, stroll around the neighborhood where you are living. If you are in a location where people have yards, what do you see in these yards? If people are in their yards, how are they dressed? What are they doing? What interactions between or among neighbors do you see? Do people leave their doors and windows open? Their curtains?

Visit a local school. A school visit is especially important if you will have children attending there. Compare the facilities and arrangements with what you would see in a school in your country. Talk with the principal, the counselor, and one or more teachers. Ask them all what role they want parents to play in their children's education. Ask them what they think parents of children from other countries need to know and understand about the school system in general and this school in particular.

Go to a drugstore, a grocery store, and a department store. See what is available for sale at each store. How does the array of merchandise compare with what you would see in a store back home? Notice how the merchandise is arranged and how the prices are marked. Find an employee and get near enough so you can hear some interchanges between the employee and a customer. What tone of voice do they use? What volume? How formal are they? How do customers behave when paying for the goods they have selected? Find some customers who have small children with them. Walk near enough so you can hear them talking. What do they call each other? How formal are they? How loud?

Attend a religious service. What are people wearing? How do they act when they enter the building? Where do they sit? Do they touch each other? What do they do until the service begins? What does the religious official (minister, priest, rabbi, etc.) say and do? How does the congregation respond? What happens when the service ends?

Attend a city council meeting. Sit next to someone who can answer your questions. Notice who else attends, what issues are discussed, and what arguments people offer to support their points of view. How formal are the proceedings? How do people treat each other? Who appears to be respected?

Who seems not to be taken seriously? Can you tell why some people are taken more seriously than others?

Visit an American home. If you can get an invitation to an American home, accept it! Notice the way the home is furnished—the types and arrangements of furniture and decorative items. How are you, as a guest, treated? Which rooms in the house do you have the opportunity to see? If you are being hosted by a couple, what can you tell about their division of labor? If children are present, observe the way they and the adults treat each other. What topics do the hosts discuss with you? What questions do they ask you? If the family has a dog, cat, or other pet that is not kept in an enclosure, notice how they treat the animal. If you are invited for dinner on Thanksgiving or Christmas, you will be able to see how an American family celebrates those holidays.

Attend a sports event. Choose baseball, football, basketball, or whatever is convenient. Notice how the other people are dressed and how they behave. Are they attentive to the game or to others in the audience? How do they display their reactions to what happens in the game? If you are watching a game you do not understand, ask someone sitting nearby to explain what is happening.

Go to a college or university classroom. Before taking this trip, identify a large class (it can be on any subject), find out who the teacher is, and ask the teacher's permission to sit in on one class session. Explain that you are new in the country and want to see how a college class operates. Then, with permission, take the trip: walk in about ten minutes before the class is scheduled to start, take a seat on the opposite side of the room from the doorway, and watch. What do the students bring with them as they arrive? In what part of the room do the early arrivals sit? What do they do while waiting for the class to begin? How do the students respond to the teacher's arrival? How does the teacher begin the class? If students enter after the class has begun, what do they do? What, if anything, does the professor say to late arrivers? Besides taking notes on the lecture or discussion, what do students do during the class? How do they behave as the class nears its scheduled ending time? What brings the class to a close and signals the students to leave? (This field trip is especially beneficial for people who will be students in the United States.)

Go to some garage sales. Garage sales (or yard sales, as they are called in some places) are lots of fun. You can find the addresses and hours of such sales in the local newspaper or tacked on a nearby telephone pole. They are usually held on weekends and start early in the morning. Notice the nature and quality of the items offered for sale. Listen to interactions between the sellers and buyers. Ask the seller some questions about items that interest you. Watch to see whether buyers bargain with the sellers. (While you are at it, you might find bargain prices on items you can use!)

Go to an "open house." A house that is for sale and has been opened for prospective buyers to inspect is called an "open house." Many people who are not prospective buyers go to open houses, and you can join them. Look at the arrangement of the rooms, the nature of the furniture, and the decorative items. If there is a bored real-estate agent present, practice your English with him or her by asking questions about the house or about the real-estate business in general.

TALK WITH EXPERIENCED EXPATRIATES

There are advantages and disadvantages to becoming affiliated with the local expatriate community (if there is one). The advantages include the sense of identity and security you feel when you are around people who resemble you in important ways and who share the experience of being a foreigner. One disadvantage is that time spent with other expatriates is time that you won't be spending with Americans. Another possible disadvantage is that you may tend to accept uncritically whatever misjudgments and misinformation is current among the people from other countries.

Try to find people who are from your country or world area, who seem to have a balanced and rational point of view, and who have been in the United States for less than one year. (Those who have been here longer than a year are likely to have forgotten much of their initial experience and so may not be as helpful to you.) Ask them about their initial experiences: What did they find the most surprising? What was hardest for them to adjust to? Who helped them the most? What field trips do they suggest? What other suggestions do they have?

You can also discuss each other's experiences of the day, sharing ideas, information, and issues. Together you can practice applying the D-I-E idea from earlier in this chapter.

Americans who have lived abroad, particularly those who have lived in your own country, are likely to prove interested and helpful. You might be able to locate such people through a college or university international education office, a local group of returned Peace Corps volunteers, or a restaurant that offers the cuisine of your country or region of the world.

KEEP A JOURNAL

Keeping a journal is a time-honored way of coping with and learning about a new culture. Writing a journal forces you to be observant and to reflect on your experience, making it easier for you to distinguish among descriptions, interpretations, and evaluations of what you see. (Refer to the earlier section about D-I-E.)

To increase your understanding of American culture, try keeping what my colleague Janet Bennett calls a "cultural curiosity journal." In such a journal, you test your cultural assumptions with someone you trust in the host culture. In each journal entry you describe an intercultural situation that puzzled or frustrated you, then try to make sense of it from your own cultural point of view.

The next step is to find a cultural informant, an American (in this case) or other person you think is able to realistically explain what happened in the situation from an American point of view. It is best to choose someone who has the appropriate cultural "credentials" to offer an explanation. For example, someone who is younger might be a more useful resource than someone older to explain the behavior of teenagers, or an African American may be better able to help you understand that culture than an Asian American would be.

Discuss the incident with your cultural informant, and ask for help in understanding what happened in the situation you wrote about. Of course, it is always best to refrain from judgments when seeking cultural understanding, so "Can you help me understand what happened last week? usually works better than "Why do these people behave like this?!" Asking more than one informant provides even richer information.

Once you hear the alternative explanation, record it in your journal, and revise your initial analysis to take into account the new perspectives you have learned.

Your journal can also address ideas you have found in this book, noting places where your experience, and what you have learned from your informants, does and does not agree with what this book says.

LEARN THE NAMES OF LOCAL AND INSTITUTIONAL VIPS

Every community has its "very important people" (VIPs), those who hold influential positions and whose names are likely to appear frequently in the news. The highest-ranking state official is the governor. Local officials include the mayor or city manager, chief of police, sheriff, and members of the city council (or whatever the local legislative body is called). Certain businesspeople will be considered "prominent," as will certain active citizens.

Each state has two members of the U.S. Senate; each part of the state has one representative in the U.S. House of Representatives, commonly referred to as "the House."

Institutions such as businesses and universities have their own VIPs— the chief executive officers and others who hold positions of power.

Local celebrities (for example, media personalities and athletes) are also considered VIPs in many communities.

You can learn the identities of these VIPs in various ways. Read the newspapers. Go to the library and either look up the information in publications or ask a librarian for help. The most direct way to obtain such information is to ask neighbors or other Americans you meet. (Do not be surprised to find Americans who cannot name their elected political representatives. You may have to ask more than one person before you get all the information you want.)

READ, REFLECT

If you are at all interested in such matters, ask a librarian to help you find some publications about local history and politics.*

Read some of the publications in the list of suggested readings at the end of this book.

Read a local newspaper reasonably regularly. A feature of local newspapers that can be particularly instructive for international visitors is the advice column, in which readers' letters about their personal problems are printed and then responded to. The readers' letters reflect the kinds of things Americans are concerned about. The advice columnist's replies imply and often explicitly state the values on which a reply is based. Notice how often the advice is to "mind your own business" or "confront the other person directly with your complaint or point of view" or "get professional help" (from a counselor or a lawyer usually). Such advice illustrates cultural assumptions about individuality, directness, and openness that are discussed in this book. What other advice do you see that you can relate to ideas in this book?

The Sunday *New York Times Magazine* carries a column called "The Ethicist," in which a writer known as an ethicist responds to readers' questions about handling ethical dilemmas. His responses invoke basic American values.**

It may be stretching the point to include "reflecting" in a list of activities. But reflection is important in learning about a new culture, so it deserves explicit attention. To reflect, find a comfortable and quiet place, arrange to be uninterrupted for a while, and think about your recent experiences with Americans. Then ask yourself questions such as these:

- What did I expect?
- How does my actual experience compare with what I expected?

---

* If the library is within a reasonable distance of the place where you are living, apply for a library card, which will entitle you to take books and other materials from the library. How complex is the application procedure? What documentation do you need? How long does the procedure take? (It's usually very simple, as long as you have some proof that you live in the area the particular library is intended to serve.)
** Some local newspapers carry this column.

- What is happening to my stereotype of Americans?
- What traits seem common to the Americans I've met or watched?
- What traits seem relatively unusual?
- In thinking about and telling others about my experiences with Americans, am I carefully distinguishing among description, interpretation, and evaluation?
- Am I judging too quickly?
- How often do I say or think the words *right* or *wrong* or *should* or *shouldn't* when I consider what the Americans do?
- Am I doing as much as I can to learn about Americans?
- Am I teaching them about myself and my culture?
- What could I do to make my experience more interesting and constructive?

The activities suggested in this chapter take time, effort, and for many people, courage. But they will be worth it. They will enhance your understanding of yourself and your own culture as they add to your understanding of Americans. They will also help you meet some local people. They will give you material for countless interesting stories to tell your friends and family. Some will become lasting memories of your experience in America.

VIEW YOURSELF AS A TEACHER

Remember that most Americans are poorly informed about other countries and about the way their own country may be viewed by those who grew up elsewhere. You can use your stay in the United States as an opportunity to teach at least a few Americans something about your country and about a visitor's reactions to America. Remember, though, that very few U.S. Americans tolerate what they call "America bashing." Even if they agree with your critical comments, they are likely to respond negatively to statements such as "You're all so greedy" or questions such as "Why can't you control your guns?" or "Can't you see that you are imperialists?"

Perceiving yourself as a teacher can help you remain patient (remember the importance of patience!) in the face of the many seemingly stupid questions Americans may ask you, questions that are often based on stereotypes, misinformation, or no information at all.

CONCLUSION

When I was working with a group of international students who were nearing graduation and getting ready to go home, I asked them to help me make a list, on the chalkboard, of those aspects of American life that they would not like to take home with them. Here are some of the many items the students called out:

- Excessive individualism
- Weak family ties
- Poor treatment of older people
- Materialism
- Competitiveness
- Rapid pace of life
- Divorce
- "Free" male-female relations
- Impersonality

Then I asked the students to list those aspects of American life that they *would* like to see incorporated at home:

- Opportunity for individuals to raise their station in life
- Efficiency of organizations
- Hard work and productivity
- Freedom to express opinions openly

- Rules applying to everyone equally
- General sense of freedom
- Women's freedom and opportunities

Finally, I asked the students to study the two lists to see if they noticed any connections between them. After several moments someone said, "Yes. American organizations are efficient because of their impersonality and fast pace, and because they have set rules to follow."

Someone else observed, "There would not be so much possibility for individuals to get better positions if family ties were stronger, and if people had to stay where their parents are. People would not move around so much to get better jobs. Maybe even divorce is related to that!"

Still another said, "Maybe it's their materialism that motivates people to work so hard." And another: "Individualism goes with the sense of freedom."

And so on. Most of the items on the don't-want list are related to items on the do-want list. So it is with the various aspects of what we call *culture*. They fit together. They overlap and reinforce each other. It is not possible to take one or two aspects of a culture and transplant them somewhere else. They will not fit.

If you make the effort to understand Americans, you will begin to see how various aspects of American culture fit together. The patterns that underlie people's behavior will become more apparent, and you will become increasingly able to predict what other people will do. Your interpretations will become more accurate, and you will be more willing to delay judgment. All this helps you to interact more constructively with Americans and to achieve your purposes in visiting the United States.

REFERENCES AND
SUGGESTED READINGS

Readers who want to pursue some of this book's topics in greater depth can look into the publications listed in this section. They are in five categories: American culture, intercultural relations, readings for students, readings for business or professional people, and English-as-a-foreign-language texts.

AMERICAN CULTURE

Note: Following this list of books and articles about American culture is a list of websites that contain frequently updated information about assorted aspects of American life, from demographic data to attitudes and practices regarding such areas as education, the media, family life, business, religion, and technology.

Books and Articles

Akst, Daniel. 2010. "America: Land of Loners?" *Wilson Quarterly* (Summer).

Asitimbay, Diane. 2009. *What's Up, America? A Foreigner's Guide to Understanding Americans*. San Diego: Culturelink Press.

Barnlund, Dean. 1989. *Communicative Styles of Japanese and Americans: Images and Realities*. Belmont, CA: Wadsworth.

Bryson, Bill. 1989. *The Lost Continent: Travels in Small-Town America*. New York: Harper & Row.

Donenberg, Geri R. 2004. "Traditional and Alternative Families: Strengths and Challenges." *www.psych.uic.edu/hd/NonTradFam_hand.pdf*

Douthat, Ross. 2010. "Islam in Two Americas." *The New York Times* (16 August). *www.nytimes.com/2010/08/16/opinion/16douthat.html?th&emc=th*

Eland, Alisa. 2001. *Intersection of Culture and Academics: The Academic Experience of International Graduate Students*. Unpublished dissertation, University of Minnesota.

Fairlie, Henry. 1983. "Why I Love America." *The New Republic* (4 July).

Fischer, Claude S. 2010. *Made in America: A Social History of American Culture and Character*. Chicago: University of Chicago Press.

Henderson, George. 1999. *Our Souls to Keep: Black/White Relations in America*. Yarmouth, ME: Intercultural Press (Nicholas Brealey).

Kim, Eun Y. 2001. *The Yin and Yang of American Culture: A Paradox*. Yarmouth, ME: Intercultural Press (Nicholas Brealey).

Loewen, James W. 1995. *Lies My Teacher Taught Me: Everything Your American History Textbook Got Wrong*. New York: Touchstone Press.

Margolis, Alan. 1994. "Key Concepts of U.S. Education." *World Education News and Reviews* (Summer).

The New York Times. 2005. "Class Matters." *www.nytimes.com/pages/national/class/index.html?scp=1-spot&sq=class%20matters&st=cse*

Patterson, Orlando. 2010. "Inequality in America and What To Do about It." *The Nation* (19 July).

Pew Research Center. 2008a. "How Religious Is Your State?" *http://pewforum.org/How-Religious-Is-Your-State-.aspx*

———. 2008b. "The New Demography of American Motherhood." *http://pewresearch.org/pubs/1586/changing-demographic-characteristics-american-mothers*

———. 2009a. "Many Americans Mix Multiple Faiths." *http://pewforum.org/Other-Beliefs-and-Practices/Many-Americans-Mix-Multiple-Faiths.aspx*

———. 2009b. "A Religious Portrait of African-Americans." *http://pewforum.org/A-Religious-Portrait-of-African-Americans.aspx*

———. 2010a. "Neighbors Online." *http://pewinternet.org/Reports/2010/Neighbors-Online.aspx*

———. 2010b. "Religion Among the Millennials." *http://pewforum.org/Age/Religion-Among-the-Millennials.aspx*

Putnam, Robert. 2002. *Bowling Alone*. New York: Simon & Shuster.

Reimold, Daniel. 2010. "Sex, Journalism and Censorship," an interview with *Inside Higher Education*. *www.insidehighered.com/news/2010/08/03/reimold*

Schlosser, Eric. 2001. *Fast Food Nation*. Boston: Houghton Mifflin.

Spock, Benjamin, & Steven Parker. 1998. *Dr. Spock's Baby and Child Care*. New York: Simon and Schuster.

Storti Craig. 2004. *Americans at Work: A Guide to the Can-Do People*. Yarmouth, ME: Intercultural Press (Nicholas Brealey).

Tannen, Deborah. 1994. *Talking from 9 to 5: Women and Men at Work*. New York: Harper Collins.

———. 1990. *You Just Don't Understand: Women and Men in Conversation*. New York: Ballantine.

———. 1998. *The Argument Culture*. New York: Ballantine.

Waning, Esther. 1992. *Culture Shock! U.S.A.* Portland, OR: Graphic Arts Center Publishing.

Websites with Results of Research on Various Aspects of U.S. American Life

- Gallup: *www.gallup.com*
- Pew Research Center: *www.pewresearch.org*
- Roper Center for Public Opinion Research: *www.ropercenter.uconn.edu/*
- United States Census Bureau: *www.census.gov*
- University of Michigan Survey Research Center: *www.src.isr.umich.edu*
- Zogby International: *www.zogby.com*

INTERCULTURAL RELATIONS

Aguilar, Leslie C. 2006. *Ouch! That Stereotype Hurts: Communicating Respectfully in a Diverse World*. Dallas: The Walk the Talk Company.

Asante, Molefi K., Yoshitaka Miike, & Jing Yin, eds. 2008. *The Global Intercultural Communication Reader*. New York: Routledge.

Barnlund, Dean. 1975. *Public and Private Self in Japan and the United States.* Tokyo: Simul Press.

Barrionuevo, Alexei. 2010. "Off Runway, Brazilian Beauty Goes Beyond Blond," *The New York Times* (8 June). *www.nytimes.com/2010/06/08/world/americas/08models.html*

Belenky, Mary, Blythe Clinchy, Nancy Goldberger, & Jill Tarule. 1997. *Women's Ways of Knowing: The Development of Self, Voice, and Mind.* New York: Basic Books.

Bennett, Milton. J., ed. 1998. *Basic Concepts of Intercultural Communication: Selected Readings.* Yarmouth, ME: Intercultural Press (Nicholas Brealey).

Brislin, Richard. 1981. *Cross-Cultural Encounters: Face-to-Face Interaction.* New York: Pergamon Press.

———. 1990. *Applied Cross-Cultural Psychology.* Newark Park, NJ: Sage.

———. 2000. *Understanding Culture's Influence on Behavior.* 2d ed. Fort Worth, TX: Harcourt Brace Jovanovich.

Burgoon, Judee K., Laura Guerrero, & Kory Floyd. 2010. *Nonverbal Communication.* Boston: Allyn & Bacon.

Davidson, Cathy N. 2006. *36 Views of Mt. Fuji: On Finding Myself in Japan.* 2d ed. Durham, NC: Duke University Press.

DeVita, Philip R. & James D. Armstrong, eds. 2002. *Distant Mirrors: America as a Foreign Culture.* 3d ed. Belmont, CA: Wadsworth/Thomson Learning.

Hall, Edward T. 1959. *The Silent Language.* New York: Anchor/Doubleday.

———. 1989. *Beyond Culture.* New York: Anchor Books.

———. 1992. *An Anthropology of Everyday Life.* New York: Anchor/Doubleday.

Knapp, Mark L. & Judith Hall. 2010. *Nonverbal Communication in Human Interaction.* 7th ed. Boston: Wadsworth.

Kochman, Thomas. 1981. *Black and White: Styles in Conflict.* Chicago: University of Chicago Press.

Kohls, L. Robert. 2001. *Survival Kit for Overseas Living: For Americans Planning to Live and Work Abroad.* 4th ed. Yarmouth, ME: Intercultural Press (Nicholas Brealey).

Mehrabian, Albert. 1981. *Silent Messages: Implicit Communication of Emotions and Attitudes.* Belmont, CA: Wadsworth.

Nisbett, Richard. 2003. *The Geography of Thought: How Asians and Westerners Think Differently . . . and Why.* New York: The Free Press.

Peterson, Brooks. 2004. *Cultural Intelligence: A Guide to Working with People from Other Cultures.* Yarmouth, ME: Intercultural Press (Nicholas Brealey).

Samovar, Larry, Richard Porter, & Edwin R. McDaniel, eds. 2010. *Intercultural Communication: A Reader.* 7th ed. Belmont, CA: Wadsworth.

Saphiere, Dianne. H., Barbara K. Mikk, & Basma I. DeVries. 2005. *Communication Highwire: Leveraging the Power of Diverse Communication Styles.* Yarmouth, ME: Intercultural Press (Nicholas Brealey).

Storti, Craig. 1999. *Figuring Foreigners Out: A Practical Guide.* Yarmouth, ME: Intercultural Press (Nicholas Brealey).

———. 2007. *The Art of Crossing Cultures.* 2d ed. Yarmouth, ME: Intercultural Press (Nicholas Brealey).

Ting-Toomey, Stella & Leeva C. Chung. 2005. *Understanding Intercultural Communication.* Los Angeles: Roxbury.

Triandis, Harry C., Richard W. Brislin, & C. H. Hui. 1988. "Cross-Cultural Training Across the Individualism-Collectivist Divide." *International Journal of Intercultural Relations* 12, no. 3.

READINGS FOR STUDENTS

Eland, Alisa, Michael Smithee & Sidney L. Greenblatt. 2009. *U.S. Classroom Culture.* Washington, D.C.: NAFSA: Association of International Educators. (Note: This is a brochure available from many college and university international-student offices.)

Hansel, Bettina. 2007. *The Exchange Student Survival Kit.* 2d ed. Boston: Intercultural Press (Nicholas Brealey).

Tinkham, Mary, Lanny Dinslow & Patricia Willer, eds. 2009. *Introduction to American Life.* Washington, D.C.: NAFSA: Association of International Educators. (Note: This is a brochure available from many college and university international-student offices.)

READINGS FOR BUSINESS AND PROFESSIONAL PEOPLE

Harris, Philip R. & Robert B. Moran. 2000. *Managing Cultural Differences.* 5th ed. Houston, TX: Gulf Publishing.

Hofstede, Geert H., Gert Jan Hofstede, & Michael Minkov. 2010. *Culture and Organizations: Software of the Mind: Intercultural Cooperation and its Importance for Survival.* 3d ed. New York: McGraw-Hill.

House, Robert J., Paul J. Hanges, Mansour Javidan, Peter W. Dorfman, & Vipin Gupta, eds. 2004. *Cultures, Leadership and Organizations: The GLOBE Study of 62 Societies.* Thousand Oaks, CA: Sage.

Scarborough, Jack. 1998. *The Origins of Cultural Differences and Their Impact on Management.* Westport, CT: Quorum Books.

ENGLISH-AS-A-FOREIGN-LANGUAGE TEXTS

Note: Most contemporary ESL texts published in the United States contain a significant amount of material about U.S. American culture. The three ESL books listed here seem particularly helpful.

Altano, Brian. 2007. *Reading Themes and Skills: A Skills-Based American Culture Reader.* Ann Arbor, MI: Michigan University Press.

Draper, C.G. 1994. *Great American Stories 2: An ESL/EFL Reader.* 2d ed. Englewood Cliffs, NJ: Prentice Hall Regents.

Williams, Jessica. 2007. *Academic Encounters: American Studies.* Cambridge, UK: Cambridge University Press.

ABOUT THE AUTHORS

Gary Althen retired after nearly thirty-five years in the field of international education. Interpreting American culture and society to people from other countries was an essential part of his work. As director of the Instituto Cultural Peruano-Norteamericano in Huancayo, Peru; as an academic adviser at the College of Preparatory Studies in Shah Alam, Malaysia; and as a foreign student adviser and director of the Office of International Students and Scholars at the University of Iowa, he interacted with thousands of people from countries all over the world. All this experience resulted in two previous editions of *American Ways* as well as dozens of articles, workshops, and presentations about intercultural communication and the characteristics of American culture. Althen served as president of NAFSA: Association of International Educators and received its Marita Houlihan Award for his contributions to the field of international educational exchange.

Janet Bennett, Ph.D., is Executive Director of the Intercultural Communication Institute and Chair of the ICI/University of the Pacific Master of Arts in Intercultural Relations program. Her Ph.D. is from the University of Minnesota, where she specialized in intercultural communication and anthropology. For twelve years, she was Chair of the Liberal Arts Division at Marylhurst College, where she developed innovative academic programs for adult degree students. As a trainer and consultant, she designs and conducts intercultural and diversity training for colleges and universities, corporations, NGOs, government, and social service agencies. She teaches courses in the training and development program at Portland State University and has published many articles and chapters on the subjects of developmental "layered" intercultural training and adjustment processes. She coedited *The Handbook of Intercultural Training*, 3rd edition (Sage Publications, 2004), and recently authored the chapter "Cultivating Intercultural Competence: A Process Perspective" for *The SAGE Handbook of Intercultural Competence* (Sage Publications, 2009).

INDEX

Boss.